BECOMING
A LEADER
THE
ANNAPOLIS
WAY

BECOMING
A LEADER
THE
ANNAPOLIS
WAY

12 COMBAT LESSONS FROM THE NAVY'S LEADERSHIP LABORATORY

W. Brad Johnson

Gregory P. Harper

McGraw-Hill
New York   Chicago   San Francisco
Lisbon   London   Madrid   Mexico City   Milan
New Delhi   San Juan   Seoul   Singapore
Sydney   Toronto

The McGraw·Hill Companies

1 2 3 4 5 6 7 8 9 0   DOC/DOC   0 9 8 7 6 5 4

ISBN 0-07-142956-5

This publication is designed to provide accurate and authoritative information in regard to the subject matter covered. It is sold with the understanding that the publisher is not engaged in rendering legal, accounting, or other professional service. If legal advice or other expert assistance is required, the services of a competent professional person should be sought.

—From a declaration of principles jointly adopted by a committee of the American Bar Association and a committee of publishers.

McGraw-Hill books are available at special quantity discounts to use as premiums and sales promotions, or for use in corporate training programs. For more information, please write to the Director of Special Sales, McGraw-Hill Professional, Two Penn Plaza, New York, NY 10121-2298. Or contact your local bookstore.

This book is printed on recycled, acid-free paper containing a minimum of 50% recycled, de-inked fiber.

Library of Congress Cataloging-in-Publication Data

Johnson, W. Brad.
    Becoming a leader the Annapolis way : 12 combat lessons from the Navy's leadership
    laboratory / by W. Brad Johnson and Gregory P. Harper.
        p. cm.
    Includes bibliographical references.
    ISBN 0-07-142956-5 (hardcover : alk. paper)
    1. Leadership. 2. Organizational commitment. 3. Responsibility. 4. Honor. I. Harper,
    Gregory P. II. Title.
HD57.7.J647   2004
658.4'092—dc22

                                                  2004006367

Dedicated to the Brigade of Midshipmen:
Past, Present, and Future

CONTENTS

CONTENTS

Acknowledgments

The views expressed in this book are those of the authors alone and should not be construed as representing the views or policies of the Naval Academy as an institution. Nonetheless, we are deeply indebted to many wonderful colleagues at USNA who have shared wisdom, offered examples, and provided encouragement along the way. Without these shipmates, the present work would be diminished. We are particularly grateful to LCDR Erick Bacho, ADM Hank Chiles, LCDR Dan Drake, LCDR Todd Finkler, LCDR Shannon Johnson, LCDR Rick McCartney, CDR Cathy Phillips, LCDR John Ralph, CDR Lee Schonenberg, CAPT Corky Vazquez, and LT Dennis Wolpe. We are also grateful to scores of USNA midshipmen and alumni who volunteered sea stories and leadership examples as we formulated various chapters.

We are particularly grateful to our spouses, Laura Johnson and Peggy Harper, for large helpings of love and support as we worked late at night and on weekends to bring this book together. And we are deeply indebted to our sons, Jacob Johnson, Daniel Johnson, and Stanton Johnson, and Captain Brendon Harper, USMC, and his brother, Captain Shawn Harper, USA, who have served so bravely and patriotically in Operation Iraqi Freedom. They are both true leaders who have exhibited great leadership qualities under combat conditions. Being fathers to these impressive young men is the thing in life we are most proud of.

Finally, we harbor abiding gratitude for the gracious support and encouragement of our acquisitions editor at McGraw-Hill, Kelli Christiansen. The idea to write this book was Kelli's, and it was her steadfast reinforcement that got us to the finish line. Thank you.

BECOMING
A LEADER
THE
ANNAPOLIS
WAY

INTRODUCTION

When Lieutenant Commander Dick Stratton (USN), a pilot aboard the USS *Ticonderoga*, was shot down over North Vietnam in January 1967, he was quickly captured and confined in Hoa Lo prison—more commonly known as the "Hanoi Hilton." He was placed in an isolation cell where he was beaten, tortured, and starved. One morning in the isolation wing shortly after his capture, one of the other prisoners, Paul Galanti, who was assigned to pick up prisoners' soup bowls and buckets of excrement, made contact with Stratton. After teaching him a coded series of coughs, Galanti's first questions were whether Stratton was Air Force or Navy and what his rank was. When Galanti, a Naval Academy graduate, discovered that Stratton was Navy, the next question he asked was, "Do you know who won the Army-Navy game?"

Navy Captain James Stockdale (USNA '47), one of the senior ranking officers among the prisoners, and later a Medal of Honor winner for his heroic leadership in prison, had created several rules that Stratton quickly learned: First, communicate at all costs. Second, when they get around to torturing you, hold out as long as you can, bounce back, and make them do it all over again. Third, don't despair when they break you; they have broken everyone. Finally, pray. Stockdale had been through it all himself: beatings, torture, starvation, and isolation. He knew what the more junior prisoners could take and he knew what they had to do to remain alive. His rules saved lives. The rules in the "Hanoi Hilton" were quite simple. "To lead was to be tortured. To communicate with a fellow prisoner was a de facto sign of leadership that resulted in torture. To fail to bow was to be beaten and tortured. To fail to do exactly what you were told when you were told was to be tortured. Medical attention was reserved for those who might have some propaganda value. Food and water were rationed out only to the extent required to keep a prisoner alive. Lenient and humane treatment was defined as permitting you to live."

As Stratton became acclimated to this hostile new world and the rules for survival put out by Captain Stockdale, he became increasingly impressed with the Naval Academy graduates, who led their peers in these most austere and dangerous of circumstances. Termed *Boat School Boys*, the "Hanoi Hilton's" academy graduates distinguished themselves as tough, resilient, and courageous leaders. Many would later say that the lessons the United States Naval Academy (USNA) taught them were played out on the Vietnamese repeatedly and to great effect. For example, Jerry Denton, a Boat School Boy, blinked out "torture" in Morse Code with his eyes during a filmed propaganda session, while another Boat School Boy showed an inverted Hawaiian Peace sign in a photo on the cover of *Life* magazine. John McCain, class of '58, seriously injured and on a stretcher, refused the offer of an early release at a time when the prisoners' own internal policy for release would have let him go with honor. For Stratton, the Boat School Boys were lifesavers because of unflinching leadership and inspiration through personal example.

The United States Naval Academy is in the business of forming a group of leaders of men and women, a class of warriors, who are willing to sacrifice their treasure, their bodies, and their very lives for the Constitution and for the citizens of the United States. After the war, Stratton reflected that the product of the Naval Academy was a person who would do the right thing for no other reason than that it was the right thing to do. The product was a person who represented the nation well, no matter what port he or she entered or what sea he or she sailed upon. The greatest accolade given the United States Naval Academy in the "Hanoi Hilton" was by the enemy camp commander, Major Bui, who told John McCain when the Major found out McCain was the son of the Commander in Chief, Pacific, and refused his early release: "They have taught you too well, McCain! They have taught you too well!"

THE NATION'S LEADERSHIP LABORATORY

In 2003 Americans watched in dismay as major U.S. companies crashed and burned in the wake of ethics scandals, illegal behavior, and mismanagement. Many organizations are reeling from declining retention of managerial talent, and still others appear adrift when it comes to crafting a vision that followers can believe in. So what's wrong with business today? War, terrorism, and recession aside, what's missing at the heart of American businesses and organizations? Some—your authors included—would say that the missing ingredient is competent *leadership*. In fact, we propose that the absence of competent and effective leadership has created a vacuum when it comes to vision, direction, and integrity in many organizations—both local and multinational. The impact of incompetent leadership can be both insidious (e.g., steadily climbing turnover, demoralized employees, declining product quality) and catastrophic (e.g., scandal-ridden bankruptcies, fatalities in employees or consumers).

But what causes incompetent leadership? Some leaders lack the necessary character virtues to lead well. Smart, well-trained, and tenacious, these leaders nonetheless fail when it comes to utterly essential moral habits such as integrity, prudence, and genuine caring. In other cases, moral men and women have poorly developed intellectual, personality, or emotional abilities. These deficits are evident when they try to lead. Send the cognitively dull, personally arrogant, or emotionally cut-off employee to as many "leadership" workshops as you want to, but you are not likely to make this person a fine leader. Many would-be leaders simply lack the tools to lead. They have not been equipped through training and experience. Blessed with the requisite virtues and abilities, these leaders now need to be trained, nurtured, and carefully developed in the leader role.

So what are the chances of finding a leader with the virtues, abilities, and focused leadership skills required for success in the world of business today? Almost none you say? Sadly, we agree that finding excellent leaders is difficult. Worse, finding outstanding junior leaders who are remarkably intelligent, impeccably honest, highly efficient, interpersonally savvy, and deeply committed to the mission of your organization may seem down right impossible.

But wait. Indulge in a bit of fantasy for a moment and imagine what it would be like if you could carefully select your new managerial talent from a gargantuan pool of the nation's most talented young men and women. Then imagine that you could send these young people to a four-year leadership-training institute designed to prepare them to become high-performing leaders in your organization. Imagine that you could bring substantial resources to bear on the task, and that the institute's sole mission was to polish and hone these young leaders morally, mentally, and physically to assume the rigors of command in the organization. And imagine the benefits to the company of generating roughly a thousand of these well-trained, competent, and highly loyal leaders each year.

In fact, this fantasy is reality for at least one major American organization. Thanks to several early Navy visionaries and a terrible leadership debacle at sea (more about this in a minute), this dream has actually been reality in the United States since 1845. An intensive leadership laboratory designed to take some of the most talented young people in our nation and shape them into profoundly effective leaders does exist.

We refer, of course, to the United States Naval Academy. For more than 150 years, where the Severn River joins the Chesapeake Bay in Annapolis, Maryland, the Naval Academy has been preparing officers to lead in the Navy and Marine Corps. In fact, building exceptional leaders for the fleet, the government, and the nation is what USNA is all about. The undergraduate college of the naval service, USNA grants bachelor of science degrees in a variety of majors to the approximately 1000 graduating officers each year.

But graduates receive a good deal more than a degree and a commission as an officer in the Navy or Marine Corps at graduation. A common refrain around the "yard" (campus) at USNA goes something like this: *Every graduate of USNA receives a degree in leadership.* Through a profoundly rigorous regimen of scholarly courses, military training, athletic participation, summer "cruises" on naval ships and operations with the Marines, and through the myriad opportunities and demands for leadership of peers and subordinates, new Naval Academy graduates are simply among the best prepared and most effective young leaders in the country today. Graduates from earlier generations hold positions of command in the fleet, as well as positions of significant leadership in government and business.

For a recent example, consider that during Operation Enduring Freedom and Operation Iraqi Freedom, three members of the USNA class of 1971 commanded the three naval fleets directly involved in those wars. Vice Admiral (VADM) Scott Fry was Commander, Sixth Fleet; VADM Tim Keating was Commander, Fifth Fleet; and VADM Jim Metzger was Commander, Seventh Fleet. Although this is not the first time that members of the same Academy class were fleet commanders, it is the first time members of the same class commanded three fleets at the same time. I (GPH) was their classmate when our leadership skills were being molded. As you can imagine, the Class of 1971 was very proud of their accomplishments and great leadership in the war on terrorism.

During another recent world event, the EP-3 incident in China, Academy grads were again directly involved in primary leadership roles. Deputy Secretary of State Dick Armitage, Ambassador to China Joe Prueher, and ADM Denny Blair, CINCPAC, all were deeply involved in the negotiations to release the crew and plane. These former midshipmen epitomize the last part of the mission statement of the Naval Academy: "...in order to provide graduates who are dedicated to a career of naval service and have potential for future development in mind and character to assume the highest responsibilities of command, citizenship, and government."

THE ANNAPOLIS WAY

The important question is this: How can modern day civilian organizations take USNA's key leader development lessons and apply them successfully in honing their own talent? And how can individual leaders, most of whom will never be midshipmen at the Naval Academy, learn the crucial components of combat leadership imbued at USNA? These questions prompted us to write this book. Our mission is simple: to translate the salient strands of the leadership development program at USNA into a set of straightforward and applied lessons for managers and organizational leaders. In this guide to leadership the Annapolis way, we offer a crash course in becoming a leader the way generations of our nation's naval officers have learned to lead. Of course, reading this book will not earn you a commission in the Navy or Marine Corps, nor do we promise that our approach to building leaders for the fleet will match your circumstances. But we do promise to tell you like it is. We'll introduce you to our approach to developing officers. We hope these leadership lessons can be employed immediately in your organization's quest to develop outstanding talent.

THE MISSION

It's all about mission. Sure, the Naval Academy gets its pick of students, the best teaching faculty in the country, and top-notch (and often combat-wizened) military instructors. Sure, USNA has the financial resources to ensure that midshipmen get the latest when it comes to cutting-edge equipment and technological training. Yet these important ingredients are only small pieces of a complicated leader-development package. When it comes to putting it all together and orchestrating the component parts into a high-functioning leader development organization, it's the USNA mission that allows thousands of faculty, military officers, staff, and enlisted service personnel to work in unison. Here is the singular mission of the United States Naval Academy:

> To develop midshipmen morally, mentally, and physically, and to imbue them with the highest ideals of duty, honor, and loyalty in order to provide graduates who are dedicated to a career of naval service and have potential for future development in mind and character to assume the highest responsibilities of command, citizenship, and government.

Brief but clear, this mission puts us all on the same page. Professors, coaches, and company officers are constantly called to account for themselves and their training activities in light of this mission. The question is this: How is this course, this duty, or this experience helping to develop midshipmen and build future leaders?

At USNA, our mission is a sobering one. We produce leaders who, on orders from the commander-in-chief, are prepared to fight and win wars anyplace in the world. Yes, our graduates often go on to assume leadership roles in government and industry, but they must always begin their careers leading military personnel—sometimes into battle. And sometimes our graduates lose their lives in service to country before they have been gone from us for long.

On the morning of September 11, 2001, I (WBJ) had just dismissed my first class and was en route to my second class of the day when a shaken colleague informed me of the attacks on the World Trade Center towers. When I entered my classroom, I managed to get CNN on the big projection screen. I watched events unfold, including the subsequent attack on the Pentagon, with my 20 stunned students. Fourteen of those killed that fateful morning (pilots, executives, and Pentagon personnel) were USNA graduates. In fact, the captain of the American Airlines flight that crashed into the Pentagon was Chic Burlingame, a member of the same Class of 1971 as the fleet commanders we already mentioned. As I surveyed the carnage on the screen juxtaposed with the bright young officers-to-be in my classroom that morning, I was troubled by the conviction that many of them would soon be participating in a military response of some sort. They would be going to war. It was likely that some of them would not be returning.

In fact, the entire history of the Naval Academy is punctuated and measured by periods of military conflict and world war. Since 1845, the Academy has been impacted by approximately one war every 20 years. In each of these military conflicts, midshipmen and graduates of USNA have been actively involved. In some instances, the Academy's schedule has drastically intensified in order to meet wartime demands for new naval officers. During World War II, for example, the USNA curriculum was compressed to three years. Although various facets of education were economized during these years, graduates of this era were imbued with the same strong leadership skills and virtues. Most recently, our graduates have gone directly into training and subsequent combat over the skies, on the ground, under the seas, and off the shores of Afghanistan and Iraq. During time of war or threat of action, the Academy's mission is painted in stark relief. Students and faculty alike appreciate the important nature of our business and the critical importance of learning to lead well.

NOT JUST ANY LEADERSHIP SCHOOL

At Navy our mission is to prepare warriors who can do it all. Writing about the sort of officer we work to produce, Admiral John Bulkeley once wrote:

> For in my mind, there is but one honorable profession [naval officership]. It requires the daily attention of all faculties, the persistence of a bulldog, the compassion of a man of the cloth, foresight entrenched in previously learned lessons, the willing-ness to sacrifice for the good of the service all that has been personally gained or earned, an unyielding belief that it is better to preserve peace than to wage war, the self force-feeding of knowledge and new technology, the ability to blend confidence and humility, and the unyielding conviction that it is far greater to serve one's country rather than oneself.

Our mission is to produce leaders that fulfill these requirements—leaders like Navy Commander William C. McCool. Graduating second of 1083 in the USNA class of 1983, he was captain of the track team and proven leader of both peers and junior midshipmen. Smart, humble, caring, tenacious, and deeply loyal to the mission of the United States Navy, CDR McCool went on to earn innumerable awards and medals as a jet pilot, and, later, as a test pilot for the Navy. Serving as an officer on board the aircraft carrier USS *Enterprise* (CVN-65) in 1996, CDR McCool learned that NASA had selected him for the astronaut program. One of NASA's rising stars, CDR McCool was selected to pilot the space shuttle Columbia on a 16-day mission. In the early morning hours of February 1, 2003, somewhere over the southern United States, this mission came to an abrupt and tragic end when the shuttle broke up on reentry and the entire crew was lost. In retrospect, those closest to CDR McCool emphasized that he died doing exactly what he loved and that his commitment to the mission of the United States Navy and NASA was unshakable.

USNA's singular mission creates a particularly profound bond among midshipmen themselves. These young leaders understand intuitively that a sobering and sacred mission binds them. They grasp the gravity and import of their call to duty and therefore become much more closely bonded than ordinary college students. When, in 1963, Roger Staubach received the Heisman Trophy, he reflected, "One of the greatest things about winning the Heisman Trophy was the pride it brought to our Navy football team in 1963 and to the entire class of 1965 at the Naval Academy. It was not my trophy; it was the team's trophy and my class's trophy."

THE PRODUCT

At Navy our mission is impressive in its clarity and pith, but a mission is only as impressive as the results it inspires. "So what has USNA actually achieved?" you ask. Over the years, the Naval Academy has turned out 1 U.S. president, 18 members of Congress, 4 state governors, 4 secretaries of the Navy, 1 secretary of the Air Force, 3 chairmen of the Joint Chiefs of Staff, 25 Chiefs of Naval Operations, 73 Medal of Honor awardees, 2 Nobel Prize awardees, 51 astronauts, 33 Rhodes Scholars, 10 Marshal Scholars, 74 Olmsted Scholars, and 619 Burke Scholars, not to mention the majority of the Navy's flag officers (admirals). Not bad for a small school that began with 50 students and even today graduates 1000 or fewer students per year. Our products include leaders like former president Jimmy Carter, Senator John McCain, NBA star David Robinson, NFL star Roger Staubach, astronaut Alan Shepard, Vietnam prisoner of war Vice Admiral James Stockdale, and famed WW II Fleet Admiral Chester W. Nimitz.

Even more impressive than these famous personalities, however, are the thousands of historically anonymous but intensely loyal officers who have graduated from USNA and gone on to serve the country with distinction. These men and women have been leaders in the truest sense—often leading subordinates into hostile waters, dangerous skies, or unnamable foreign lands as commanders of ships or submarines, pilots, or special forces officers; leaders who understand how to commit to a mission and inspire followers to get the job done.

STARTING WITH THE RIGHT STUFF

In order to generate products such as these, we admittedly stack the deck when it comes to selection. "Plebes" (first-year Academy students) are some of the very brightest (and toughest) high school graduates in the country each year. With average SATs well over 1300, the vast majority are extremely fit varsity athletes, ranked at or near the top of their high school classes, and nominated by a U.S. congressman. These are sharp folks. Representing every state and territory of our great nation, our students have shown a strong propensity for leadership, self-motivation, ambition, and service to others even before arriving at our gates.

It goes without saying that any young man or woman who selects USNA over the nation's other elite undergraduate schools is looking for something different. They are drawn by the promise of extreme challenge— mentally, physically, and personally. They are turned off by the mundane, the routine, and the ordinary. Although not certain they have what it takes to persevere and graduate USNA, they revel in the quest.

When we set out to create a specific kind of leader in our graduates, we have a different sort of motivation from most colleges around the country. We are contributing to the future of our own organization. The men and women sitting in our classes and marching the hallowed grounds around Annapolis today will be our commanders, captains, and admirals of tomorrow. We remember one superintendent who, in his annual briefing to the faculty, said that we should look around the Yard at the midshipmen as we walked to class, for somewhere out there were 12 to 13 future four-star admirals who would be leading the fleet one day. Writing just after USNA's centennial in 1946, R.S. West wrote this about the unusual perspective of USNA superintendents:

> In many ways their job parallels that of dozens of presidents or superintendents of civilian technical colleges. But unlike the latter, they feel a much more keen and justifiably selfish interest in the success of their graduates…. They may someday be junior officers under him in battle.

BORN OF A LEADERSHIP FAILURE

Although the Naval Academy was not founded until 1845, "midshipmen," or apprentice officers, were first appointed to American ships in 1775. The term *midshipman* was borrowed from the British fleet. On Britain's monstrous wooden ships of the 1700s, specialized seamen were stationed amid ships for the purpose of relaying orders between officers on the bow and in the stern. Regarded as having more authority than ordinary seamen, midshipmen came to be seen as junior officers, and this became the apprentice route to a commission in the Navy. In the early American Navy, midshipmen had no formal education and those in command often neglected their training and preparation for commissioning. Until 1845, the lives of midshipmen were often painful and left to the whims of hardened sea-going veterans of the service:

> The first midshipmen of the regular navy came under the command and influence of men who were products of the hardest kind of experience the sea could offer. Their officers had come up through service in the British Navy, in colonial naval vessels, in privateers, and the merchant marine. They were men, toughened by years before the mast, who did not hesitate to enforce their orders with their fists or to have a man's back laid raw by the cat-o-nine-tails. The life was rugged, the duty was hard, and the chances for learning enough to win a commission depended almost wholly on the individual midshipman's determination to make the most of his opportunities.

Even without any formal program of education or training, however, midshipmen of the United States Navy established themselves as capable and courageous young men—often earning the respect of senior naval officers. One of these midshipmen was James Jarvis, assigned to the *Constellation* in her battle with the British ship *Vengeance*. Historians note that: "Jarvis clung to his station in the ship's maintop, even though the rigging had been destroyed and the mast left unsupported. When warned of the danger, he said 'If the mast goes, we go with it.' It fell and Jarvis and his men were lost."

It is a credit to the quality and tenacity of midshipmen of this era that so many of them weathered the harsh and disorganized system of training then prevalent in the fleet, successfully dispatched their duties as midshipmen, and went on to positions of leadership in our nation's early navy. In fact, this entirely informal system of leader development might have persisted for quite some time were it not for the U.S. ship *Somers* and the tragic events that unfolded on her decks in the fall of 1842.

On September 13, 1842, the *Somers* set sail from Brooklyn, New York, to the shores of Africa. On board were 7 midshipmen and 114 other crew members. In November, as the ship made its way home, 19-year-old Philip Spencer (the son of the U. S. Secretary of War, John Canfield Spencer) was accused by the ship's captain, Commander Alexander Slidell Mackenzie, of plotting a mutiny in collaboration with at least two other sailors. Notes written in Spencer's own hand appeared to confirm these mutinous intentions. In a hastily assembled court of inquiry, Spencer and his two seamen associates were found guilty of an attempt to commit mutiny. The three men were hanged to death at the ship's yardarm later that very day.

Upon the return of the *Somers* to the United States the following month, there was a strong outcry from members of Congress, the Secretary of War, and others regarding the wisdom of sending midshipmen directly aboard ship to learn in the school of hard knocks. In fact, the entire country was shocked by the hanging of a midshipman, and in spite of the continuing conviction of some senior naval officers that formal education was entirely irrelevant to the training of officers, the country, the government, and the Navy understood the risks of failing to prepare midshipmen for the strains and demands of leadership at sea.

Through the efforts of then secretary of the Navy, George Bancroft, the Naval School was established at an old Army post named Fort Severn in Annapolis on October 10, 1845. With 50 students and 7 professors that first year, the school began preparing officers versed in navigation, seamanship, gunnery, steam propulsion, chemistry, mathematics, English, philosophy, and French. In 1850 the institution was formally named the United States Naval Academy and a curriculum was established that required midshipmen to study at the Academy for 4 years and train aboard ships in the fleet each summer. Although the current student body numbers more than 4000, and although the Academy grounds cover more than 338 acres, this early idea of blending academic and applied training has never changed.

LEADERSHIP THE NAVY WAY

Many institutions of higher learning these days are reluctant to claim leadership as an academic specialty or as an area of applied training. Some are embarrassed to claim expertise when it comes to building leaders. Others lack a view of the field of leadership or experience in producing leaders with a track record of success. This is not the case at Navy. Leader building is the bedrock of what we do. Creating the finest leaders in the military and the country at large is what we are all about. After more than a century and a half, and after countless worldwide conflicts and successful naval operations, we are convinced of one thing: Naval Academy graduates are prepared to lead.

At USNA we have learned that to be successful, leader development cannot be accidental or incidental; successful leader development is deliberate and intentional. We understand that leadership is complicated, yet we are unabashed in our assertion that we create leaders. Excellent leadership does not come easily to most. Sometimes painful, it requires profound effort and commitment. Learning to lead often requires a few notable failures and inevitable periods of self-doubt. Leadership is not the result of good genes, good luck, or divine intervention (though we suppose any of these factors might help). Yes, IQ and leader-oriented personality traits help make leading easier, but these are not enough. Leadership competence requires training, modeling, and frequent experience "trying on" or practicing the various skills inculcated in class, in readings, and in lectures. We see our share of "natural" leaders come through the gates at Annapolis, but even this fortunate minority requires direction; their inherent leader skills require honing and polishing.

Although nobody graduates from UNSA with an academic major in leadership, neither does anyone graduate from USNA without proving himself or herself capable of leading well. The father of the American Navy, John Paul Jones (now interred in the basement of the USNA chapel), once described the qualities of the naval officer USNA endeavors to produce in this way:

> He [a leader] should be the soul of tact, patience, justice, firmness, and charity. No meritorious act of a subordinate should escape his attention or be left to pass without its reward, even if the reward is only a word of approval. Conversely, he should not be blind to a single fault in any subordinate, though, at the same time, he should be quick and unfailing to distinguish error from malice, thoughtlessness from incompetency, and well-meant shortcoming from heedless or stupid blunder.

More simply, President Harry Truman, a strong advocate of USNA, thought of leadership as "that quality which can make other men [and women] do what they do not want to do and like it."

In our courses and applied leadership training experiences at USNA, we work to inculcate future officers with knowledge of themselves, others, and the demands of various situations. We work on moral responsibility, self-discipline, judgment, analytical ability, communication skill, honor, integrity, and loyalty. We deliberately set about creating naval officers who have mastered the art of influencing and directing others and creating a vision that spurs followers to reach peak performance. We want officers who have both technical expertise and the proven capacity for applying this expertise to good effect. Although USNA is among the most academically challenging of all undergraduate institutions, it is USNA's reputation as a laboratory for the next generation of leaders that gives the institution its international reputation. In the end, our organization, like yours, will rise or fall on the quality of its leaders.

THE GOUGE

Becoming a Leader the Annapolis Way is a guide for those who want to build leaders in any organization. Even if your leaders are not destined to command multibillion-dollar naval vessels, fly bombing sorties, or lead platoons of Marines into combat, we believe that the lessons for leadership learned by all USNA midshipmen will be of value to your personnel. The leadership lessons contained in this guide can also be self-applied. We hope that you find them useful in your own effort to become a more effective and productive leader.

Throughout this book, we attempt to distill the key ingredients of excellent leadership. We have taken the best leadership lessons from the four-year curriculum at the Naval Academy and summarized them for immediate use. This book will give you an insider's look at how leadership can be nurtured and developed, and how great men and women can become competent leaders through hard work and attention to detail.

In the pages that follow we cover the making of leaders, the importance of commitment, learning to follow, character development, creation of vision, inoculating leaders for stress, learning loyalty, the importance of preparation, leading by example, the importance of emotional competence, empowerment-focused leadership, and prizing diversity.

We end each chapter with a section titled "The Gouge." In Navy-speak, the *gouge* is the synopsis or abbreviated version—the executive summary or the crucial take away. Although we hope each chapter offers some new insight when it comes to training leaders, you will get a sense of the crucial lessons midshipmen learn in each area of leadership by scanning the gouge.

A FEW WORDS ABOUT YOUR AUTHORS

I, Brad Johnson, am a professor in the USNA department of Leadership, Ethics, and Law. A psychologist by profession, my job is to blend cutting-edge research from the behavioral sciences with the Academy's tried-and-true approach to building naval officers. A former Navy Lieutenant, I was stationed at Bethesda Naval Hospital and Pearl Harbor Naval Medical Clinic. My years as an officer, psychologist, and professor to midshipmen have given me a unique academic and consulting vantage point from which to observe the process of leader building.

I, Greg Harper, am a Naval Academy graduate and was a career Naval Officer before retiring as a Captain. I spent my operational tours in the Patrol Aviation (VP) community culminating as Commanding Officer of Patrol Squadron Sixteen. During my career, I served two tours at the Academy teaching both times in the History and Political Science departments and also served as the First Battalion Officer in Bancroft Hall. Recently, I served three years as a civilian as the Leadership Fellow teaching in the Leadership Department.

I have taught midshipmen leadership both in the classroom and in Bancroft Hall, where classroom lessons learned are exercised in real life. I have observed midshipmen practice leadership both in and out of the classroom and like Brad have a unique vantage point for watching midshipmen become leaders the Annapolis way. Of course, everything in this book is a product of our own experience and perspective. Nothing herein reflects any official policy of the United States Naval Academy.

In our humble opinion, USNA is simply tops when it comes to turning out leaders. We hope our experiences have combined to make us able guides in the territory of shaping leaders. We hope the lessons we share in the pages that follow make the task of building leaders for your own organization—or becoming a stronger leader yourself—more transparent, rational, and applicable.

1

ON BUILDING COMBAT LEADERS

The scene is a crowded seminar room at the famed Wharton Business School at the University of Pennsylvania. The speaker, an esteemed professor of leadership and management at Wharton, is launching into a summer lecture to leaders from a range of organizations and businesses. To kick things off, the professor inquires of the audience: "I wonder whether most of you think leaders are born or whether they are made? Those who think leaders are born, raise your hands."

The vast majority of the audience members send their arms skyward. There are nods and smiles all around and emphatic murmurs of agreement as it becomes apparent that most in this group concur—excellent leadership is innate. Undeterred, the professor continues, "And does anyone feel that leaders are primarily made?"

In the front row of the hall, several white-sleeved arms shoot up. The crowd gawks in surprise, but these front-row occupants keep their hands aloft. Each arm belongs to a uniformed naval officer—a leadership instructor from the Naval Academy's Department of Leadership, Ethics, and Law. The group has come to glean the latest in leadership research and practice. They are accomplished junior officers who spend their days teaching midshipmen the mechanics of good leadership. Most of them are graduates of USNA themselves and all of them have seen midshipmen with apparently low aptitude for leading become outstanding leaders in the fleet. Their experiences at USNA and beyond have convinced them that, given the right mix of ability and aptitude, excellent leadership can be dramatically shaped and developed.

This true story from a recent Wharton seminar highlights an important assumption undergirding all that we do at USNA. The assumption goes something like this: Aptitude is important but it's not enough. Becoming an excellent leader requires hard work, intensive training, careful coaching, and deliberate feedback from seasoned leaders. Yes, certain traits seem to make leader-development easier for some, but traits alone will never make a leader.

The classic trait approach to leadership assumes that some people are simply natural born leaders. Unfortunately, massive research efforts in psychology and management have failed to elucidate these crucial personality characteristics—traits that reliably predict success in the leader role. Although personality features may make leadership somewhat more comfortable and effective, there are other important questions to ask about potential leaders than "What are they like?" For example, what do these people actually do in different situations? How do they spend their time? What are their priorities? How do they gain and use power? What are their interpersonal relationships like? How do various situations and contexts influence their leader behaviors? These are important variables and we have observed them at play in a vast number of naval leaders over the course of our careers.

Of course, we do not mean to ignore the importance of ability and aptitude when selecting leaders. Requiring one of the nation's most arduous collegiate application procedures, USNA enjoys the profound luxury of selecting only a small percentage of applicants from among a wide pool of remarkably bright and multitalented students. One cannot ignore the importance of choosing leaders who are intellectually bright, highly motivated, and imbued with positive personality traits. Still, these characteristics do not ensure excellent leadership. It takes more than capacity.

We don't always "get it right" when it comes to selecting future leaders. Occasionally, one gets by us. I (GPH) recall one young plebe that entered USNA when I was a battalion officer. On Induction Day (I-Day), which is probably the most intensive day of any midshipman's career, one young man went through the process of having all of his hair cut off, getting shots, collecting a sea bag full of uniforms, and undergoing the first intensive scrutiny of the upper-class in charge of the new plebes. Finally, after surviving all the rigors of I-Day and just before he was to say goodbye to his parents, he asked his squad leader for permission to speak "freely." When the second-class midshipman asked him what he wanted, the young plebe said, "Sir, I didn't know this was a military school!" Needless to say, when he met his parents, he informed them of his mistake and left after the first day. Although both the plebe and the admissions board missed the boat in this case, we are generally confident that if a young man or woman is motivated to learn to lead at USNA, we can help him or her to get there.

In an important *Harvard Business Review* article titled "Leadership in a Combat Zone," W.G. Pagonis reflected that leadership is only possible when the ground has been carefully prepared in advance. He noted that the military goes to great lengths to groom and prepare leaders for the demands of leading in combat. A complex mixture of careful selection, formal education, informal mentoring, and systematic rotation through a range of settings is used to prepare officers to effectively lead across contexts and conflicts. Through it all, our objective is to challenge without overwhelming.

FIRST, FORGET WHAT YOU'VE BEEN TOLD ABOUT LEADERS

In this chapter we debunk a few common leadership myths often propagated as common sense or "givens" whenever leadership is discussed. The worst of these myths include:

- Leaders are born, not made.
- Good leadership is all common sense.
- The only school that teaches leadership is the school of hard knocks.

Before becoming an effective leader in the military or anywhere else, you had better work at recognizing these statements as mythical and as antithetical to the hard work required to rise in the ranks of outstanding leaders. In the balance of this chapter we dispatch each of these pernicious myths.

LEADERS ARE MADE (THOUGH APTITUDE SURE DOESN'T HURT)

A particularly ridiculous yet maddeningly enduring leadership myth is that excellent leaders are simply born that way. Although most of us have heard this statement so many times that we tend to believe it on some level, it is actually quite a laughable idea. The statement that leaders are born implies that the world is full of leaders and nonleaders, that you either "have it" or don't in the leadership area. The fact is that each of us has a unique blend of emotional, intellectual, and behavioral talents and proclivities that place us somewhere on the continuum from poor to excellent leadership. And most important, one's location on the continuum is not static but fluid; leadership is responsive to a range of factors such as motivation, new learning, maturity, and experience. People often become more effective leaders. One alumnus shared with us an experience that we think illustrates this point very well. Robert Niewoehner, Class of '81 recalled

Fall of my 3/c [second] year, I was a struggling member of the Lightweight Crew team. Because the team was not comprised of an even multiple of eight, several guys were left at the boat house every day to train by themselves. It seemed my number came up 2–3 times per week to stay behind. It was pretty discouraging, and I really wrestled with sticking it out.

Thursday afternoons, after practice, the coach would pull four upperclassmen aside to pick boats for Friday's practice, an hour-long race from USNA around Holiday Island and back. This process was much like picking teams for sandlot baseball or soccer in elementary school. One Thursday after boats were picked, one second class took me aside and told me,

"Rob, I think you're the most underrated member of the team. I specifically wanted you in my boat, and I want to see you make big puddles for me tomorrow." All the discouragement from the previous weeks was lifted by that one remark. He could certainly not have known the extent of my discouragement.

I exhausted myself the next day on the end of that oar, determined not to disappoint his trust. I was staunchly his supporter when he was elected Team Captain the following year, for in my eyes he could do no wrong.

His remark set the tone and the path for my entire Naval Academy experience.

I committed to crew and resolved that I was going to letter by graduation.

Though I finished second in my class, held five stripes, and finished a Master's in Electrical Engineering before graduation, I am far more proud of my "N" (varsity letter) for it came at a far greater price. Encouragement is a very powerful thing. Make a point to notice the quiet ones standing in the back, tentative about whether they can fit in or contribute. It may not take much to move them.

But what about personality? Don't people with specific personality traits make better leaders? The answer appears to be: Certain traits help, but they are not enough. Positive personality features assist excellent leadership but don't guarantee it (later in this chapter we highlight some of the primary personality characteristics among those who lead well). For evidence that innate personality features do not alone predict leadership success, one only needs to consider the case of two famously successful World War II admirals.

We refer, of course, to Vice Admiral William F. "Bull" Halsey and Rear Admiral Raymond Spruance. This is one of our favorite examples for letting midshipmen know that officers with different personalities really can become effective leaders. Following the Japanese attack on Pearl Harbor and a series of Japanese naval victories, morale in the service was at low ebb. With the Japanese planning a bold attack on the U.S. naval base at Midway Island, America's ability to survive in the Pacific depended upon the success of an aircraft carrier task force led by the notoriously charismatic and outgoing VADM Halsey. A gung-ho leader who personified extroversion and was fond of large informal meetings, Halsey was interpersonally affable and prone to intuitive decision making. He was inspirational and popular among the enlisted ranks. Halsey was also a "brown shoe," a naval aviator, who was outgoing, bold, and sometimes maybe even a little too daring.

When Halsey became seriously ill shortly before the Midway battle, he was ordered hospitalized by Admiral Chester Nimitz and was quickly replaced by RADM Spruance. Now, Spruance was a "black shoe," a surface warfare officer. "Black shoes" traditionally have been quite different in their view of fleet operations when compared to their "brown shoe" brethren.

"Black shoe" officers had long clung to the doctrine that battleships were the capital ships of the Navy and the carriers and naval aviators were only to be used to scout out the enemy for the battleships. The "black shoes" would then engage in the classic surface action in the tradition of the Battle of Jutland. "Black shoes" sailed at 30 knots, whereas "brown shoes" flew at 300 knots. Of course Pearl Harbor changed all of that.

Differences in the personality constellations between Halsey and Spruance were immediately noticeable. In fact, the two men appeared to be polar opposites on many dimensions of personality. In contrast to his predecessor, Spruance was quiet, reserved, and preferred reflection over constant interaction. More comfortable with small meetings and individual conversations, he was notorious for sifting through facts and analytical decision making. Officers in the carrier task force must have wondered how this introverted surface warfare officer could possibly succeed in replacing one of the most popular and admired naval aviators in history just before the most important battle of the war. Could Spruance possibly be as effective a leader? Sure enough, the wardroom had great difficulty adjusting to Spruance. Halsey had been outgoing; Spruance preferred quiet channels. Halsey paid minimal attention to detail; Spruance was compulsively focused on details and facts. Halsey was a free spirit; Spruance was deliberate and methodical.

In the end, Spruance led Carrier Task Force 16 to one of the greatest naval war victories of all time. It marked the crucial turning point in American resolve and morale in the Pacific theater. History shows that Spruance was a superb combat leader, as was his predecessor VADM Halsey.

It appears that nondescript introverts can lead as effectively as gregarious extroverts. This is a lesson learned over and over at USNA and in the Navy at large. Although certain personality traits may fit certain tasks and contexts better than others, personality will always be secondary to leader knowledge, skill, and attitude.

EXCELLENT LEADERSHIP REQUIRES MORE THAN COMMON SENSE

Related to the myth that leaders are born is the equally unsupportable notion that leadership is a matter of common sense. Translation: Anyone who is not a total flake can lead well because the keys to good leadership are self-evident. Again, we disagree. If leadership were common sense, it is unlikely that there would be so many problems with ineffective leadership in everyday life. Even the Navy suffers from its share of less than sterling leadership.

When USNA graduate CDR Michael Abrashoff, USN, became the commanding office of the guided missile destroyer USS *Benfold*, he immediately set to work reading exit interviews from crewmembers who had recently departed the ship. He wondered why so many had been departing this ship and the Navy prematurely. What he found appalled him.

> I assumed that low pay would be the first reason, but in fact it was the fifth. The top reason was not being treated with respect or dignity; second was being prevented from making an impact on the organization; third, not being listened to; and fourth, not being rewarded with more responsibility.

Either Abrashoff's predecessor had no common sense or good leadership is more complex and demanding than most realize. As he set about listening to his sailors and seeking creative means to inspire and motivate them to turn the *Benfold* into a fighting community defined by high morale, Commander Abrashoff employed more than common sense. Aware of Gallup poll research showing that 65 percent of those who leave their companies are actually seeking to escape their direct managers, Abrashoff drew from science-based principles of reinforcement, organizational models of team building, and four years of intensive practice for leadership at the Naval Academy.

Commonsense leadership is rooted in the erroneous assumption that *if most people believe it, it must be right*. Of course, throughout history, the majority of military leaders have at times held to clearly false beliefs such as: "Unless your men fear you, they won't respect you," and "Good leaders know when to break some china!" Further, many forms of common sense are clearly incompatible. For example, if counseling a sailor about going to sea and leaving his girlfriend behind, which common sense advice would you give: "Absence makes the heart grow fonder," or "Out of sight, out of mind"?

It comes as no surprise that research in psychology and business consistently shows that people (including would-be leaders) frequently assume they know more than they actually do; we overestimate our understanding of how to lead. When students enter the Naval Academy, many are immediately thrust into leadership roles in their company, in their classes, and in the larger brigade of midshipmen.

I (GPH) remember very clearly an example of this during my own plebe summer. On I-Day, I was assigned to a company and an upperclass midshipman marched the company's new plebes to our rooms in Bancroft Hall where we were to meet our roommates. When I arrived at my room, my roommate was already there. He was a *Napster*, a midshipman who had attended the Naval Academy Prep School for a year prior to coming to the Academy, and the Napsters had arrived the day before the plebes (the majority of whom are fresh out of high school). After a very hectic day and following evening meal, we were allowed to return to our rooms and start stowing all our gear. My roommate, Marc, because of his experience at NAPS, had been informed by the upperclass that he would be Company Commander beginning the next day. Anxious, nervous, and a little overwhelmed at this new leadership position being thrust upon him, Marc started practicing his commands. He wanted to make sure that he had that "command voice." So for the rest of the evening, Marc stood in front of our open window shouting commands out into the empty Midshipman Store parking lot. He went on all evening until finally, much to my relief, we had to hit our racks and Taps was played over the Bancroft Hall intercom.

THE SCHOOL OF HARD KNOCKS IS NOT
THE BEST WAY TO LEARN LEADERSHIP

A final myth bearing on leadership training holds that the best way to train a naval leader is to send him or her directly to sea where leadership will be inculcated in the raw and unforgiving school of hard knocks. Of course, we think the late midshipmen Philip Spencer of the USS *Somers* would disagree (see Introduction). We have shown that the Naval Academy was brought to life as a result of the profound failures of this "hard knocks" approach. In fact, long before USNA, the father of the American Navy, John Paul Jones himself, was one of the earliest and staunchest supporters of a well-rounded education for naval officers. This is particularly important in light of the fact that Jones was a product of the old "hard knocks" system. Jones wrote:

> It is by no means enough that an officer of the Navy should be a capable mariner. He must be that of course, but also a great deal more. He should be, as well, a gentleman of liberal education, refined manners, punctilious courtesy and the nicest sense of personal honor.

Experience has proven John Paul Jones correct. In fact, the curriculum at USNA is rooted in the assumption that formal education and seagoing training are naturally complementary and equally important. Academic preparation accelerates learning in the fleet. Midshipmen learn models of leadership and behavioral principles for motivating and influencing others and then apply them in the context of pervasive feedback—both around the yard and during summer assignments with the Navy and Marine Corps.

John McCain recently recounted his first class cruise and some of the lessons he learned:

> I boarded the USS *Hunt* to begin my first class cruise to Rio de Janeiro in June 1957. The *Hunt* was an old destroyer. It had seen better days. It seemed to me a barely floating rust bucket that should have been scrapped years before, unfit even for mothballing. I spent most of the cruise on the bridge, where the skipper would order me to take the conn. There is a real mental challenge to running a ship of that size, and I had little practical experience for the job. But I truly enjoyed it. I made more than a few mistakes, and every time I screwed up, the skipper would explode, letting loose an impressive blast of profane derision. "Dammit, McCain, you useless bastard. Give up the conn right now. Get the hell off my bridge. I mean it, goddammit; I won't have a worthless S.O.B. at the helm of my ship. You've really screwed up this time McCain. Get the hell out of here." As I began to skulk off the bridge, he would call me back. "Hold on a second, come on back here, Mister. Get over here and take the conn." And then he would begin, more calmly, to explain what I had done wrong and how the task was done properly. We would go along pleasantly until I committed my next unpardonable error, when he would unleash another string of salty oaths in

despair over my unfitness for service, only to beckon me back for a last chance to prove myself worthy of his fine ship. One beautiful afternoon, the flagship of the Destroyer Division to which the *Hunt* was attached, flying the ensign of the commanding Admiral, approached us for the purpose of replenishing the *Hunt's* depleted stores. The skipper gave me the conn, and without a trace of apprehension, made me bring her alongside the Admiral's flagship. He told me to bring her up slowly, but offered no rebuke when I ordered, "All engines ahead two-thirds." At precisely the right moment I ordered, "All engines back full." A few moments later, again well timed, I ordered, "All engines ahead one-third." Thrillingly and to my great relief, the *Hunt* slipped into place so gracefully that any observer would have thought the skipper himself, master shiphandler that he was, had the conn. The skipper was proud of me, and I was much indebted to him. He had given me his trust, and I had had the good fortune to avoid letting him down. After the two ships were tied up, he sent a message to the Admiral. "Midshipman McCain has the conn." The impressed Admiral sent a message to the Superintendent of the Naval Academy informing him of my accomplishment.

Deliberate training and education equip new officers for the range of leadership challenges they will certainly encounter in the fleet. The school of hard knocks has proven inadequate as a leadership laboratory. More than 230 years of American naval experience has taught us this lesson: If you want great leaders, prepare them to lead. And never assume that hard knocks alone produce leadership skills.

If leadership is more than personality, common sense, and experience born of hard knocks then what do leaders need to learn? Our answer is lots. In fact, the remainder of this book is dedicated to highlighting the range of leadership lessons inculcated at USNA. But here is a summary of some key things midshipmen (and other fine leaders) learn to do—not just as students, but also as a way of life.

- Manage time effectively.
- Make commitments to tasks and organizations and be faithful.
- Recognize that following well is a prerequisite to outstanding leadership.
- Actively seek out opportunities for leadership.

- Observe and critically evaluate one's own leadership performance. Reflect on outcomes and explore alternatives for use in future situations.
- Understand that character matters; leadership requires virtue.
- Correctly diagnose leadership situations and select the most appropriate leader style for the situation.
- Constantly and tenaciously work at increasing both technical and interpersonal expertise and competence.
- Become inoculated to stress and capable of maintaining emotional equanimity during difficult situations; maintain focus without disturbance.
- Develop interpersonal skills and communication savvy; heighten emotional intelligence.
- Empower and praise always.
- Be an intentional model; lead by example.
- Take care of your people first.

PERSONALITY AND LEADERSHIP: SOME HELPFUL TRAITS

Although our premise here, and throughout this book, is that leaders are built, it is no secret that certain personality characteristics are positively correlated with a proclivity to seek out leadership roles and succeed. Those with specific personality traits appear to have an easier time becoming effective leaders. Personality traits are enduring trends or regularities in a person's behavior. Personality tends to be established early in life and remains remarkably consistent across time and context. In fact, the hallmark of a personality trait is that it is evident in most situations and interactions. Our demonstrated traits help our colleagues, loved ones, and subordinates very reliably predict our future behavior.

Research aimed at connecting personality and leadership reveals clearly that certain traits are *leadership-facilitative* while others are *leadership-inhibitive*. Still, this research shows that personality is only one ingredient in successful leadership. Possessing certain traits may simply make it more likely that a leader will take certain actions, behave in certain ways and, as a result, become more successful in the leader role. Below we highlight some of the most helpful personality traits for leaders—those we hope to find among our midshipmen at USNA—as well as those most likely to detract from excellent leadership.

DRIVE

Great leaders often exhibit a high need for achievement, an ambitious edge, and a tendency to compete in a variety of contexts. They are energetic and likely to take initiative in new situations. They are proactive and often described by others as tenacious, persistent, and likely to work hard at overcoming obstacles. This is true in all the services, but we've seen it firsthand in the Navy and Marine Corps. The goal of every naval officer should be to assume a position of command, to lead men and women in the fleet and, when required, into combat. After all, that is why USNA exists, to prepare leaders for command in combat. It takes hard work, stamina, dedication, and drive to become a commanding officer.

INTELLIGENCE

By intelligence, we do not mean simply IQ, but imagination, curiosity, and creative potential. Good leaders show a capacity to organize, synthesize, interpret, and strategically apply a range of data. They are also naturally curious and broad in their interests and intellectual explorations. Not surprisingly, USNA midshipmen are among the brightest potential leaders anywhere. Able to think on their feet, they are notorious for sharp wit and creativity. Consider the following real-life final exam answer written by a midshipman who had forgotten the material relevant to one question on the exam in his advanced leadership class, but who nonetheless wanted to offer the professor something interesting to read:

> Here's the thing, I'm suffering from this huge memory lapse on this one. I only recall parts of Maslow and pretty much none of Herzberg. So, even if I get zero points for this, I thought at least I could be somewhat entertaining and not leave the page blank. This even relates to leadership in some way....
>
> I'm not opposed to war. War may be a lot of things, but it is never a bad show. It's the original Greatest Show on Earth. But I realize not everyone feels this way, so I've come up with a couple of solutions. It's the least I could do.

My first idea was folk dancing. Nonstop, year-round folk dancing. It would be required that everybody in the world be dancing 24 hours a day. When it was offered that this might be impractical, I compromised and said half the world has to be dancing all the time. Of course this led to the distinct possibility that while half the world is folk dancing, the other half is robbing their homes. So I scaled it down. Now for 24 hours, one day a year, the world will be required to dance. Anything they want: rumba, minuet, mazurka, cakewalk, Peabody, mashed potato. Doesn't matter. Shut-ins, old, sick, they all dance. And if you're too sick to dance then you just die while the doctors and nurses are dancing. This is a good way to weed out the weak. It's natural selection with a beat! Not only that, but it will significantly reduce world violence because for the six months after the dance people will be too busy talking about what a great time they had. And for six moths after that they'll be too busy planning what to wear for next year's dance.

My other plan for peace is meeting the world through formal introductions. That's right; every person would meet every other person in the world, look him or her in the eye, shake their hand, repeat their name, and try to remember one outstanding physical characteristic. I figure it would be a lot harder to fight someone you already know: "Who? The Malaysians? Are you kidding?! I know those people!" Obviously the problem with this would be the logistics. How would you do it? Line the people of the world up single file and have the person at one end start moving down the line? Not to mention that babies would be born during the introductions and you'd have to meet them too. Also, due to the length of their names, some nationalities would move through the line more slowly than others. If you've ever bought an ID bracelet for a Russian, you know what I'm talking about. "Nikolai Aristolov Bartovski, meet Yevgeny Dimitri Smolovyebgeny. Yevgeny Dimitri Smolovyebgeny meet Nikolai Aristolov Bartovski." Major delay! On the other hand, the Chinese tend to have shorter names: "Chin Lu, Wu Han. Wu Han, Chin Lu." Bang! Done, moving along. Which explains why there are so many Chinese people. Less time saying hello. Just a couple of thoughts. Sorry I couldn't recall Maslow, although I thought this was more interesting and fun to write anyway.

LEADERSHIP MOTIVATION

It is easier to become a leader when one is strongly motivated to lead. Personality research confirms that those who prefer to influence others and are willing to exercise power over subordinates are best suited for leader roles. They are not afraid to seek power as a means of accomplishing goals. Persons who are more emotionally mature tend to use power for the community, not for self-aggrandizement. Of course USNA students are selected because they have been drawn to leadership in schools, athletics, and community organizations long before applying to the academy.

HONESTY AND INTEGRITY

In study after study, followers prefer leaders who are open, truthful, straightforward, and reliable. A given among USNA midshipmen, integrity is in many ways an absolute prerequisite for effective leadership. Naval Academy students understand that to lead men and women into combat, they must first demonstrate that they are worthy of trust; even a hint of incongruence or deceit can be fatal.

I (GPH) remember when I was stationed at the Anti-Submarine Warfare Operations Center in the Azores. We had responsibility for tracking Soviet submarines in the mid-Atlantic and I was in charge of these prosecutions. During one particular prosecution, we had two allied flight crews working with us and, at the time, they flew an old, slow airplane. It flew at about 150 knots but it could stay on-station a long time. I was on the mid-watch (1830-0630) and had briefed the crew to give me a call when they were about 100 miles away from where they were prosecuting the submarine on their way back to the Azores. This went against our established communications procedures, but if I didn't tell them to call and report, the following two P-3 missions would have no updated data and we would waste their flights. Well, they called when they got 100 miles away from the submarine and I was able to successfully update the P-3 missions. When I was getting off watch the next morning, one of the other officers conveyed the ominous news that the captain, my boss, had called and wanted to see me before I left. As I entered the captain's office I could sense that he was not happy. He asked me if anything unusual had happened on my watch. I couldn't think of anything unusual (I didn't think what I did with the crew was unusual at the time, only common sense) and said, "No sir." He then asked me if we had done anything different the previous night. The only thing I could think of was that I had told the crew to call me and I said to him, "Well, sir, I did have to break our communications policy last night." I then explained to him what had happened and why I had done what I did. He then informed me that his boss in Norfolk had called earlier and was quite upset—fearing my decision had compromised the prosecution. His final comment made a great impression on me concerning honesty and integrity. He looked at me and said, "Thanks for being honest and up front about breaking the rules and for what it's worth, I would have done the same thing myself."

SELF-CONFIDENCE

Again, we at USNA are spoiled when it comes to a student body at the high end of the continuum on this salient personality trait. Self-confident people are willing to effectively take control and guide others. Free of leadership-threatening hesitancy or self-doubt, they are calm, graceful under pressure, and confident enough to make a decision and move ahead. Self-confident people are not easily threatened and, for this reason, are seldom irrational, defensive, or impulsively angry. All things considered, you are likely to have an easier time leading others if you feel good about yourself and confident in your abilities. Any USNA instructor who has had a bright and self-assured midshipmen challenge him or her on a fact or perspective in class can vouch for the confidence among these future leaders.

Personality research on USNA midshipmen shows that, compared with the general population, our students are more extroverted (they direct their attention outward and receive energy from external events, experiences, and interactions) as opposed to introverted, and they tend to be more ambitious, intellectually curious, and sociable than the typical young person. However, this research also shows clearly that personality alone is a very poor predictor of successful graduation from the Naval Academy. That is, introverted, tender-hearted, and feeling-oriented students frequently succeed both at USNA and in the fleet as officers.

UNHELPFUL LEADER TRAITS

Just as some traits are facilitative of good leadership, so are other traits counterproductive or *inhibitive* when it comes to leading effectively. Sometimes called *dark-side* personality traits, they include:

- *Argumentativeness*—the leader is suspicious, defensive, and extremely sensitive to criticism.
- *Interpersonal insensitivity*—the leader is detached, aloof, and apparently unable to take the perspective of others or empathize with the plight of a subordinate.
- *Narcissism*—the leader is arrogant, self-absorbed, grandiose in self-appraisal, and prone to exploiting others for the purpose of self-aggrandizement.
- *Fear of failure*—the leader is paralyzed by fear of negative evaluation and subsequently refuses to take needed risks or try innovative strategies.
- *Perfectionism*—the classic compulsive, this person is bound by unreasonable demands for flawless performance in self and others and is often rigid and micromanaging.
- *Impulsivity*—this leader is focused on self-gratification at the expense of appropriate behavior, keeping commitments, and respecting boundaries and limits organizationally and interpersonally.

When we look at all the inhibitive traits listed above it reminds us of one of the videos we use in class to make the point about uphelpful leader traits. It's called *The Caine Mutiny* and it's a classic movie about the captain of the USS *Caine*, Captain Queeg, during World War II and his paranoid leadership style. Queeg exhibited many of the dark-side traits—ultimately leading to mutiny by several of his officers.

Although each of these personality characteristics can be corrosive to good leadership just as there is tremendous variability among those with positive personality features, so does the intensity and severity of dark-side traits vary widely. The perfectionist may be good natured and aware of his or her compulsive side, or may lack insight altogether and rule with an angry, fearful determination to avoid even the smallest mistake. At USNA, midshipmen personalities vary widely. Rarely will a person with severe personality problems perform well enough in high school to gain admission.

The vast majority of future officers at Navy possess a unique mix of positive and less positive personality features. Rather than limiting where they can finish as leaders, these traits merely define where they begin the process of learning to lead. Tenacity, intelligence, experience, and training will become the other key ingredients in creating top-notch leaders.

THE GOUGE

So, what's the gouge for Chapter 1? We do not believe that leaders are born, nor do we believe that good leadership comes only from common sense or that leadership can only be learned in the school of "hard knocks." At the Academy, our leadership curriculum is built on the premise that leaders can be taught how to lead. At USNA, we accomplish this not only in the classroom, but in the leadership laboratory called Bancroft Hall with its midshipmen leadership organization. We accomplish leadership training during summer cruises with the fleet where midshipmen see examples of Naval/Marine Corps leadership in action. Midshipmen learn leadership firsthand during plebe summer by being both followers as plebes and leaders as upperclassmen. Midshipmen learn leadership through athletics and team play. Most importantly, midshipmen learn leadership from the examples offered by officers, coaches, and faculty assigned to the Naval Academy.

The Naval Academy has been teaching leadership for over 158 years and the proof of its effectiveness is in the quality leaders it has produced. The balance of this book rests on the firm premise that leadership can be developed. At Annapolis, it happens every day.

2

TAKING OATHS AND MAKING COMMITMENTS

Imagine that you are a USNA plebe—a first-year midshipman—who has just arrived for Induction Day (I-Day) in Annapolis. Graduated from high school for only two or three weeks, your parents have (probably tearfully) deposited you at Alumni Hall on the Academy grounds some time just after the crack of dawn. Of course, you didn't get any sleep the night before and couldn't put anything in your stomach I-Day morning—perhaps a glass of water or orange juice if you were lucky.

Like everyone else standing in line outside Alumni Hall that morning, you worked like crazy to secure an appointment to USNA. Now, standing in line with 1200 of your new best friends, you wonder what you've gotten yourself into. Walking into Alumni Hall I-Day morning is like walking into the middle of a hurricane. About one minute after sitting in the barber's chair, you lose all your hair (or if you're a woman it's cut very short), you are given a duffle bag and start filling it with various uniforms and essential equipment, you get poked, prodded, and immunized with what seems like dozens of shots, and most importantly, you begin the process of "training" by squared-away upperclass midshipmen. At first they seem nice enough, but once they get you out of Alumni Hall and away from your family, a strange metamorphosis occurs. Previously mild-mannered detailers become crazed drill sergeants.

You will quickly begin to question your own sanity. What were you thinking when you signed up for this? Courtesy of your committed trainers, you will immediately learn to stand at attention, keep your eyes "in the boat" (focused straight ahead), "brace up" (chin tucked into your neck at attention until it makes your neck sore), and respond appropriately when asked a question. There are only four responses a new plebe needs to know ("Yes sir/ma'am"; "No sir/ma'am"; "No excuse sir/ma'am"; and "I'll find out sir/ma'am"). The upperclassmen don't want to hear anything else. You're a plebe now and plebes don't have opinions. They certainly don't speak what's on their minds.

Within the first hour you learn how to render a salute, count cadence, and march as a member of a military squad. After leaving Alumni Hall you are marched to Mother "B" (Bancroft Hall) and your company area, meet your new roommates, and begin to stow all your new gear. You will get a demonstration on how to fold everything you own from skivvies to socks. You are amazed that you are expected to fold your socks into precise blocks and that your underwear must be stowed in a square stack. Everything in your closet must be lined up in a very precise order as well as your shoes. Your civilian clothes are put into a box and you are told to get into your "white works," the classic uniform denoting plebe status. You are hot, sticky, sweating profusely, and your new white works feel like they are made out of heated canvas—only making matters worse on a hot, humid, mid-Atlantic day.

During any short breaks in this first arduous training day, you will be required to memorize essential facts and figures bearing on naval history, officership, and the structure of USNA from the "Plebe Bible" called *Reef Points*. From the moment you are given *Reef Points* it will never be out of your possession. On I-day most plebes can be seen standing at attention holding their *Reef Points* directly out in front of them memorizing Navy facts. At times during this first day you will feel exhausted and overwhelmed. You may have doubts about your capacity to endure and concerns that you are an imposter who will soon be discovered as incapable of handling the rigors of life at USNA.

As the afternoon of this first day winds to a close, your entire class (all of you now looking like white-washed deer in the headlights) will be solemnly marched into the expansive stone courtyard fronting Bancroft

Hall—your residence for the next four years. The courtyard is surrounded by thousands of people—parents and family members—who have come to watch the final public event of I-Day, administration of the oath of office. To your great relief, your class will be marched to rows of folding chairs and you will be allowed to sit at long last. The sensation will be luxurious.

After the day you just went through, it's hard to avoid the temptation to just fall asleep right there in a gray folding chair, but the sight is impressive: twelve hundred of the nation's brightest high school graduates from all 50 states and U. S. territories, and several foreign countries, now looking remarkably transformed, like impossibly young officers of the Navy. It becomes evident at once that this is a solemn occasion, one dripping with meaning and consequence. After a few welcoming comments from the Superintendent (always a three-star admiral), the newest USNA class is called to its feet. Warning students that the oath about to be taken is sacred and thoroughly binding, the Superintendent will then ask each of you to raise your right hand.

Standing in historic Bancroft court with your family and thousands of additional witnesses looking on in reverent silence, you take the following oath:

> I, _____, having been appointed a midshipman in the United States Navy, do solemnly swear (or affirm) that I will support and defend the Constitution of the United States against all enemies foreign and domestic; that I will bear true faith and allegiance to the same; that I take this obligation freely, without any mental reservation or purpose of evasion; and that I will well and faithfully discharge the duties of the office on which I am about to enter, so help me God.

You may be surprised at your own visceral reaction to this event. For many young plebes, this is the first oath ever taken. It is solemn and meaningful. Imbued with a powerful symbolism, the midshipman oath of office casts one's military obligations into full view. Freely taken, these obligations place the new midshipman in the service of the people of the United States and under the direct command of the president. The oath of office will be affirmed both in writing and in word on several occasions during the journey through USNA and every time you are promoted throughout your subsequent military career. The oath of office is nothing short of a full commitment. Upon taking the oath, the midshipman is irrevocably committed to defending and protecting the Constitution, the country, and its citizens.

COMMITMENT AS A WAY OF LIFE

So what's so important about taking oaths and making commitments? Wouldn't these young men and women be just as successful at USNA and beyond without the oath? And aren't we just making a lot of a silly tradition? We are convinced that one of the palpable problems with business today is lack of organizational commitment. Employees come and go in the blink of an eye—constantly lured on by more pay or extra enticements. Sometimes young leaders are committed to excellent performance, but too often this is really a commitment to self—a commitment to look good at all costs in hopes of garnering attention and securing further promotions or external offers.

Over two centuries, the Navy has discovered a secret about commitment that modern day business would do well to take seriously. To keep your best and brightest young leaders, make the organization part of them; find ways to help them personally identify with the organization and its mission.

This deliberate process of identity formation is a cornerstone of life at USNA. Midshipmen wear uniforms and insignia of the naval profession. They are introduced to the long legacy of heroism and service rendered by their predecessors. As they walk the halls of various USNA buildings named after famous naval and marine heroes, they pass photos, plaques, monuments, and statues rendering the images of midshipmen who have gone on to become president, congressmen, and medal-of-honor recipients. These experiences will become part of the fabric of the young naval officer's psyche.

Although certain of these rituals may sound quaint to the civilian observer, they create powerful and emotionally charged memories for those who pass through them. Researchers refer to these as *flashbulb memories*. These are extremely vivid and long-lasting memories—typically related to very distinctive, unexpected, and strongly emotional events. Life at the

Naval Academy is rife with flashbulb experiences. Most of them result in good memories, things the midshipman goes on to cherish.

Of course, most modern day organizations do relatively little to foster and ritualize organizational commitment at this level. Few CEOs take time to consider strategies for helping their young leaders bond effectively to the company. Compensation packages are fattened while spiritual/emotional connections are ignored. It has always been true that bright young people thirst for meaning in vocation; they want to feel connected and committed to something important and enduring, something noble.

After the Iraq war started, I (GPH) was discussing events one day with my class when one of my students made a statement that struck to the heart of the significance of commitment. He said that watching the war on television and seeing the responsibility of command unfold in front of him was intimidating. The thing that struck him most was that while he was watching the news, a reporter showed a young Marine 1st Lieutenant who was calling all the shots. He called for more firepower, brought in tanks, and radioed for close air support. The midshipman (who planned to go Marine Corps) said it was then that he realized that one day marines would be relying on him to lead them into battle, keep them safe, and complete the mission. He said he had to rededicate his time remaining at the Academy so he could learn how to become a better leader—one who would make the right decisions during the worst of times. He truly saw his calling as something enduring, something noble.

At USNA, midshipmen are deliberately welcomed into the proud community of naval service. At each juncture in their journey through the Academy, they are officially and publicly invited, welcomed, and approved. In fact, at each of the most momentous of these milestones, the entire community stops, takes note, and honors the accomplishments of these young men and women. On Induction Day, the Herndon Climb, the Ring Dance (where they finally get to wear their class rings), and Commencement, the community halts and pays homage. Midshipmen come to feel a strong attachment to the USNA mission. They sense that they are part of something much larger than themselves, something infinitely honorable. It is not uncommon for USNA alumni to refer to current midshipmen as "standing the watch," or as being "on patrol"—a reference to the fact that naval service is both an honor and an obligation and that naval officers throughout history have taken their turn shouldering the burden of defending our nation.

For this reason, the phrase "I stand relieved" is used at change-of-command and retirement ceremonies to emphasize the lifting of the sworn responsibility of service and command. Sometimes, that phrase is extremely difficult to utter. I (GPH) remember at my own change of command, when my executive officer said, "I relieve you, Sir," I didn't want to hear it. I don't think any Commanding Officer who is being relieved wants to hear those words. However, there are other naval officers and midshipmen waiting their turns to do their duty and assume positions of command, and they have to be given that opportunity. So, "stand relieved" you are.

The lesson for those invested in creating loyal and emotionally attached organizational leaders is this: Find ways to help your young talent identify with the company. How can you make them feel invited and endorsed? How can you instill a sense of purpose and noble mission? What rituals, ceremonies, and traditions might be employed to help celebrate and honor commitment and service?

I (GPH) know one submarine commander who had a unique way of accomplishing this. Whenever a sailor on his boat got an award or advanced to a higher rank, he would have the command master chief read a citation from a World War II submarine hero during the ceremony. He was connecting that young sailor to an age of courage, heroism, and valor in the submarine fleet, making him feel a part of an honored and brave tradition.

WHY COMMITMENT MUST BE INTRINSIC

At Navy, we are careful to build intrinsic or internal motivation for service to country. And this is not a difficult task. Our students are often internally driven by a sense of service and patriotic obligation, especially after 9/11. These flames are usually ignited before they arrive in Annapolis. Our job is to fan them and provide plenty of fuel. But we are careful never to apply extrinsic rewards (e.g., monetary incentives or extra benefits) to a midshipman's internally driven commitment.

A fascinating strand of behavioral science research shows that when people are financially (extrinsically) rewarded for activities or commitments that provide intrinsic satisfaction, they paradoxically begin to take less pleasure in them. So, when people who love to paint are suddenly paid to do it, intrinsic joy and pleasure in the painting diminish; what was a source of delight becomes mundane and obligatory. Far too often, business leaders assume that only extrinsic incentives will heighten performance and commitment. To this we say, "Fooey."

Consider the spartan conditions in Bancroft Hall where 4000 midshipmen languish in the mid-Atlantic summer heat and humidity without air conditioning. Or consider the work tempo of the typical Navy ship or submarine where our graduates toil in rough and sleep-deprived circumstances for months on end. And consider the comparatively low salaries our officers enjoy in comparison to their civilian managerial counterparts. Are extrinsic rewards critical to the abiding commitment of these men and women? No way.

I (GPH) remember a particular time in the Azores when we were prosecuting three submarines over a six-month period. The entire command was on port and starboard 12-hour shifts, seven days a week for six months, and we didn't get overtime. But it was very satisfying knowing we were doing our jobs well and keeping our country safe. We found meaning in the work, if not more money.

At USNA, we foster intrinsic motivation. Yes, we meet our students' basic needs and even cover all expenses associated with their education, but we generally offer nothing more than praise and recognition for the kind of commitment and loyalty these officers-in-training exhibit. Midshipmen harbor a sense of meaning and purpose about their work that most businesses seldom seem to conjure up from employees. Midshipmen understand that they are part of something important, something larger than themselves. This understanding allows them to make considerable sacrifice en route to becoming Navy and Marine Corps officers.

When I (GPH) was a 2/C midshipman, I recall another experience that galvanized my commitment to the naval service. Apollo 13 Astronaut and USNA alum, James Lovell, addressed the brigade of midshipmen a little more than a month after he returned from aboard the ill-fated Apollo 13 flight. He gave a firsthand account of the explosion onboard, the sorrow of passing around the moon without landing, about their daring repairs, and the frightening descent wondering if their heat shield would keep them from burning up. When he described telling his crew, just prior to entry, that no matter what happened, it had been a pleasure serving with them, it sent chills down every midshipman's spine. It made me feel not only proud but challenged. Challenged to meet his expectations and follow this shipmate's example. It made me proud to be a midshipman.

THE PARADOX OF DOING DIFFICULT THINGS

Interestingly, the degree of sacrifice required merely to graduate from USNA often makes attainment of this goal deeply meaningful to alumni. Research confirms that a goal is much more highly esteemed if it is difficult to achieve. It comes as no surprise then to discover that after the intense demands, the bonding rituals, and the profound internal commitment required to be graduated from USNA, our alumni are among the most fervently committed and eternally connected graduates anywhere in the country.

The class of 1971 is a prime example. During our plebe year there was one company in the Brigade that was more demanding and merciless on its plebes than any other company. Plebes from other companies would deliberately go up or down two flights of stairs to avoid having to pass through that company area because any plebe was fair game for scrutiny and torment. As legend went, a few that did pass through never returned. In fact, of the 40 or so plebes that started plebe summer, 12 survived the ordeal and made it to the end of plebe year. Although that kind of attrition is no longer considered evidence of good training, back in 1967 and 1968 it was much more accepted. It was considered a rite of passage to endure a scarcely manageable plebe year, as any class will tell you. Those 12 survivors named themselves the "Dirty Dozen" and through the years became somewhat infamous in our class. At our 30th reunion, the Dirty Dozen were reunited and had a great time. But that Dirty Dozen bond, along with the bonds of the members of our class as a whole, remain extremely strong.

It is a paradox of sorts that the harder one must work to achieve membership in a group, the more thoroughly one will own and cherish it. Similarly, when we sacrifice or suffer for a cause or commitment, the suffering appears to intensify our allegiance. It is this phenomenon that has sustained USNA prisoners of war through unbearable torture and everyday naval officers through the trying circumstances of long deployments and exhausting operational schedules.

The questions for leaders are these: "Can you help your people find meaning in the midst of adversity?" "How can suffering be reframed as a challenge?" And "How can adverse circumstances lead to heightened commitment from junior talent?" Here is a lesson learned well at USNA: If you want your new leaders to be deeply committed to the organization, make entrance difficult and dependent on some hard work and meaningful sacrifice.

COMMITMENT THRIVES WHEN NEEDS ARE MET

The famous military recruiting slogan "Be all that you can be" highlights one foundational belief at Navy. One of our premier missions is to create the right conditions in which young leaders can maximize potential and achieve remarkable things. Study after study supports the notion that when organizations address employee needs for achievement, creativity, and growth, these employees are more satisfied and loyal in the long term. In other words, to heighten commitment in your organization, you had better consider more than financial needs.

Nearly half a century ago, psychologist Abraham Maslow proposed that too few people ever have the opportunity to do as the Army commercial suggests; they do not become all that they could become. Maslow proposed his now famous *hierarchy of needs* and suggested that people must have basic needs satisfied (biological needs, needs for security, and needs for belongingness) before they can become motivated by higher-order needs such as esteem and self-actualization.

At USNA, midshipmen are constantly nourished biologically, and they exist within the secure walls of the Academy and under the watchful eyes of round-the-clock Marine sentries. Belongingness needs are met at a level rarely found in a civilian college. From the day midshipmen take the oath of office, they enjoy the camaraderie and instant loyalty of over 1000 "shipmates" and peers in their classes and companies. More than classmates, these fellow midshipmen are thoroughly committed to protecting and assisting one another to succeed. Midshipmen quickly learn that success only comes when units work together.

Needs for esteem are addressed as midshipmen find success in academics, military performance, and athletics. Some midshipmen receive special recognition for performance in these areas or for volunteerism, leadership excellence, musical or theatrical performance, or independent research. Esteem needs are further met through association with an institution and a group of peers that make the midshipmen proud and grateful.

With these preliminary needs addressed, midshipmen are encouraged to explore dreams, think creatively, and consider where their own careers and life paths will take them. Yes, they will all become military officers, but how will they serve? What contribution will they make and how will they employ their unique talents and interests both to enhance the Navy or Marine Corps and to become the people they were intended to be? They are free to become self-actualized. And when a person can become self-actualized, he or she is considerably more likely to be a loyal and committed organizational member. Too few organizations work at explicitly addressing needs of belonging and esteem and, subsequently, too few employees are encouraged to explore their own unique gifts and aspirations.

A prime example of this occurred during the Vietnam War. During that time in the Rotunda in Bancroft Hall, there was a large display of photographs of Academy graduates who were killed or missing-in-action in Southeast Asia. After the child of a POW dined in King Hall in the fall of 1970, two members of the Class of 1972, Joe Glover and Rick Rubel, decided to help out the children of other POWs and started a campaign to raise money to buy them Academy sweatshirts as Christmas presents. They raised over $5000, and over Christmas distributed the presents to the children. This got Glover and Rubel more interested in promoting attention to the POWs, so Glover contacted Ross Perot, an Academy alumnus.

Together, the three of them started a letter-writing campaign to inform citizens of the POWs' plight, to show the North Vietnamese that Americans cared about their POWs, and to encourage them to follow the Geneva Convention concerning POWs. A POW exhibit was set up in Smoke Hall and the letters that were received were placed on display in the exhibit. Tens of thousands of letters were received. At the Army-Navy game, the

Secretary of the Navy, John Warner, arranged a half-time ceremony in which a mail truck delivered the letters to midfield as millions on television watched. The letters were presented to wives of the POWs and were later airlifted to North Vietnam. Although it didn't directly result in the release of the POWs, Glover and Rubel did something that was meaningful to them, to the POWs, and to their wives.

Not only do we consider the motivational needs of midshipmen when helping them to form a commitment to the Navy and to the mission the Navy serves, we also teach our graduates to lead with the motivation of subordinates in mind. Excellent leaders consciously diagnose the location a follower occupies on the need hierarchy. The reason is simple. Unless lower-level needs are satisfied, a follower cannot successfully achieve the kind of growth and development likely to further the organizational mission.

Perhaps the best example of the *need-conscious* leadership we are referring to comes from a scene in the civil war movie *Gettysburg*. Prior to the battle, Colonel Chamberlin, commander of a regiment from Maine, is tasked with guarding an entire company of Union soldiers who were also from Maine. These were soldiers who had seen more than their share of combat, taken heavy losses, and become demoralized. They had effectively gone AWOL and Chamberlin was to treat them as treasonous prisoners. Just as he was presented with the mutinous company, members of which he was told he could shoot if he wanted to; a messenger arrived and gave him orders to move his men along a ridge at Little Round Top and take up position. Chamberlin was thrust into a dilemma regarding how to handle this mutinous group of soldiers. He offered them a hot meal and then decided to talk to them.

In the speech, he informed them that he was given permission to shoot them if he wanted to, but assured them that he wouldn't do that (safety needs). He allowed them to finish their meals because they had not been fed in quite some time (biological needs). Then he told them about their great opportunity. He sympathized with their losses but reminded them of the great act of love they were undertaking (esteem). He told them that they were in a unique Army, an Army that was not fighting for land, for women, or for material gain, but for a noble cause—to set a people free. Their cause was one of the most noble (self-actualization) that any army in history had undertaken.

He went on to praise their dedication and courage and remind them that his men were also from Maine (belonginess), and that they had a lot in common. He invited them to join his unit, which they did. The Maine regiment went on to save the day at Gettysburg. Chamberlin was awarded the Medal of Honor for his valorous conduct that day.

CREATING A CLIMATE OF COMMITMENT

When it comes to building committed leaders, nothing may be as important as creating an organizational climate that fosters commitment-making. Most young men and women enter military service prepared to believe and follow. They are impressionable and seeking models to emulate. Unless leaders destroy trust through exploitation of power, coercion, or lying, young people are typically willing to trust and commit.

Jonathan Shay, a popular leadership expert and business consultant, describes the centrality of trust in organizational commitment as *vertical cohesion*. Vertical cohesion or cohesion between followers and leaders emanates directly from trust in immediate leaders. Shay suggests that trust and cohesion in the workplace are a direct result of the leader's competence, consideration, and moral integrity as he or she deploys institutional power.

Vertical cohesion is rooted in trust and contributes more than any other factor to the command climate—a military unit's atmosphere of support, confidence, and cohesion. Not only do subordinates watch a leader's behaviors and example in interactions with followers, cohesion and climate are also heavily dictated by the leader's interactions with other leaders. In the Navy, when senior officers treat one another with dignity and integrity, they help to induce a climate of social trust. These officers help subordinates to become bonded and committed to the organization. In the same way that children feel "safe" with respectful parents, new members are heartened and emboldened by leaders who demonstrate congruence and integrity in all of their relationships—personal and professional.

At USNA, we have learned that the golden rule is central to creating a culture of commitment. That is, to build loyal and committed leaders it is important to be loyal and committed to them first. Stephen Covey might refer to USNA faculty and staff as *inside-out* leaders in the sense that they are typically men and women with a habit of making and keeping promises to themselves and others. They see themselves as stewards of our nation's most precious resource—its most gifted young men and women. They recognize the need to use these resources for positive purposes and fully expect to be held accountable. One of the essential ingredients in helping midshipmen to learn to commit is first to commit to them.

Many faculty members at USNA have signs on their doors or decorating the walls of their offices that say something like this: "Midshipmen are not an interruption. Midshipmen are my reason for being here today." And they mean it. For the past several years, the prestigious *Princeton Review* ranking of American colleges and universities has listed the Naval Academy in the top 10—and typically in the top 1 to 5—of more than 350 schools in the category of faculty availability. At USNA, faculty have three overarching objectives: admit top quality candidates, put them through an arduous course of study and training aimed at producing combat leaders, and, above all, help each one of them get to the finish line. This commitment means class sizes of 20 or fewer, frequent one-to-one interaction with officers and civilian faculty, extra instruction whenever a midshipman is struggling with material, and genuine personal concern expressed by both faculty and senior midshipmen leaders.

THE GOUGE

Oaths and commitment are important. To retain, motivate, and challenge your best and brightest young leaders, you must make them feel not only part of the organization, but part of something larger than themselves. Whether that comes from tradition, rituals, or an oath, an organization must make young leaders feel that they have become part of the fabric of an organization. They must feel that they are inheritors of something good and noble, something to be treasured. Through commitment you will create loyalty, unleash talent, and provide intrinsic satisfaction.

But commitment is rarely achieved through financial means. It comes through instilling a sense of meaning and purpose about the work itself. These ingredients allow young leaders to make considerable sacrifices en route to attaining their goals, and this sacrifice heightens commitment. At Navy, the oath of office introduces midshipmen to something beyond themselves. It offers a meaningful mission to which they can firmly commit. Although not all graduates will serve for an entire naval career, on Induction Day, they will make a commitment to a mission and a vision of service that typically lasts a lifetime.

3

FOLLOW FIRST

If the Navy's ships close swiftly upon enemy positions, its submarines prowl undetected, and its aircraft project power with efficiency and surprise. It is safe to say that excellent followership is a primary reason why. No organization succeeds without outstanding followers and no one rises to lead effectively without first learning to follow.

Because every leader in the Navy is also subordinate to the commander-in-chief, every leader in the Navy must practice followership. In the Navy, we call this following the *chain of command*. Every naval and marine officer is both a follower and a leader at the same time. Every officer at one time or another will be in charge of a branch, platoon, division, department, and, if they show the "right stuff," will become the commander of a battalion, ship, squadron, or submarine. But that officer always reports to someone senior. Throughout this whole process, one thing becomes perfectly clear—those officers who advance have learned how to follow effectively. Even if an officer rises to the top and becomes the Chief of Naval Operations, he or she still has someone to report to.

Although an outstanding followership plays an essential role in an organization's success or failure, it is quite common for both organizational members and outside observers to erroneously attribute success or failure exclusively to the executive savvy of a single leader. It is easy to become obsessed with leader traits and behaviors. We are tempted to attribute unusual talent to leaders who succeed, just as we are tempted to attribute malignancy or inadequacy to the character and personality of the leader when an organization underachieves. The obvious problem with this view is that quality of subordinate behavior ("followership") often has as much, if not more, to do with an organization's ultimate success or failure.

WHEN "FOLLOWERSHIP" FAILS

Nowhere is "followership" more important than on naval vessels at sea. When I (WBJ) was a lieutenant stationed at Pearl Harbor, one of the ships, an oiler, became notorious for a series of embarrassing mishaps. This ship carried a complement of competent officers and enlisted crew; she had all the capabilities of other oilers in the fleet; and her commanding officers (coming and going in rapid succession as each was fired) were well-trained ship handlers. Nonetheless, the ship accidentally managed to ram a tugboat into the pier and sink it. Just off the coast of Hawaii, the ship's anchor was dropped too quickly, snapped off, and sank to the bottom, necessitating an expensive salvage operation. Entering the harbor one fateful day and heavily loaded with fuel, the ship maneuvered too close to a sand bar and ran aground. Coming out of dry dock with brand new engines, the ship's leaders ignored warnings about a lubrication problem. Hoping to avoid a time-consuming repair, the crew kept the ship at sea. The engines burned up, an even more costly repair period ensued, and the "Ramit," as the ship was now known by crews from other ships around the harbor, lost yet another commanding officer.

So what was wrong with the "Ramit"? What is the probability that the performance woes of this ship were exclusively—or even primarily— the result of a string of incompetent commanding officers? The Navy brass at Pearl Harbor seemed convinced this was the case. Thus, after each new embarrassment, the ship's CO was promptly (and often in humiliating fashion) relieved of command. In the eyes of top leaders, performance failures were always directly linked to leadership failures. But there is a problem with this reasoning. Quite often, "leadership failures" are actually failures by subordinates; disengaged, inadequate, or sabotaging followers can indeed sink ships (and commanding officers it seems). Leaders can fail grandly when followers resist directives, fail to share the leader's vision, or refuse to do the work required for mission accomplishment.

I (GPH) saw this play out tragically in one of my fellow P-3 squadrons on the West Coast. A young, very popular pilot couldn't seem to play by the rules. He regarded the chain of command with disdain and ignored essential protocol. He consistently broke flight rules, acted without regard to numerous regulations in the Navy's flight manual, and even took his father flying in his aircraft without permission.

Unfortunately, this behavior remained unknown to the commanding officer. Trusting the pilot's judgment, the CO gave the pilot's crew a great assignment to fly to an air show in the south Pacific and drop some Navy parachutists over a beautiful bay as a public relations gesture. After he dropped the parachutists, and contrary to his instructions, the pilot maneuvered his aircraft around the bay to watch the parachutists and fly over them. What he didn't know was that there was a tramline running from a hotel on the beach to a mountain across the bay. Unwittingly, his plane hit the line and the tail was completely severed from the aircraft. The plane crashed into the hotel and he and his crew were lost.

During the subsequent investigation, it became apparent that numerous people in the squadron knew the pilot had consistently broken rules, yet no one had ever said anything to the commanding officer about it. Of course, the CO was responsible for what went on in his command and suffered the consequences. Had he known, he most certainly would have taken swift, corrective action. This young lieutenant was a poor follower, and in this case (and others like it), he paid for it with his life and his crew's. This is one of the lessons we try to impress firmly upon midshipmen: You had damn well better learn how to follow if you want to lead.

NOT EVEN THE BEST COMMANDING OFFICER GOES TO SEA ALONE

A Navy ship or submarine is an astonishingly complicated piece of equipment. Typically requiring several hundred men and women, all thoroughly trained for their jobs and all giving 100 percent of their attention to the details of the mission, these monstrous war machines cannot possibly be maneuvered away from the pier, let alone used effectively in combat, without full participation from the crew. At the very least, common sense and experience suggest that leaders and followers always share in the ultimate responsibility for a unit's success or failure.

As a psychologist stationed at the medical clinic a few blocks from the "Ramit's" pier, it came as no surprise to me that the frequency of mental health visits from the ship's crew far exceeded those of other ships in the harbor. Morale on board during those years was horrendous. Enlisted sailors applied for transfer or discharge in droves. Alcohol-related incidents and other behavior problems were rampant. The picture was clear that from the lowliest seaman recruit to the commissioned officers, the crew was failing to get the job done. Yes, the commanding officers made some mistakes, but they had very little to work with. Without the active support of loyal followers, it is quite likely that these COs were doomed from the start.

THE USNA PLEBE: FOLLOWING TO LEAD

At USNA, midshipmen must prove themselves impeccable followers before they are trusted to lead. In fact, the entire plebe year might reasonably be called a crucible of followership. Plebes learn to follow orders precisely and thoroughly. They learn to attend to the details when given a mission. Officers and upperclassmen develop the plan of the day (POD); plebes sweat the details and make it happen. Those who cannot follow seamlessly and loyally do not survive plebe year. We've already talked about learning *rates* (naval history and technical data that all midshipmen are required to have memorized) from *Reef Points*, but there's another quite unique ritual plebes must undergo for the entire year, and this is called the "chow call."

Chow calls are another method used to enhance the followership training in Bancroft Hall. The scenario goes something like this. Exactly 10 minutes before each meal formation, plebes are required to recite from memory the following:

Sir/Ma'am, you now have 10 minutes to evening/morning/noon meal formation. The uniform for evening meal is Tropical Whites. The menu for evening meal is tossed green salad, grilled New

York steak, mashed potatoes and gravy, sautéed vegetables, bread, milk, and butter. For dessert, Apple Brown Betty. The Officers of the Watch are: The Officer of the Watch is Lieutenant Thompson. The Assistant Officer of the Watch is Lieutenant Lee. The Midshipman Officer of the Watch is Midshipman First Class Pera. The movie in the yard is "Crimson Tide." There are now 66 days until Army, 79 days until Christmas leave, and 167 days until graduation. Sir/Ma'am, you now have 10 minutes.

Five minutes before formation the call is repeated again, and finally at two minutes before the appointed time for formation, the plebes shout:

Sir/Ma'am, you now have 2 minutes before evening meal formation. Time, tide and formation wait for no one. I am now shoving off. You have one minute Sir/Ma'am!

After this final call the plebes go rushing off to get to formation on time. It is a ritual that goes on every day, in every company area, all year long. As soon as that particular "chow call" is over, the plebes are immediately responsible for knowing the menu for the next three meals. The plebes who cannot master this ritual usually have trouble in other areas. Former President Jimmy Carter put it this way:

The memories of my years at the Naval Academy remain especially vivid. Plebe Year in my day was quite severe, to put it mildly. I became highly proficient on a commando course, could easily do 94 push-ups—that's twice my class of '47—and set some speed records in changing uniforms inside a cruise box. We never ate a peaceful meal. There were constant questions, research, songs, poems, reports, and recitations. I must say this turned out to be good preparation for service in elected office.

The year of followership at USNA is so significant that its ending is marked by one of the most storied traditions at the Academy: the charge of 1000. On the first day of commencement week each spring, a cannon blast signals the start of the Herndon climb, also known as the plebe recognition ceremony, to 1000 or more anxious plebes. Having been cordoned off near Bancroft Hall awaiting the final task of their plebe year, these eager midshipmen sprint across campus and quickly encircle the 21-foot gray monument known as Herndon.

Their task seems easy enough: Remove a plebe Dixie-cup hat that has been affixed to the top of the monument and replace it with an upper-classmen's hat. These are largely engineering students. A simple human pyramid comprised of about four levels of students standing on shoulders should allow one of them to reach the top. Easy, right? Only one problem, the thoughtful upperclassmen have applied roughly 200 pounds of pure lard to the monument, making it nearly impossible to touch without slipping, let alone climb, and the upperclass have taped the cap solidly to the top of the monument. Additionally, as the plebes begin the climb they are hosed down with water, making the ground around Herndon a muddy trench.

As bodies crush in around the monument and the first waves of climbing midshipmen slide off the monument and tumble onto shipmates below, it quickly becomes clear why this final plebe class effort requires large doses of teamwork, tenacity, and courage to complete. Although the record is three minutes (1962) and the longest recorded climb was four hours, five minutes (1995), most classes require about two hours of well-orchestrated effort to get the job done. When the upperclassmen's cap finally rests atop the monument, the class erupts in celebration. Plebe year is over. These followers must now assume roles of increasing leadership in the brigade and, eventually, in the fleet.

FOLLOWERS IN THE FLEET: WHAT EXCELLENT JUNIOR OFFICERS DO

At Navy, we prepare commissioned officers for combat leadership in the fleet and Marine Corps. But we understand that our graduates will be judged on the basis of their followership first. Any commanding officer will tell you that competent, innovative, and deeply loyal junior officers can make life in command both thoroughly satisfying and delightfully successful. Look at the high-performing units in the Navy and you will typically find great leadership coupled with smart and dedicated followership.

A study of the distinguishing characteristics of junior officers on board the Navy's top-performing ships revealed some interesting trends in the behavior and personality of these excellent followers. In comparison to junior officers aboard average or low-performing ships, junior officers on the most successful ships were significantly more likely to:

- *Work as a cohesive unit.* Excellent followers work as a team. They have more interaction and more positive expectations of one another.
- *Support top leadership.* These officers were loyal to the captain. They were enthusiastic supporters of their captain's policies and directives and they never allowed enlisted personnel to sense division among officers or lack of advocacy for the captain's orders. In other words, these excellent followers were *congruent.*
- *Raise concerns with leaders.* Outstanding followers in the fleet did not hesitate to raise questions and concerns with their commanding officers. They brought bad news to the CO and pointed out shortcomings of the captain's plan-of-the-day or plans for battle before problems could result in failure. But they never voiced criticism in front of the crew.
- *Take initiative.* Junior officers on board top-flight ships are self-starters and hard-chargers. Always searching for ways to enhance the ship's readiness for action, they took action when a need or problem was discovered. They didn't wait to be told.
- *Take responsibility for team performance.* Excellent followers own a pervasive sense of responsibility for the ultimate success or failure of the ship's mission. Unlike the more passive or disengaged junior officers on ships that repeatedly fail to compete for performance prizes, these officers felt personally responsible for their unit's ultimate success.

This survey of junior officers on the nation's best-performing Navy vessels reveals a good deal about what it takes to follow well. Although each of these officers—many of whom are USNA graduates—are also leading large numbers of enlisted personnel, the hallmark of their leadership is their continued proclivity to follow superbly. They understand that in order for the ship to do its job in the most demanding of circumstances, combat at sea, they must be proactive, committed, and loyal to the commanding officer. Paradoxically, in serving the commanding officer well, these officers are models of follower excellence for their own subordinates. Effective followers are more likely to create good followers in their own people.

THE "DAMN EXEC"

In our plebe leadership textbook, we have a reading called "Damn Exec." The story is about a captain who came to his ship one morning and noticed that one of his sailors standing sentry duty wore a foul weather jacket that was faded, frayed, dirty, and spotted with red lead. Later that morning when the captain was going over some charts with the ship's executive officer, he mentioned the sailor's attire and told the XO that from now on he'd like to see his sentries wear the traditional navy peacoat when it was cold outside. The XO said "Aye, aye" and went to find the senior watch officer to pass along the CO's wishes. Rather than pass along the order as the captain's, the XO passed along the order as his own. When the senior watch officer departed, the order was passed as the XO's, not as his own, and it blossomed into complaints about not only wearing peacoats, but shining the brass work throughout the ship and numerous other onerous tasks. Of course, to the crew all of this extra work was the result of the "Damn Exec" (XO) or that's how it was passed down. Toward the end of the day, the Captain overheard some of his seamen talking about the "Damn Exec" and he was extremely surprised. Concerned, the CO called all of his officers into the wardroom and said:

> Gentlemen...,whether you're cleaning boilers, standing bridge watch, or administering a training program, it's easy to say, "The Exec wants, or the Exec says." That's not the way it should be. You can sometimes discuss or even argue with an order, but when you give it to a subordinate make them think it's coming from you. Giving lazy orders is like a drug. Once you start doing it, you will find yourself doing it more and more until you can't get a thing done any other way. Your people will pass along orders that way, too, and it will become part of your organization right down to the lowest level. When some problem arises you will get, "Who wants this?" or "Why should we?" Now ask yourself if that order really originated with the person who gave it to you, or did he receive it from someone higher? We never really know do we? But why should we even care? Let's push the "Damn Exec" all the way down and out of our vocabulary, and then we will have a damn good ship!

When I (GPH) taught the second class leadership class, it was amazing to me that the one story they remembered from the plebe class was

"Damn Exec." Midshipmen resonate with the idea that to pass an order off as someone else's is lousy followership. And this makes for lousy leadership.

THE ANCHORS OF OUTSTANDING FOLLOWERSHIP

We now offer the primary components of being an outstanding follower. These important *anchors* are the lessons we hope midshipmen learn; these are lessons they must learn to be successful in the fleet and in life beyond. Ask any commanding officer in the Navy or Marines what they want in USNA graduates and you will get a list containing most of these salient habits.

I (GPH) remember vividly when I checked aboard my first squadron and had my check-in interview with the XO. When he discovered that I was from USNA he said, "I expect more out of Academy graduates and I better get it." In the section that follows we synthesize some excellent scholarship on followership with lessons midshipmen learn on their journey through Annapolis.

MANAGE YOURSELF

At the Naval Academy, first-year students find unrelenting physical, academic, and emotional challenge. They find seemingly impossible demands for new learning, precise adherence to detail, and achievement in an environment that can be punishing and unforgiving. They do not find babysitters. Midshipmen learn almost at once that survival, let alone success, demands self-management. Those who make it through plebe year are those who learn to take initiative and get the job done without waiting for direction and without being issued an order.

One of the most important things you have to learn right away at the Naval Academy is time management. During plebe summer, midshipmen rush from event to event at a hectic pace. One hour plebes march, the next they swim, the next they are sailing knock-abouts, and it goes on all day long until plebes finally fall into bed exhausted. When do plebes get a chance to shine their shoes, polish their brass belt-buckles, get haircuts, and do all the other mandatory things a plebe must do, much less study *rates?* Plebes have to learn quickly how to prioritize and figure out what's important and what's not.

Excellent followers think for themselves and take initiative for creatively and enthusiastically accomplishing tasks required for the organization's success. Nobody wants to lead robots. Sure, they can be programmed to perform rote tasks, but robots don't take initiative; they can't be trusted to see a problem and create innovative solutions without direct oversight. This is the hallmark of the excellent follower. Followers at Navy have what Rotter termed *internal locus of control*. The internally controlled follower is self-directed. This follower believes in his or her own capacity to direct effort, organize activity, and accomplish specific tasks. They are independent critical thinkers who assume they can make a good decision. Those with an internal locus of control reject the idea that they are dictated to by luck, fate, or the wishes of others. Yes, they are respectful of authority and take orders effectively, but they do not require constant direction and reassurance.

In many instances, the self-managing follower makes decisions without first seeking approval or direction from the boss. And this is not because he or she has trouble with authority or difficulty in following. These followers are willing to take initiative when it counts; they make good decisions and then brief their bosses when they can. In a pinch they ask themselves what the commanding officer would do, make a move, and live with the consequences. Over time, a track record of initiative and good judgment combine to build the CO's trust. These followers enjoy increasing latitude and freedom in the follower role.

LEARN YOUR JOB

The outstanding follower intuits the value of learning a subordinate role well. This follower sees the junior roles in one's career trajectory as valuable, meaningful, and contributing to both the follower's own development and the superordinate organizational mission. The great follower pursues the followership role with intensity and thoroughness—often working at length with no special recognition or star billing.

In fact, this is the life of the USNA plebe or the junior officer in the fleet. Promotion to higher rank is slow and sequential, typically requiring excellence in many follower roles along the way. In the P-3 community this is evident in the progression to become a patrol plane commander. The new "nugget pilot" arrives in the squadron fresh out of flight school and is called a Zero-P. He or she is starting from scratch. As the months go along the new pilot progresses through his or her syllabus and becomes a 3P, or third pilot; then becomes a 2P, or copilot; and after approximately two years is made a patrol plane commander, or PPC.

They accomplish all of this while still expected to perform at the highest level in their ground jobs. Passing that PPC flight is a day of great accomplishment because it means the commanding officer has placed enough trust and confidence in you to let you take a plane and crew out under your own command. Later, only the very best of the PPCs will be selected as squadron instructor pilots. This is the ultimate achievement a young lieutenant can attain in his or her first squadron and it is the mark of a very special pilot.

Stellar followers approach their roles with enthusiasm and commitment to establish and maintain competence. Competence is an elusive quality in business these days. Competence demands more than acquisition of several competencies or microskills. Midshipmen at USNA can get strait A's in engineering classes, yet lack real competence in the sea-going engineer role. Competence is the capacity to integrate knowledge, experience, and contextual factors in order to function smoothly and effectively in the real world. That's why every summer midshipmen are required to go to sea and serve with real fleet units or with the Marine Corps. Before they graduate and are commissioned, they get to see what it's like in the fleet.

Competent followers start by doing their homework. They become intentional students of the organization, literate in the organization's mission and objectives, and very aware of the CO's philosophy and leadership style. Because they anticipate problems and questions, they acquire all the information their superior requires to make well-informed decisions. In fact, they routinely go above and beyond minimum expectations in this regard. They are proactive in seeking opportunities for enhancing job knowledge and practical competence.

I (GPH) remember a young lieutenant who worked for me in my second squadron. His ground job was to ensure that every officer and chief remained current in required reading material for a special mission the squadron was assigned. It seemed that the officers were always too busy to come into his office, sit down, and do the reading. So this young lieutenant took his job "on the road." He went to all the individuals in their offices, briefed them thoroughly on the material, and waited while they read it themselves. He even took it a step further. He administered a test (which was not required) to each individual after they read the material so that everyone not only did the required reading, but understood what they read. Needless to say, it was very time intensive for him, but while he had that job the squadron passed each inspection with flying colors.

Finally, competent followers are self-aware. Familiar with their primary strengths and weaknesses, they volunteer for those tasks for which they are especially well suited and exploit their strengths for the benefit of the unit. They only make promises when they know they can deliver.

BE LOYAL TO THE COMMANDING OFFICER

At Navy, as in other top-flight organizations, outstanding followers are loyal to their immediate bosses and ultimately to the CO. It matters not how popular or likeable the commanding officer happens to be. Disloyalty in the ranks always sabotages the mission. Most junior officers know how profoundly tempting it can be to seek popularity and favor from their own subordinates by letting it be known that they dislike or disagree with the policies or decisions of the "old man" running the ship. Whether this message is delivered with overt hostility or subtle sarcasm, it is lousy followership.

Underachievement at sea is oftentimes traceable to this sort of followership among junior grade officers. At USNA, midshipmen learn to pass orders to their subordinates as though the orders were their own (see "Damn Exec"). This includes the most unpopular orders (e.g., loss of liberty, or extra "fun" physical fitness training on Saturday morning). When a follower shows distaste or regret at passing on a leader's order, the net impact of the CO's intent is compromised.

However, leaders have a responsibility not to give their followers a reason to fail them. In my (GPH) first squadron, the CO and XO really did not get along well but the XO was loyal to the CO and carried out his directives with great enthusiasm. One Monday morning, we arrived to find that the CO had relieved the XO over the weekend for cause. When we found out the facts, many officers felt that the XO had been relieved more out of animosity than for cause. The wing commander conducted an investigation and exonerated the XO. He offered him the choice of returning to the squadron or accepting assignment as the XO of another squadron. The XO elected to come back to the squadron.

Upon his return, however, the wardroom was virtually split down the middle in their loyalty to the CO and XO. I never forgot this lesson: Although it is the subordinate's job to demonstrate real loyalty, it is the leader's job to fuel this loyalty. Junior officers inevitably struggle with loyalty to cruel, vindictive, or grossly incompetent leaders.

SPEAK YOUR MIND BUT NOT IN PUBLIC

In the story of *The Emperor's New Clothes*, a self-absorbed king suffers the indignity of walking naked through the streets of his kingdom—all because his most trusted advisers refused to tell him the truth. They were tight-lipped when he most needed honest feedback and straight advice. These disloyal followers placed their own fear of reprisal or embarrassment above the requirements of excellent followership. Sometimes such withholding is intentional and aggressive. The follower seeks to sabotage the leader. More often such failure is born of anxiety, self-doubt, or an unwillingness to risk disfavor.

In the leadership laboratory of Bancroft Hall, midshipmen learn that failing to take care of one's boss is a grievous failure in one's own leadership. Excellent followers are straightforward, forthright, transparent, and thoroughly honest when asked for an answer or opinion. Nowhere is a "yes" person rejected more quickly than on the deck of a ship or submarine. With the mission at stake and lives in the balance, real leaders learn to jettison any adviser or subordinate whom they cannot trust to be 100 percent straight—even when this means the boss will hear things that make him or her enraged or wounded. Of course, the best followers are judicious about when to confront the boss. Criticism or questioning is never appropriate in public, yet when delivered behind closed doors, it may contribute more than anything else to mission achievement.

WHEN YOU BLOW IT, TELL THE TRUTH
AND ACCEPT RESPONSIBILITY

Admiral Bud Edney, formerly the distinguished leadership professor at USNA, would tell midshipmen the story of two jet pilots who served under his command on a carrier at sea. During one routine patrol flight these young pilots decided to imitate a scene from the movie *Top Gun* and take photographs of each other while flying their aircraft at close range. Their attention diverted by photography, they misjudged the distance between them and the planes made contact, causing substantial damage to one of them.

Back on the carrier, the pilots made a much more grievous error. They decided to lie about the incident. The pilots reported that a sudden wind sheer and poor visibility had caused the collision. They withheld information about the photography. During the extensive post-event investigation, evidence about the real cause of the mishap was revealed and the disenchanted admiral confronted the pilots. Little did the pilots know that their radio conversations about how best to lie and cover up evidence of their photography had been heard aboard the carrier. Both pilots were immediately fired and removed from the ship. The lie was career-ending.

Would the outcome have been more favorable for the pilots if they had come clean? The admiral would tell midshipmen there was no doubt of this. Aircraft can often be repaired. Damage to integrity is often permanent. Excellent followers tell the truth, precisely. They reject opportunities to alter reality or protect themselves from the repercussions of their behavior. They are courageous in the sense of sticking to their beliefs and ethical commitments even when these commitments might require some suffering. Solid followers accept the fact that they will make blunders. Leaders will inevitably admire followers who tell the truth—even when they don't like what they hear.

When I (GPH) was a battalion officer at USNA, Captain Joseph Prueher, later a four-star admiral, was commandant and assigned me duty on the Women Midshipmen's Advisory Committee. The Committee was tasked to investigate the "climate" at the Academy regarding women's issues and report to him. During our work, we discovered many things wrong with the climate for women at USNA. Some of these things were difficult to hear, and we might have been reluctant to commit some of them to our report, but Admiral Prueher insisted on getting all the details and hearing it straight.

TAKE NECESSARY RISKS AND
ADDRESS PROBLEMS IMMEDIATELY

Few things are worse than risk-phobic followers. Midshipmen quickly learn that smart initiative and appropriate risk-taking are prerequisites to making the company run. As followers, they learn that every member of a crew is responsible for keeping the ship afloat and moving. If you spot a problem, fix it. And fix it right away. Yes, there is a chance you might screw it up. There always is. Yet if you wait to move, you may slow the ship's progress—or worse, put shipmates at risk.

One of the salient experiences midshipmen often have during summer cruises on board Navy ships around the world is training in shipboard damage control. When a hole is created below the water line, a ship is in immediate danger of sinking. A rapid response is required of all the ship's personnel—especially those closest to the breach. Any delay to find someone "more qualified" or to protect oneself from the responsibility involved in making a risky decision about how to respond could easily cost time that might save lives and equipment.

One of our Leadership guest speakers in 2003 was the commanding officer of the USS *Samuel B. Roberts*. While deployed to the Persian Gulf, the *Roberts* sailed into an Iranian minefield and hit a mine. The blast almost tore the ship in half. The skipper told the midshipmen a story about a sailor who performed above and beyond the call of duty. This sailor had been to Captain's Mast (a formal proceeding to adjudicate violations of military rule and order) twice for serious infractions. His master chief had recommended both times that the sailor be booted out of the Navy, but the CO saw something in him and kept him aboard. During the mine incident, the sailor was below-deck and when the explosion occurred he was alone in the pump room. Knowing that the ship needed the pumps to survive, he remained in the pump room, even though the water was rising, repaired one of the pumps when it broke, and kept the pumps running.

Without the pumps in operation, the ship would most certainly have sunk. After the ship was saved, the CO asked the XO when they had sent the young sailor to school to learn about operating and repairing the pumps. It turned out that the sailor had never been to school but explained to the CO that he knew how serious the damage was and how important the pumps were to survival. He knew he was taking a risk trying to fix the pump alone, but also knew that the situation was dire and if he didn't try to fix it, they would all end up in the water. He had seen the numerous sea snakes in the Persian Gulf when he was on deck, and told the CO he didn't relish having to undertake that experience, so he fixed the pump.

In the military, leaders want subordinates who take appropriate risks without seeking reassurance or permission. Many problems can be corrected immediately and locally without the commanding officer's attention. It is the rare captain who wants to have a hand in every decision on board a ship. Captains sleep well when assured that their followers assume responsibility for problems and move quickly to correct them.

FOLLOWERS WHO FAIL

There are a few approaches to followership that always lead to failure. Sometimes these dysfunctional strategies are rooted in personality style. At other times, they are linked to performance anxiety or insecurity. And occasionally, the approach to followership is quite malignant and reflects more serious pathology in the very character of the follower.

Whatever the cause, certain problems related to followership nearly always lead to adverse outcomes, not only for the follower, but also for the leader and everyone else in the chain of command. Although these problem patterns are rare among midshipmen, they occasionally rear their heads and must be addressed expeditiously. A midshipman who cannot overcome disordered followership behavior cannot follow in the fleet and cannot be expected to lead. Here are the most common profiles of disordered followers.

ANXIOUS/IMMOBILIZED

Everyone gets scared. Fear is an innate human response with important evolutionary value. It primes our bodies for flight or self-defense. Anxiety, on the other hand, is a state characterized by chronic worry and apprehension. People who live with ongoing anticipatory anxiety about the potential for bad events or negative outcomes are more likely to suffer emotional and physical problems. Constant anxiety-based vigilance is exhausting.

Although everyone in a new work situation experiences some minor anxiety about performance and acceptance, some never seem to get past it. These anxious followers place the mission at risk. Because anxiety actually inhibits performance, they are prone to becoming immobilized.

In one of our leadership classes we show the scene from *The Caine Mutiny* when Captain Queeg becomes immobilized by anxiety during a typhoon and cannot make the right decision to turn the ship back into the enormous waves. His junior officers know that running from the waves will lead to disaster. His XO must step in, take command, and give the correct order to turn the ship.

The anxious follower can become the proverbial "deer in the headlights" when crisis strikes. Nowhere would immobility of this sort be more life-threatening than on a ship, submarine, or aircraft when the stuff hits the fan. For example, when a fire breaks out on a submerged submarine or when an engine fails on a P-3, commanders need followers who act. That's why followers are perpetually trained to react in these crisis situations. When bad things happen, personnel need to react instantaneously and reflexively—as if they are going robotically through a drill. At USNA, midshipmen are rewarded for taking initiative and moving quickly to resolve problems. They learn early on that hesitation is never rewarded; stepping back from a tough problem usually makes it worse.

STICKY/DEPENDENT

Few things are as unpleasant for leaders as a high-maintenance follower. This is the subordinate who requires copious quantities of reassurance in order to get the job done. So lacking in self-esteem is this follower that he or she feels painfully inadequate. The dependent follower waits passively for leadership. His or her locus of control is external; this follower will not take initiative or show autonomy. The dependent is usually happy to follow orders, but feels so insecure that the leader must give detailed instructions for each task and then reassure the follower that his or her work is acceptable.

Dependent followers are to leadership as black holes are to the universe. They drain the leader's time and energy and usually don't perform at a level that justifies this expenditure of resources. In the Navy, dependent followers are always a liability. Like the anxious/immobilized follower, they can place others at risk and distract leaders from their primary objective. They never make good leaders themselves and are usually ineffective in any context requiring innovation or tenacity. Dependent personalities rarely gain admission to USNA. When they do, they are among the first to drop out.

ARROGANT/GRANDIOSE

Who likes a narcissist? Nobody we know. One of the toughest challenges in leadership is guiding an arrogant and self-absorbed follower. This is a subordinate who expects to be noticed as special and unusually gifted.

Although we have emphasized the importance of self-starting confidence in good followers, the narcissistic follower is overconfident. Egotistical and self-absorbed, these followers see themselves as equal to or even better than their bosses. They may come across as smug and superior; perhaps suggesting that they could rather easily do the leader's job, and do it better. Such a follower is often preoccupied with fantasies of grand success and glory while on the outside performance is probably average. When extreme praise and recognition are not forthcoming, the narcissistic follower may become sullen or even enraged.

Although junior naval leaders may join the Navy with some narcissistic features, these are typically stamped out rather dramatically during the boot camp or indoctrination phases of training. Plebe summer quickly puts every plebe on the same level. Plebes find out that they are at the bottom of the totem pole and will be there for an entire year. At USNA, a plebe with serious arrogance problems would become a lightening rod for negative attention from the upperclassmen. Life for the narcissist would be hell in Bancroft Hall. Humility combined with a sober assessment of one's actual abilities is an essential virtue among midshipmen.

RIGID/COMPULSIVE

One thing is certain in the Navy and Marines: Nothing is certain. Deployment schedules change in the blink of an eye and a routine 1-month training cruise may become a 10-month combat operation. Operating procedures may change daily and swift reactions to enemy activity may require a new plan every few hours. At times, a unit may have to make do with less—to improvise and innovate outside the manual.

The trait that will make all this possible is flexibility. The best followers are careful and attentive to detail, but they are simultaneously able to switch gears quickly and adapt to handle adversity or sudden changes to orders. Unfortunately, some followers are better defined by rigid and compulsive demands for rules and standards at all costs. When faced with demands for flexibility or change, these followers become anxious or hostile. They are typically perfectionists and quite harsh in their evaluations of self. Although perfectionists can do a great job with the details in any command, their preoccupation with details causes them to lose sight of the larger mission at times.

THE GOUGE

You have to learn how to follow if you want to excel as a leader. There are no shortcuts here. The entire four-class system at the Academy is built on the premise that leadership hinges on followership. From day one, midshipmen learn how to follow first.

One of the great benefits of this system is that midshipmen can observe those more senior to themselves having a go at leading; they can watch and learn. Midshipmen have the advantage of seeing both stellar and mediocre leadership at play during their four years. Both the successes and failures of superiors can teach the followers a great deal about being a leader. As midshipmen advance in their responsibilities, they learn to become self-managing and internally driven. They learn their jobs and strive for competence in the subordinate role. Midshipmen learn to be loyal to the CO and to deliver the CO's orders as their own.

Excellent followers speak their minds and safeguard the commander's best interests by delivering accurate, if unpopular, news. Finally, midshipmen learn to act expeditiously when trouble breaks out. They never pass the buck. And afterward, they take full responsibility for the outcome.

4

THE CRUCIBLE OF CHARACTER

Were a professor from another university to visit the Naval Academy, he or she might be startled by a few notable oddities in the USNA culture. Faculty and midshipmen alike often leave their doors open or unlocked. Wallets, purses, and valuables are commonly left in plain view, and thefts are remarkably rare. Midshipmen, whether individually or in groups, often take unproctored exams and professors take a midshipman's word at face value. In fact, lying, cheating, and stealing are so rare at USNA that when any form of deceit comes to light, it generally constitutes big news.

There is a reason for this institutional culture of integrity and trust. Midshipmen know it as the Honor Concept. Formalized in the 1950s, the brigade honor system serves to develop midshipmen who possess a clear sense of moral conviction and the ability to articulate personal moral commitments.

The classes of 1950 through 1953 created the Honor Concept to ensure nothing related to honor and integrity ever brought discredit to the Academy. The Honor Concept holds that midshipmen are persons of integrity; they stand for that which is right in light of moral values such as respect for human dignity, respect for honesty, and respect for the property of others. As one former midshipman described it:

The Honor Concept was presented to us as the ultimate standard of a midshipman's character and conduct. As far as the Academy was concerned, it seemed to outrank even the Ten Commandants. One thing about the Honor Concept—it's simple. "Midshipmen are persons of integrity. They do not lie, cheat, or steal." It was drilled into us that the Honor Concept was the minimum standard. We were to judge all facets of our lives by its requirements. If we couldn't function acceptably in accordance with it, we could rest assured that we were not "fit to hold a commission in the Naval Service" and might jeopardize our privilege of being members of the Brigade of Midshipmen. The plebes soaked it up like sponges. We had expected the Academy to demand the best, and we viewed the Honor Concept as the ultimate example of the price we were willing to pay to pass muster. We were beginning to understand why greatness was the rule, rather than the exception, for Annapolis graduates.

Corny as an honor code may sound to outside observers, the purpose of the code is profoundly sober. USNA admissions material informs applicants that after four short years at Annapolis, our graduates will begin assuming responsibility for the priceless lives of many men and women and multimillion (sometimes billion)-dollar machines. These graduates must be above reproach when it comes to personal honor. The President of the United States and the Secretary of Defense place complete and unfettered trust in the integrity, courage, and commitment of each of our graduates. If trust is ever compromised, so too is the capacity for leadership. Excellent leadership assumes personal honor. John McCain said this about his father's sense of honor as a midshipman:

> ...neither would my father have considered for a moment committing a violation of the Academy's honor code. Honor codes were something he had been raised from birth to respect, and I truly believe he would have preferred any misfortune to having his honor called into question for an offense he committed. His profile in the class yearbook commended his character with the following description: "Sooner could Gibraltar be loosed from its base than could Mac be loosed from the principles which he has adopted to govern his actions."

HONOR AS A WAY OF LIFE

In the system of education at Navy, one finds substantial attention to ethical and moral education; there is a concerted effort to shape the character of midshipmen. Midshipmen learn that if either the ends of leadership or the methods of achieving it are immoral or unethical, then the leader's credibility and ultimate objectives are compromised.

As one of USNA's most illustrious graduates, Vice Admiral James Stockdale, puts it, "Students [midshipmen] need to understand that without personal integrity, intellectual skills are worthless. Education steeped in honor and the promotion of moral character must be certain to shed light on values, not marginalize them in the quest for academic or athletic stardom."

It is interesting that enforcement and maintenance of the honor concept occurs nearly exclusively at the peer level. That was the result of Commandant Robert Pirie's suggestion that classes create their own honor committees. It was decided by midshipmen that reports of honor violations would be reported to class honor committees that would investigate honor violations and report to the Brigade Honor Board.

Committees composed of elected upperclass midshipmen are responsible for education and training in the honor concept. Midshipmen found in violation of the code by their peers may be separated from USNA. In fact, midshipmen are often harder on one another when it comes to violations of honor than senior officers might be. On more than one occasion, a midshipmen honor board has recommended expulsion of a midshipman, only to have the commandant or superintendent ultimately decide against such a severe sentence.

PRINCIPLES AND VIRTUES IN THE LIVES OF LEADERS

At times, purveyors of moral education advocate teaching ethical principles as the primary means of creating leaders with sound ethical reasoning and decision-making skills. We refer to this approach to moral education as *principle ethics*. Principle ethics is a method for addressing moral issues with the goal of solving a particular ethical dilemma. The idea here is that teaching young leaders to use a deliberate ethical decision-making template will help them to make the right decision in a tough ethical bind. Decision makers learn to consider essential ethical principles when deciding how to proceed.

So, when an enlisted sailor discloses a personal struggle with very serious depression, the ethically astute officer may first consider the nature of the quandary (protecting the service member's privacy, acting in his or her best interest, and simultaneously considering how this admission will impact the ship's crew and the command's preparedness). The officer might then consider important ethical principles such as justice, love, and honesty. Finally, having considered ethical obligations, ethical principles, and the unique or ticklish aspects of the present quagmire, he or she is ready to render a decision.

One of the realities of assuming command is the fact that an officer will face this challenge often. I (GPH) didn't fully understand that until I was in the position of making these choices for some of my sailors. Sometimes it's very difficult.

I had a young single mother in my command who, while on deployment, bounced about $1000 worth of checks at the Navy Exchange. I was given the choice of giving her a courts-martial or taking her to Captain's Mast. The problem with giving her a courts-martial was that I knew she would be thrown out of the Navy and given a bad conduct discharge. She and her little girl would be out on the street with little probability of finding employment. The problem of taking her to Captain's Mast was that I knew I would have to take money away from her (and she obviously was already strapped for money) or place her on 45 days restriction. She had no one to take care of her child for 45 days if I put her on restriction. It was a difficult choice. Fortunately, she had a loyal department head who stood up for her and got someone to take care of her daughter. I gave her the 45 days restriction, suspended her demotion to a lower rank based upon her conduct for the next six months, and admonished her for what she had done. Fortunately, everything worked out well. We got her financial counseling; she got out of debt and turned into a model sailor after that.

Examples of revered and age-old ethical principles include

- *Fidelity*—fulfilling one's responsibilities and telling the truth
- *Beneficence*—acting in the best interests of others
- *Justice*—ensuring equitable distribution of burdens and benefits

Of course, these are good principles and most of us agree they are important ethical touch points when considering how best to resolve a prickly moral quandary.

The paramount question from the principle ethics perspective is always this: "What shall I do?" A principle-based decision tree can help a leader analyze a dilemma. And the purpose of this analysis is always the solution of the dilemma in a fair and just manner.

ETHICAL PRINCIPLES: NECESSARY BUT NOT SUFFICIENT

Ethical principles are important. Midshipmen at USNA find readings and discussions bearing on principles nested throughout the ethics and character development curriculum. We have no quarrel with principle ethics and most business leaders today would do well to have a stronger, more internalized sense of ethical awareness. Clearly, many senior leaders at Enron, WorldCom, Tyco, and other morally imploded companies failed when it came to basic adherence to ethical principles.

They could have used the lecture given to midshipmen by one of our guest speakers in the Leadership course: Warrant Officer Hugh Thompson. He was the helicopter pilot who has been described as the hero of My Lai. Thompson was the one who stepped in to stop his fellow soldiers who had gone over the edge at My Lai and murdered hundreds of Vietnamese.

Thompson was flying his helicopter that morning in support of U.S. troops. As he flew over My Lai, he saw American soldiers gunning down Vietnamese civilians. He heroically placed his helicopter between the surviving Vietnamese from the village and the American troops who were trying to shoot them. He got out of his helicopter and told his gunner to open fire on the Americans if they continued to fire. He then went to the aid of the civilians who had taken refuge in a bunker. For many villagers, Thompson was too late. After coaxing the frightened civilians from the bunker, he discovered that there were too many of them to take away in his helicopter, so he radioed a fellow helicopter pilot for help. Thompson then returned to his base and reported the slaughter to his seniors who immediately ordered the local commander to stop the onslaught. Warrant Officer Thompson certainly was the hero that day because he adhered to moral and ethical principles, even when he had to confront, challenge, and threaten fellow American soldiers.

The problem with principle ethics is simply the ultimate inadequacy of this approach. Learning good ethical reasoning strategies is not enough. Something salient and integral to the leader's essential being is missing here. In short, a course in leadership ethics is not enough to produce ethical leadership. "What's missing?" you ask. We say the missing component is the very person of the leader. More specifically, the leader's character—a structure or quality that has its beginning long before a student applies for admission at USNA and long before a manager begins an ethics workshop.

BECOMING A VIRTUOUS LEADER

The complement to principle ethics is *virtue ethics*. Virtue ethics assumes that ethical leadership is about more than just moral actions. In other words, it's not always about solving a moral dilemma and ultimately doing the right thing. Right moral outcomes are good, but ethics based on virtue move beyond moral obligation to moral ideal.

Virtue ethics calls upon individuals to aspire toward ideals and to develop virtues or traits of character that enable them to achieve these ideals. When a leader is described has having "moral virtue," we suggest that he or she has certain qualities or aspects of character that guide decisions or habits of right and wrong conduct. Thus, virtue ethics takes into account the very person of the leader. Rather than focus exclusively on the prescribed rules or ethical principles governing a decision, the virtue approach focuses just as intensely on the motivations, moral habits, and foundational character of the actor.

Warrant Officer Thompson considered ethical principles but he was also a virtuous man; he was instantly troubled by a clear injustice. The commanding officer of the USS *Morton* offers another example of virtuous leadership.

In February 1982 the USS *Morton* (DD 948) was en route to a six-month deployment in the western Pacific. During a brief stop in Guam, the squadron commander assembled his five commanding officers and issued an order that Navy ships were no longer allowed to pick up Vietnamese "boat people." The reason for this order was that Navy ships had been deterred from their basic missions by picking up boat people, and those countries that had accepted the boat people were becoming overwhelmed with refugees. Additionally, rescue at sea only encouraged more refugees to flee Vietnam. If Navy vessels were to encounter refugees in boats, they were to provide only food, fuel, water, and directions to the nearest land.

As the USS *Morton* was sailing toward the Philippines, it encountered heavy seas as it entered a storm. The radar shack reported a small boat contact. In those days, some COs avoided the moral dilemma of boat people by altering course. Out of sight—out of mind. The CO of the *Morton*, however, did not rationalize that this was a fishing vessel.

As the *Morton* approached the boat, those on board saw a 35-foot boat with 52 men, women, and children on board. Without hesitation, the *Morton* took them aboard. Trying to house the additional people on his ship was a monumental task for the CO, but the ship finally sailed to the Philippines and all the refugees were accepted. This CO faced an ethical dilemma—follow the squadron commander's policy, including verbal orders, and people might possibly die, or ignore the orders and save lives. Like Warrant Officer Thompson, he decided to take the road his character virtues required.

WHEN LEADING, WHO SHALL I BE?

What are the virtues upon which this approach to moral leadership is based? At USNA, we think of moral virtues as the internal composition of one's character. These are distinctly good and admirable human qualities that denote moral excellence or uprightness in the way one lives. Virtues do not require a religious framework; they clearly exist in virtuous human beings who claim no religious worldview.

The question we want midshipmen to ask themselves when decisions must be made is this: "Who shall I be?" That is, what sort of agent or leader will I be? Not simply "What shall I do?" Although the second question must be answered day-to-day, the first question is more basic, more foundational, and more critical to ensuring excellent moral leadership among the young officers we generate for the fleet.

And being virtuous is harder than it sounds. Notre Dame ethicist Naomi Meara suggests that a virtuous agent is one who

- Is motivated to do what is good
- Possesses vision and discernment
- Realizes the role of emotion in assessing or judging proper conduct
- Has a high degree of self-understanding and self-awareness
- Is connected with and understands the traditions of his or her community

Using this understanding, we might say that a virtuous leader is driven by virtuous intent, wise and discerning, well acquainted with him- or herself, insightful regarding personal motivations and emotional reactions, and both bonded to and deeply respectful of his or her primary group or community. This is a leader who is driven by strong character virtues and seen by his or her subordinates as virtuous as well. This congruence between reality and the perceptions of others is critical. Unless subordinates experience the leader as moral, his or her leadership will lack moral authority.

Former Commandant of Midshipmen, Colonel John Allen, USMC, wrote his *Commandant's Intent,* an 8½ page essay for the midshipmen, to let them know where he stood when he became commandant. In it he said

> War exacts great personal sacrifice from the officers of the naval service. Preparing for this sacrifice requires that we learn to live to be ready at all times to lead at the point of impact.... Combat conditioning brings home the reality of combat in our own preparation for the moment of truth and spans comprehensive, inextricably linked moral, intellectual, and physical preparations. The midshipmen must understand their moral obligation...their duty. At the moral level, the midshipmen must understand the centrality of the role of character, integrity, and ethics in the demands of leading sailors and marines at the point of impact. I am not interested in teaching any of these concepts to the midshipmen in order to make them good midshipmen; I am interested in preparing them to be ready for commissioned service and their leadership responsibilities for war.

When it comes to character virtues, we again like to stack the deck in selecting midshipmen. We deliberately consider evidence of character qualities when selecting high school students for admission to USNA. Any evidence of moral turpitude or questionable integrity is typically grounds for denial of admission. Why take chances with character when there are so many equally qualified applicants in the pool? If sound character is the bedrock on which leadership operates, it simply makes sense to find future leaders with sturdy footings.

CORE PRINCIPLES OF THE UNITED STATES NAVY

In the balance of this chapter, we want to present the Navy's core values or code of honor. These core principles must be memorized and practiced by every USNA midshipman. These values are simultaneously simple and profound. Their brevity and pithy elegance can be deceptive.

The honor concept specifies that every midshipman at the Naval Academy must adhere scrupulously and unconditionally to three vital and immutable principles. Actually, they are virtues of character, but they are also conscious values—explicit principles for living and leading with honor. Although the core values are memorized quickly during the first hours of life as midshipmen, the gravity of commitment to this code becomes more salient in the days and months that follow.

The honor system specifies three absolute moral imperatives: honor, courage, and commitment. That is all. If this sounds easy enough, some elaboration is required. It is important to understand how each of these virtues is articulated and defined in practical life of a future officer in the Navy or Marine Corps. As we reflect upon each of these principles below, we encourage you to consider how your own business or organization would be influenced and altered if each generation of new managerial leaders came to work fully and unequivocally committed to these simple principles.

HONOR

"I will bear true faith and allegiance…." Accordingly, we will: Conduct ourselves in the highest ethical manner in all relationships with peers, superiors, and subordinates; Be honest and truthful in our dealings with each other, and with those outside the Navy; Be willing to make honest recommendations and accept those of junior personnel; Encourage new ideas and deliver the bad news, even when it is unpopular; Abide by an uncompromising code of integrity, taking responsibility for our actions and keeping our word; Fulfill or exceed our legal and ethical responsibilities in our public and personal lives 24 hours a day. Illegal or improper behavior or even the appearance of such behavior will not be tolerated. We are accountable for our professional and personal behavior. We will be mindful of the privilege to serve our fellow Americans.

If there is a common theme in this vow of honor, it is the virtue of integrity. To have integrity is to be somehow incorruptible in the moral sense. An officer with integrity would not perform wrong actions or perform any actions for the wrong reason. To say that a leader has integrity conjures a variety of related attributes—qualities of the honorable person. These include honesty, fairness, respectfulness, self-awareness, reliability, and even flexibility.

Perhaps the most precious and foundational component of integrity is truthfulness. During an address at the Naval Academy in June of 1996, President Jimmy Carter (USNA class of '47) quoted from his Navy *Bluejacket Manual*—an officer manual issued on his first day as a plebe in 1943.

Those who serve on ships are expected to exhibit obedience, knowledge, fighting spirit, reliability, loyalty, initiative, self-control, energy, courage, justice, faith in ourselves, cheerfulness, and honor, but above all comes absolute truth, the final test of a man.

There is something utterly correct about this advice from the post-World War II Navy. Above all comes truth. Truth is the very heart of integrity and nothing compromises an officer's integrity more thoroughly and instantaneously than telling an untruth. The commanding officer of a ship or submarine must assume with unflinching certainty that his or her officers will never compromise on this score. Give me bad news and give me all of it, but never ever twist or withhold the facts.

In my (GPH) second squadron, we had a lieutenant who, after he completed his initial tour, wanted to get out and fly for the airlines. In order for it to look like he had a lot of flight experience, he doctored his flight log, adding flights that he never flew. No one knew this until another lieutenant (instructor pilot) checked his log book one day before giving him an annual qualification check-ride. Upon discovering the doctored book, he immediately took it to the operations officer, who took it up the chain of command, and an investigation was conducted. It was discovered that the pilot had indeed doctored his flight log. He had lied in writing and he had compromised his honor. He was finished in the squadron. No one would trust him after that and he was quickly taken off flight status and released from active duty. How could the Commanding Officer ever trust this man with an airplane and the lives of a crew again? Even now, whenever I fly on a commercial airliner, I look at the pilots in the cockpit and make sure that this man is not piloting the plane. I still wouldn't trust him!

Of course, truthfulness is a prerequisite for trust. Originating in the German word *trost*, which means comfort, trust suggests a state of confidence and comfort in relation to one who habitually tells the truth. Trust is further enhanced when a leader respects privacy and protects confidence in interpersonal relationships. Honor and integrity hinge upon trust.

HONOR IS NONNEGOTIABLE

In a recent speech to the brigade of midshipmen, Admiral J. Paul Reason reminded midshipmen that at USNA and in the fleet, it is an absolute imperative that you rely on your fellow officers' sense of honor and that they rely on yours. When a new USNA graduate reports aboard a sea-going command with sparkling new ensign bars, the ensign trusts the experience, wisdom, and integrity of the senior officers. Simultaneously, senior officers put their faith in the new ensign. Interestingly, most skippers in the U.S. Navy will tell you that they can tolerate some inconsistency in aptitude and professional competence among USNA graduates, but they unanimously insist on new officers that follow and lead with honor and unquestioned integrity.

Perhaps the most compelling evidence for the importance of ensuring the character virtue of honor in new military leaders comes from the experience of several USNA graduates who have survived periods of captivity as prisoners of war. One of the most thoughtful and reflective Navy POWs to return from Vietnam is Vice Admiral James B. Stockdale. A USNA graduate and career naval aviator, then Commander Stockdale was shot down over Vietnam in 1965. He served as the senior leader among American POWs for eight years—four of which were spent in solitary confinement. Following his repatriation, Admiral Stockdale received the Congressional Medal of Honor. In Stockdale's experience, integrity is a person's most precious asset in an environment of constant torture and threat of death. Read Stockdale's words regarding honor:

> Integrity is one of those words that many people keep in that desk drawer labeled "too hard." It's not a topic for the dinner table or the cocktail party. You can't buy or sell it. When supported with education, a person's integrity can give him something to rely on when his perspective seems to blur, when rules and principles seem to waiver, and when he's faced with hard choices of right or wrong. It's something to keep him on the right track, something to keep him afloat when he's drowning; if only for practical reasons, it is an attribute that should be kept at the very top of a young person's consciousness.

Stockdale recounts the case of an American officer who sold out his integrity early in the POW experience. Unwilling to tolerate discomfort and torture, the young officer became a willing participant in recording anti-America propaganda in exchange for special favors and privileges. These tapes were used against other prisoners. Although he eventually experienced regret and remorse at his behavior, rejected his captor's appeals for further cooperation, and rejoined his countrymen entirely, Stockdale noted that the officer's integrity was permanently damaged in the eyes of his comrades: "Those who lose credibility with their peers and who cause their superiors to doubt their directness, honesty, or integrity are dead. Recovery isn't possible."

Loss of honor can be terminal when it comes to leadership. Moral leadership demands unquestioned evidence of virtue; followers need to trust and trust is deceptively fragile. This officer never really recovered. After his return from Vietnam, he died in an "accident" that strongly resembled suicide.

It is interesting that the enemy understands the salience of integrity for leader effectiveness. Get the officers to compromise and you've got the entire crew. In Vietnam, captors went to great lengths to get men to compromise their own moral code, even if the compromise appeared minuscule or petty at first:

> The linkage of men's ethics, reputations, and fates can be studied in even more vivid detail in prison camp. In that brutally controlled environment a perceptive enemy can get his hooks into the slightest chink in a man's ethical armor and accelerate his downfall. Given the right opening, the right moral weakness, a certain susceptibility on the part of the prisoner, a clever extortionist can drive his victim into a downhill slide that will ruin his image, self-respect, and life in a very short time.

To succeed as leaders, midshipmen learn from day one that integrity is nonnegotiable. Evidence of lying or dishonesty is grounds for separation. No argument.

When I (GPH) was battalion officer, I recall a female midshipman who came before the commandant on an honor violation. She was in her room one Saturday night when she got a call from some of her friends to come out to McGarvey's, a popular bar in Annapolis. She agreed, and on her way out saw her roommate's ID card on the desk. Because she was not 21, she picked it up. Although she did not ever drink alcohol, she thought she would need it to get into the bar. Well, the doorman saw that the card wasn't hers, took it from her, and later returned it to the Academy.

The midshipman was brought up on an honor violation, was found guilty, and went before the commandant. There she was, her whole career on the line, for falsely using her roommate's ID card. The commandant upheld the Board's recommendation and she was dismissed. But the commandant did tell her that after her class graduated, if she applied for readmission, he would champion her cause. After her class graduated, she returned to the Academy and graduated after finishing her courses.

Although this kind of punishment policy may seem harsh to outsiders, the outcome is a leadership environment second-to-none when it comes to trust. Midshipmen trust one another to follow-through, tell the truth, respect property, and confront any behavior incongruent with the honor code. They're being prepared for what is expected from them in the fleet.

COURAGE

"I will support and defend...." Accordingly, we will have: Courage to meet the demands of our profession and the mission when it is hazardous, demanding, or otherwise difficult; Make decisions in the best interest of the navy and the nation, without regard to personal consequences; Meet these challenges while adhering to a higher standard of personal conduct and decency; Be loyal to our nation, ensuring the resources entrusted to us are used in an honest, careful, and efficient way. Courage is the value that gives us the moral and mental strength to do what is right, even in the face of personal or professional adversity.

On his second patrol as the skipper of the American submarine USS *Parche* in July 1944, Commander L. P. Ramage (USNA class of '31) came upon a large and heavily protected Japanese convoy near the Philippines. Rather than submerge and look for an easy target, Commander Ramage pursued the convoy and engaged in an extended night-time battle with the heavily armed Japanese warships. Ramage managed to fire 19 torpedoes—often at close range—and ultimately sank three large tankers and crew transport ships.

Ramage pursued his targets through wilting fire, several near misses from enemy torpedoes, and attempts to ram his submarine. By refusing to submerge, by relentlessly pursing his targets, and by conducting an entirely unconventional and unanticipated surface attack, Commander Ramage left the Japanese war ships in total disarray and the convoy largely destroyed. The commander's courage and audacity resulted in one of the greatest submarine attacks of all time. Commander Ramage became the first living submariner to receive the Congressional Medal of Honor.

Colonel John Ripley, USMC (USNA class of '62), was the first Marine graduate of the Academy to receive the Distinguished Graduate Award. During the 1972 Easter Offensive in Vietnam, then Captain Ripley was attached to a Vietnamese unit that was attacked by a large North Vietnamese contingent with over 200 tanks. If the North Vietnamese took the capital of Quang Tri province, nothing could stop them from capturing the ancient capital of Hue.

One strategic bridge over the Cam Lo River was the only obstacle standing in their path. Under continuous fire, Ripley made a dozen trips with explosives loaded in his backpack, hand over hand, to the center of the bridge. By the time he was finished, Ripley had placed over 500 pounds of explosives under the bridge—enough to destroy the bridge and stop the invasion. After Ripley detonated the explosives and destroyed the bridge, the North Vietnamese were trapped on the far side of the river, where they were attacked and destroyed by naval gunfire and air strikes. For his heroic action, Ripley was awarded the Navy Cross.

We would like to quote from the Medal of Honor citation given to one more hero during World War II who displayed exceptional courage for his boat and his men.

> For conspicuous gallantry and valor above and beyond the call of duty as Commanding Officer of the USS *Growler* during her Fourth War patrol in the Southwest Pacific. Boldly striking at the enemy in spite of continuous hostile air and antisubmarine patrols, Commander Gilmore sank one Japanese freighter and damaged another by torpedo fire, successfully evading severe depth charges following each attack. In the darkness of night on 7 February 1943, an enemy gunboat closed range and prepared to ram the *Growler*. Commander Gilmore daringly maneuvered to avoid the crash and rammed the attacker instead, ripping into her port side at 17 knots and bursting wide her plates. In the terrific fire of the sinking gunboat's heavy machine guns, Commander Gilmore calmly gave the order to clear the bridge and, refusing safety for himself, remained on deck while his men preceded him below. Struck down by the fusillade of bullets and having done his utmost against the enemy, in his final living moments, Commander Gilmore gave the last order to the deck, "Take her down." The *Growler* dived; seriously damaged but under control, she was brought safely to port by her well-trained crew inspired by the courageous fighting spirit of the dead captain.

These are some of the USNA graduates who have helped to define what honor and courage mean. It's a lot to live up to, but then, we expect a lot of our graduates.

COURAGE BEGETS COURAGE

Observing or reading about courage in action, such as that displayed so prominently by Commander Ramage, Colonel Ripley, and Commander

Gilmore, often inspires others to courageous behavior as well. Followers of courageous leaders often borrow from the courage of their leaders as they face the anxiety that accompanies new challenges, unfamiliar demands, and perhaps even torture or death. In this way, a leader's stores of courage can sustain and embolden those that follow—even in the face of daunting odds. In Colonel Allen's *Commandant's Intent*, he cites the famous passage from *Henry V* in which the king exhorts his friends:

> *Once more into the breach dear friends, once more;*
> *Or close the wall up with our English dead.*
> *In peace there's nothing so becomes a man*
> *As modest stillness and humility;*
> *But when the blast of war blows in our ears,*
> *Then imitate the action of the tiger;*
> *Stiffen the sinews, conjure up the blood,*
> *Disguise fair nature with hard-favor'd rage;*
> *Then lend the eye a terrible aspect.*

Of course, courage is a virtue of character and it cannot be constructed entirely from scratch. Midshipmen come to USNA having demonstrated courage academically, athletically, and as young leaders in their lives before the Navy. Our job is to sharpen this virtue, and sharpening happens when courage is exercised—typically in the course of challenges designed to provoke anxiety and exhaustion.

The word *courage* stems from the French *coeur*, or heart. Thus, the expression "take heart" is a call to courageous belief and action in the face of dismaying odds. In the excellent World War II submarine movie *U-571*, the submarine's executive officer faces the awful task of ordering a young enlisted sailor to dive into a flooded compartment to seal an air valve critical for operating the torpedo tubes. The lives of the remaining crew depend on it. The problem is simple: Both officer and enlisted seaman understand that the task is life-threatening. As members of the audience, we feel the intense anxiety that nearly always accompanies courage under fire. While the seaman is terrified of dying, the officer is terrified of ordering this seaman to his death as a means of saving the crew and achieving victory. The young man in this story does die; courage never guarantees safety or success. Yet, we understand that the actions of both men were undeniably courageous.

Of course, courage is expressed most often in day-to-day leadership behavior. Thankfully, few of us routinely require courage in the face of life-threatening combat. In organizations around the world, courageous leaders demonstrate courage when they:

- Accept and tolerate their own shortcomings and failures
- Pursue insight and self-awareness—even when this is painful
- Adopt a realistically (versus naively) optimistic view of the future, and a particularly optimistic view of what their own unit or team can accomplish
- Empower followers through consistent and well-timed application of resources, opportunities, and motivation
- Infuse followers with faith and optimism as circumstances become more trying.

In business as in the military, courageous leaders stand up for their people, show an abiding belief in their unit's ability to get the job done, and make tough decisions without passing the buck.

COMMITMENT

"I will obey the orders...." Accordingly, we will: Demand respect up and down the chain of command; Care for the safety, professional, personal, and spiritual well-being of our people; Show respect toward all people without regard to race, religion, or gender; Treat each individual with human dignity; Be committed to positive change and constant improvement; Exhibit the highest degree of moral character, technical excellence, quality and competence in what we have been trained to do. The day-to-day duty of every Navy man and woman is to work together as a team to improve the quality of our work, our people, and ourselves.

The third and final principle or virtue undergirding the Navy's approach to leadership is commitment. It could just as easily be called caring. Excellent leadership demands integrity and truthfulness, courage to face whatever challenges present themselves, and a sturdy commitment to caring for those we lead. Once again, the capacity for care and commitment to the well-being and best interest of those who depend on us is a fundamental virtue of character. Not every person is capable of caring.

Sociopaths, for example, lack the inherent ability to comprehend fully the feelings and concerns of others. They lack a fundamental skill we call empathy. This is why the sociopathic criminal can so easily commit violent offenses against others. The perspective of the other (e.g., horror, pain, injustice) never fully registers in the sociopath's awareness.

And subordinates know when a leader cares for them. The caring leader takes time to know and understand subordinates—particularly those most directly in the immediate chain of command. Outstanding leaders devote concerted attention to discerning subordinates' primary talents and vulnerabilities in order to showcase and reinforce talents and augment and develop areas of relative weakness. Excellent leaders communicate commitment and caring through authentic respectfulness. If genuine, respect is not difficult to convey to followers.

Simply pausing to speak with an enlisted serviceperson, asking questions about his or her life, provides convincing evidence to a ship's crew that the CO gives a damn about them. I (GPH) learned this lesson when I was in my department head tour. We had a CO who learned the first name of every sailor in the squadron and when he saw them around the hangar, he would talk to them and address them by their first names. Not only that, but at squadron picnics and get-togethers, he would meet the spouses and families of the sailors and remember their names too. Whenever he saw a sailor around the hangar, he would say hello, greet them by first name, and then ask about the family members by name.

The effect this had on the sailors was amazing. It was a morale booster like none other I had ever seen. And it didn't cost a dime. Those sailors thought they were really something special because the CO knew their names and inquired about how their families were faring. You could literally see their faces light up. When I became a CO, I swore I would do the same thing. It was hard to remember all those names, (around 350 in a squadron with one third leaving and another new one third replacing them each year) but it had the same effect on my squadron that it did on my former CO's.

Finally, the virtue of caring and commitment rings forth whenever a leader follows through with a promise made to the crew. When the skipper makes a promise, he or she had better deliver the goods—particularly when the promise bears on the interests and personal needs of the crew. Although followers appreciate adversity and unexpected changes in the battle plan, they will quickly lose respect for the leader who neglects commitments for reasons of expedience, laziness, or personal gain.

MORAL LEADERSHIP IN IMMORAL PLACES

At times, midshipmen at the Naval Academy have behaved immorally; their behavior has been incongruent with their commitment to the Navy's guiding principles, their own fundamental character virtues, and the honor system for midshipmen. The most notorious and well-publicized example of such behavior was a cheating scandal that rocked the class of 1994, when several midshipmen obtained an advance copy of the electrical engineering examination. As Vice Academic Dean William Garret related in a speech delivered on Character Development at the Academy:

> Late in the fall of 1992, about 650 of the second-class midshipmen, or those in their third year, took a final examination in electrical engineering. Within a few hours of the end of the examination midshipmen started to report to their chain of command that the examination had been compromised and that some midshipmen had a copy of the examination prior to exam time. I recalled thinking, "This is not possible." But I was mistaken. The investigation revealed that some midshipmen did indeed have a copy of the examination, had shared it with others, and had studied it, strictly contrary to the principles, concepts, and traditions of the Naval Academy, contrary to Midshipmen Regulations, and in contravention of the Midshipmen's Honor Concept that stated "A midshipman does not lie, cheat or steal."

Although a few midshipmen appeared to be deliberate and intentional about obtaining the exam and achieving unfair advantage in their exam performance, many others were taken by surprise—having used the "gouge" provided by shipmates only to be honestly shocked that the material mirrored the questions on the actual exam perfectly. Approximately 29 midshipmen were dismissed and 76 others did not graduate on time but stayed at the Academy for two months after graduation for an Honor Remediation course.

When a leader has well-developed character virtues, behavior that goes against these value commitments is distressing. Psychologists refer to this phenomenon as *cognitive dissonance*, and few internal emotional states are as unpleasant. Human beings are inherently motivated to reduce the incongruence and emotional unrest that accompanies inconsistency between belief and behavior. Many of the midshipmen who participated in cheating on the engineering exam began to flounder under the weight of cognitive dissonance. Of course, the only solution to this state of distress is admission of the incongruence, seeking restitution, and a renewed determination to maintain consistency between moral commitment and behavior.

In the real world of both military and organizational leadership, leaders will frequently discover practices and traditions that appear to violate core principles and virtues. For example, the infamous "pinning" ceremonies in many military communities have been officially banned yet continue in various forms "under the radar" of top leaders. This unseemly "tradition" was exposed on Dateline several years ago and was depicted as a brutal, demeaning, and tortuous practice.

Pinning occurs when a service member achieves an important milestone qualification such as becoming warfare qualified as a submariner or a Marine Corps parachutist. He or she is awarded an insignia to wear that is pinned onto the uniform on the left chest. The pin is held in place with buttons attached to sharp barbs on the back of the pin. In some instances, pinning ceremonies became violent and traumatic hazing rituals in which those pinned would be bloodied as a rite of passage by having the insignia beaten and pounded into their chests without the buttons in place. Although officially banned, such ceremonies still crop up now and then.

Graduates of USNA must be able to lead with consistent character even in environments or situations that appear fundamentally immoral. If the ethics and character curriculum at USNA are about anything at all, they are about turning out leaders with precisely this sort of courage. Leaders willing to honor and enforce the organization's core principles—particularly when unpopular and unpleasant.

THE GOUGE

Midshipmen must be honorable people. Midshipmen and Naval and Marine Corps officers are expected to be people of integrity—no exceptions. From the day midshipmen take the oath of office, it is expected that they will not lie, cheat, or steal. It really is that simple.

As Deputy Secretary of State Richard Armitage (class of '67) told the midshipmen and guests at the Naval Academy's 2003 Leadership Conference, the leadership experience midshipmen will have to face differs significantly from that of their civilian peers. At an early age, midshipmen will be placed in charge of men and women, whose welfare and maybe even lives will be in their hands. It is an awesome responsibility. And it demands that they be mature as persons of integrity early in their careers. That's why the Academy is dedicated and designed to show midshipmen at the beginning of their careers that honor, courage, and commitment are immutable virtues and essential for excellent leadership.

5

CREATE
TRI-LEVEL VISION

During the 2000, 2001, and 2002 football seasons, the USNA community languished through 1-10, 0-11, and 2-10 records. The mention of football around campus began to conjure up universally morose and downcast expressions. In class, our student football players often appeared depressed and sullen following weekend games that frequently featured blowout losses. To make matters worse for these athletes, tradition requires the team to gather before the brigade of midshipmen and sing the venerable "Navy Blue and Gold" alma mater song following each game. The midshipmen had not won a home game in three long years. This singing ritual became very painful to perform after all those losses.

As we sit down to finish this book, we are happy to report that the U.S. Naval Academy football team pulled off a Cinderella season. Finishing 8-5, they appeared in their first bowl game in seven years. More than achieving a winning record, however, the team played with intensity and confidence. Previously unknown players made big plays and showed some "swagger." The entire team played as though it expected to win each and every game. In fact, "Expect to win" has been adopted as the team's motto. They have become a formidable force on the football gridiron, and teams on our schedule next year, including Notre Dame, are speaking with some anxiety about this "new" Navy team.

Although a sudden turnaround in the fortunes of a football team may not sound all that relevant or interesting to those who are not avid Navy football fans, we find this turnaround striking in light of three important facts. First, in terms of returning players, this was largely the same team that lost nearly every game during the past two years. Second, the team fielded more freshmen than any Navy team in modern history. Third, as a small service academy, USNA is severely hampered in the competition for the best high school recruits. Our athletes must be exceptional academic performers and, in most cases, willing to forgo prospects for professional sports careers. Our graduates must serve a minimum of five years as commissioned officers following graduation. For this reason, many blue-chip athletes shun service academies.

So how do we account for the dramatic turnaround in Navy's football fortunes? Vision. Second-year coach Paul Johnson had this team of freshman and previously downtrodden upperclassmen believing they could play against anybody and win. This collection of undersized (and underrated) scholar-athletes adopted Johnson's vision of themselves as a team that could play with the best and win in a big way every Saturday. In his own calm and unassuming way, Johnson is a master when it comes to crafting a team vision. It is no surprise to us that his teams at Georgia Southern (the Division I-AA university where he coached for the last several years) won national championships twice. Nor is it surprising that Johnson himself is consistently nominated for coach-of-the-year honors. The proof of Coach Johnson's success in leading with vision is in his Navy team's remarkable turnaround.

LEADING WITH VISION

Whether leading a football team, a major corporation, or the crew of a Navy destroyer, leaders have got both to create and successfully communicate a vision. Excellent leadership hinges on the leader's capacity to construct the right vision for a unit or organization at just the right time. By *vision* we mean an ideal image or picture of what the unit can become. Successful visions are clear, compelling, and carefully articulated. Such a vision is a primary key to creating real organizational change. The outstanding leader is a fine storyteller in the sense of creating an ideal, yet realistic story of what the group or organization could ultimately become and achieve.

The vision should have meaning to the group members; in a real way it must captivate their interest and their faith.

A graduate from the USNA class of '65 relayed his experiences in fashioning a command vision and getting subordinates committed to his ideas. He was fortunate, however, because he held three different commands during his career. He had the opportunity to try it again and get it right. As commanding officer of a fighter squadron, he developed a two-to-three page "Command Philosophy" document and drilled it into his officers and chiefs. It was cumbersome and lacked a clear vision. The end-goal was not simple and transparent. His squadron failed to achieve their goal of becoming the top-rated squadron on the West Coast.

His second command was a large amphibious ship. This time, he simply placed a banner heading on the printed Plan of the Day that read "The Best Amphibious Ship in the Fleet." He took some ribbing from his crew about the banner but finally explained to them that it wasn't just a catchy phrase—it was their goal. It worked. They won the Battle Excellence E award for being the most efficient and effective ship of their class in the Navy that year. He ultimately assumed command of a nuclear aircraft carrier with a crew of 6000 sailors. By that time he had a clear vision of what it took to lead and win. After assuming command, he first met with the XO and department heads, then with the entire chief's mess, and finally with the entire crew on the flight deck and explained his vision. It was simple. He told them that each crewmember should consciously select one thing he or she had to do each day and be commited to doing it a little bit better than it had ever been done before. The CO made this the ship's motto, "Get a Little Better Each Day." He reinforced it constantly with chats on the ship's intercom system and visits to workshops. His philosophy was that if you get thousands of little improvements each day, you will end up with dramatic improvements around the entire ship. His ideas paid off—his carrier won not only the Battle E, but also the aviation safety award for that year.

"VISIONING" LEADERS NEED NOT BE "VISIONARY"

Please notice that we are not talking about "visionary" leaders here. A leader who can predict future trends and anticipate cultural or economic shifts may indeed be a credit to any organization, but such visionary abilities mean little if the leader cannot craft a convincing picture of what the immediate group can become.

In the Navy, we need leaders who can take the helm of everyday military teams and mold them into high-performing combat crews. This seldom demands futuristic vision (although the Department of Defense employs a host of wonderfully visionary engineers, scientists, and strategists), but rather, the capacity to create vision at the level of the local unit. Although Coach Paul Johnson could well be a visionary when it comes to innovative offensive plays and defensive schemes (time will tell), the Navy football team needed him to provide vision on their level—a vision that told them they could compete and win.

When a leader creates a motivating vision for his or her people, the vision itself conveys a powerful message of affirmation and faith in the ability of the team to rise to a higher level. Shaskin referred to this process as *visioning*. Visioning requires the leader to deftly construct a potent and stirring image of the organization and its culture. This image offers followers a vivid picture of what they can corporately achieve.

When USNA alumnus Captain Michael Abrashoff took the helm of the USS *Benfold*, it is fair to say he walked into an organizational climate devoid of vision. With sailors leaving the ship in droves, it quickly became apparent to Abrashoff that the crew had no sense of meaning and purpose related to their roles on the ship. They desperately needed vision. So CDR Abrashoff gave them one: instead of remaining the dysfunctional doormat of the entire fleet of guided missile destroyers, why not become the best damn ship in the Navy? Why not win the coveted battle excellence awards and rise to the top of the "can-do" ships in the eyes of the admirals? Of course, Abrashoff's crew responded magnificently to this vision and the rest is history.

THE CHALLENGE OF COMMUNICATING VISION

It is one thing to create a vision for the crew; it is quite another to find a way to describe and sell the vision to the masses effectively. An outstanding corporate vision will have little impact if the leader fails to show courageous and complete commitment to the vision. Nothing sabotages a plan like lukewarm buy-in. We suspect that Coach Johnson did not tell his team that they "might" have what it takes to secure a winning season, and no sailor about to enter battle takes comfort from a commanding officer who communicates tentative confidence or outright trepidation about the unit's capacity to prevail. The visioning leader is an utter believer when it comes to the vision and is genuinely committed to bringing the crew along to this ideal end point. An excellent vision must also conform broadly to the larger organization's mission and directives. CDR Abrashoff had to guarantee that his vision for the *Benfold's* crew was congruent with the policies and command intent of his own superior officers.

Both my (GPH) sons are military officers: Brendon is a Marine and Shawn is an Army officer who participated in Operation Iraqi Freedom. Of course I'm very proud of them both, but worried all the time. My Marine son, Brendon, was with the 1st Marine Expeditionary Force in March waiting on the Kuwaiti border for the invasion orders to be issued. Just prior to launching the attack, their commanding general, Major General Mattis, issued a message to all of his Marines that is well worth quoting because it gave the Marines a clear vision of their mission:

> For decades, Saddam Hussein has tortured and imprisoned, raped and murdered the Iraqi people; invaded neighboring countries without provocation; and threatened the world with weapons of mass destruction. The time has come to end his reign of terror. On your young shoulders rest the hopes of mankind.
>
> When I give you the word, together we will cross the Line of Departure, close with those forces that choose to fight, and destroy them. Our fight is not with the Iraqi people, nor is it with members of the Iraqi army who choose to surrender. While we will move swiftly and aggressively against those who resist, we will treat all others with decency, demonstrating chivalry and soldierly compassion for people who have endured a lifetime under Saddam's oppression.
>
> Chemical attack, treachery, and use of the innocent as human shields can be expected, as can other unethical tactics. Take it all in stride. Be the hunter, not the hunted: never allow your unit to be caught with its guard down. Use good judgment and act in the best interests of our nation. You are part of the

world's most feared and trusted force. Engage your brain before you engage your weapon. Share your courage with each other as we enter the uncertain terrain north of the Line of Departure. Keep faith in your comrades on your left and right and Marine Air overhead. Fight with a happy heart and strong spirit.

For the mission's sake, our country's sake, and the sake of the men who carried the Division's colors in past battles—who fought for life and never lost their nerve—carry out your mission and keep your honor clean. Demonstrate to the world there is "No Better Friend, No Worse Enemy" than a U.S. Marine.

Marines have a way of putting it directly, succinctly, and to the heart. My son reported that you could feel the power the general's message conveyed all the way down to the lowest enlisted person. It had a profound impact on all of them. He gave them the proper vision of what they were there to accomplish. After hearing this message, they were " pumped up" and ready to go.

Although most discussions of visioning start and stop with consideration of generating a unit or organizational vision, this is only one slice of the visioning process. In fact, we would say that an effective leader must possess vision in at least three dimensions—we call this *tri-level vision*. For midshipmen and officers to thrive in the visioning role, they must construct and fully embrace three important domains of vision: (1) self-vision, (2) follower vision, and (3) unit or command vision. In the balance of this chapter, we suggest that a capable leader must create and endorse vision effectively in each of these areas.

CREATING A VISION OF SELF

USNA graduate Jimmy Carter once described his first submarine skipper, J.B. Williams, Jr., of the USS *Pomfret*. This is what he said.

He was a man of stern discipline; we all knew exactly where we stood, but he never had to chastise us. He was a man of gentleness. He shared with us our problems and our ideals; our fears; our concerns; our hopes and dreams. We tried never to fail him, not because we feared punishment but because we didn't want to let our skipper down. That made a great impact on my life.

So how did Captain Williams manage to so successfully and thoroughly capture his men's loyalty and commitment? He delivered a vision of his men and their capability as a submarine crew that inspired and elevated them. But long before Captain Williams rose to command a submarine in the U.S. fleet, he had to create a vision of himself as an officer and leader. This vision of self would serve as the base from which all of his leader behavior would emanate over the course of his career.

Leaders are self-acquainted. The first, and perhaps the most fundamental, element of visioning is building and sharpening a vision of who you are as a leader. At USNA, we call this "knowing thyself" and plebes are indoctrinated with this idea in their first-semester leadership course. A key premise of the USNA leadership curriculum is that no leader gets far without a clear view of his or her primary strengths and weaknesses. So, plebes get personality test feedback. They get 360-degree leadership performance feedback from their peers, their subordinates, and their senior midshipmen leaders. They receive evaluations and ratings from the company officer. Some of Navy's most famous graduates have undergone this system of exhaustive scrutiny. Here's what one of Ross Perot's classmates said about him:

> Every year, people in the academy were ranked by their peers. If I was in a bunk sleeping, how happy would I be to have this guy on the bridge on watch? Leadership quality is the number one factor, and decision making ability is number two. Ross certainly wasn't the biggest guy, and he didn't look like a military guy, but he was always from day one, a standout—someone you would accept as a leader. Three times a year, all midshipmen were evaluated by classmates, students in the class above, and their company officers. Based on the evaluations, combined with grades and athletic achievements, stripes (up to six) were awarded. Perot earned four stripes, which was remarkable considering his grades were average and he had no athletic accomplishments.

SELF-AWARENESS SOMETIMES HURTS

Self-awareness, sometimes painfully accrued, is the first step toward outstanding leadership. It is nearly impossible to build a vision of self-as-leader without first knowing the self. And we mean really knowing the self. One of the great shocks for midshipmen during their plebe year at USNA is the experience of mediocre or even substandard performance in some area—perhaps even in most areas. This may be the first time in the young person's life that he or she has not been at the top of the class with every exam or at the top of the list when class rankings occur.

In my (GPH) plebe leadership class, I always reminded them that it didn't matter where they stood in their high school class—half of them would be in the lower half of the class once their first grades were posted. Grades are an extremely important factor in determining midshipmen class standing, which impacts their career choices during their last year at the Academy. Where you stand in your class will dictate what your chances are for entering specific professional communities, such as flight school or submarines, after graduation. It is very hard for plebes to accept that half of them won't be in the top of their class. Failing to be the "best" among peers is a huge "know-yourself" shock for many of them. The problem is this: USNA is full of stars. To shine here, you have to be a real gem in a sea of talent. Bright students fail classes, athletic standouts get cut, and high school leaders become "just another plebe."

We often notice that students suffer a crisis of identity shortly after reporting for plebe summer. Overwhelmed, exhausted, and barely able to keep treading water physically and academically, the plebe is cut off from all sources of external support. One of more than a thousand talented students, the plebe must painfully relinquish his or her hard-won high school identity and begin scrambling for a view of self that fits the new situation.

I (GPH) entered plebe summer directly from high school where I had excelled academically, athletically, and in student government. It didn't take long into plebe summer though until I dreaded being noticed. I wanted to blend into the woodwork and become anonymous. I didn't want upperclassmen to single me out because that usually meant I wasn't performing up to their standards. I just wanted to become part of the background. I think every plebe feels that way at some point or another during plebe summer and during the first part of plebe year when the entire Brigade returns. However, you slowly start to learn the ropes and discover how you fit in as a midshipman.

Understandably, many plebes develop what we call an *imposter syndrome.* Here one begins to question whether one is cut out for the demands of life at USNA. Doubt sets in and even the most highly achieving plebes begin to wonder if they somehow slipped in through the admission cracks accidentally. Perhaps the admissions committee missed some crucial indicator of inadequacy and this will certainly come to light soon—probably in a public and deeply humiliating way.

In his book, *Plebe,* Hank Turowski describes what happened to one young plebe after going through the *imposter syndrome.*

> Plebe Summer had a strange effect on me. Like a quiet evening rainstorm, the Academy sneaked up on me and thoroughly drenched me with its outpouring. And once the traditions and ceremonies soaked in, I found I could not and would not separate myself willingly. One bright morning nearly at the end of Plebe Summer, I awoke and discovered that I was no longer a civilian proto-plebe. Suddenly—and surprisingly—I found myself a full-fledged, heart-and-soul, into-the-breach, damn-the-torpedoes member of the Brigade of Midshipmen. I had joined the fleet.

Healthy and adaptive young leaders move beyond the imposter phase, begin to accept themselves as imperfect human beings, and then set about constructing a self-concept or identity as leader that will get them through their careers. Moving beyond this imposter phase demands an evolving vision of self, based on consistent and realistic feedback.

Some of the essential questions midshipmen will have to ask and answer for themselves include: What is my main interpersonal style? How am I when it comes to confrontation? What motivational approaches seem to work for me? Do subordinates like me? Do subordinates respect me? Do I enjoy interacting with others or would I prefer to close the door and work with facts and figures? When I get fatigued, overwhelmed, or scared, how do I respond? When answered, each of these questions will provide an important window into each midshipman's main leader qualities and styles. One of my (GPH) second-class midshipmen put it this way:

> I noticed something the other day that crystallized for me some of the differences between what goes on here as opposed to what goes on at civilian college with regard to leadership. I was

walking down the hall and one of my plebes was doing something he wasn't supposed to. I honestly don't recall what it was but it was something like not tucking his shirt in. I stopped him of course and corrected him. I wasn't mean or loud or scathing, and I didn't act out of meanness or because "by God I had to tuck my shirt in when I was a plebe" but because I felt responsible. I subconsciously realized it was one of "my plebes." To me that is a fundamental concept of leadership. That most basic accountability. Being responsible for more than yourself—that is an absolute necessity of real leadership. It is something we get here, and it's often overlooked.

Although developing a clear and accurate picture of self as leader can be painful, it sets the stage for self-understanding and growth. Armed with a realistic view of self, the midshipman can now begin acquiring and sharpening those skill areas that need extra attention. And this is essential for the next level of visioning—developing a vision of one's followers. Only a secure, confident, and self-aware leader will really take the time to know and affirm followers.

CREATING A VISION OF FOLLOWERS

When I (WBJ) was a lieutenant at Pearl Harbor, I worked with an 18-year-old seaman who had become depressed and involved in an alcohol-related incident shortly after reporting to his first ship. A shy and self-conscious young man, he stared quietly at his shoes as he sat in my office during our initial meeting. He fought back tears as he described feeling that he really didn't belong in the Navy and that he was not "good enough" to make it very far. After an hour it became clear that he was both depressed and defeated. He saw himself as worthless and incapable of achieving anything significant in the Navy.

I learned that this young man's father was a harsh and domineering taskmaster. During 18 years under this man's roof, my young patient got one message loud and clear: "You are a sorry excuse for a son and you'll never amount to anything." Of course, he had adopted this as accurate; he failed a number of classes in high school, barely graduated, and had trouble securing even part-time employment. Because he was not suicidal, I cleared this young man to go to sea, and I recommended that he follow up at the clinic after his return. I informed the CO of the seaman's diagnosis, an adjustment-related mild depression, and told him he would have to decide whether to keep the sailor on board or not. Considering the boy's bleak presentation, I felt the prognosis for long-term success was poor.

Imagine my surprise when the same young man, advanced to the rank of petty officer, came to my office a little more than a year later as part of a routine security clearance evaluation. I was stunned. Gone were the slumped shoulders, the downcast eyes, and the tearful demeanor. Before me sat a model sailor—upright, eyes locked on, self-confident, and smiling. The contrast was so striking, I kept double checking his chart and trying to recall whether I had truly seen this man before. Sure enough, my hand-written notes described the depressed seaman I evaluated only a year earlier. Although I entertained the fleeting thought that my skill as a psychologist had cured the man with a single diagnostic interview, I soon discovered that the reason for his change lay elsewhere.

The day after our initial meeting the sailor had deployed with the ship feeling morose and hopeless. His department head on board the ship, a lieutenant commander and a USNA graduate, met with him, listened to his concerns, and then took him completely off guard by saying, "Okay, I understand what you're saying, but when are you going to stop lying to me about what you are capable of?"

Taken back and befuddled, the seaman just stared as the LCDR produced his aptitude test scores taken during recruiting. These placed him at roughly the 98th percentile in terms of achievement and intellectual capacity. The department head continued, "See, I don't know what you were told about yourself growing up. That's really not important now. What matters is that you are one of the smartest young men I've ever supervised. With scores like these, you should be learning your job faster than anyone on the ship. I want you to start acting like the bright guy you are."

Shaken but inspired by this perception of himself as "bright" and capable, the young seaman began to respond accordingly. He got qualified more quickly than any seaman in his rate, began tackling more collateral duties, and began to see himself as smarter than most of his peers. Upon the urging of his department head, he sat for his petty officer exam at the earliest opportunity and passed with flying colors. The department head then handed him material on college correspondence courses and said, "These should be a breeze for a guy like you. Start taking some classes and bring me your grades." He did.

During the next year, he completed a variety of college courses, earning straight A's. He began to see himself as a very capable student. In fact, he became an informal tutor to several peers on the ship. The department head continued to show this young man a vision of himself as smart, talented, and promising. Word of this fellow's turnaround reached the CO, who made it a point to put him in for an achievement medal for his performance on the ship—he had established himself as one of the sharpest and most effective junior enlisted leaders in the command.

The following year, this petty officer became one of the few enlisted service members each year who gain admission to the Naval Academy. Again, his department head, recognizing the sailor's abilities, encouraged him to take the SAT (his scores were well above the mean for most top-tier universities), and make application to the Academy. Having fully adopted the department head's view of him as intelligent, talented, and worth paying attention to, he never flinched during the arduous application process. This young man graduated from USNA several years ago. He was near the top of his class. He may very well be an admiral one day. If so, I hope he recalls the power of creating a vision for subordinates.

DELIVERING VISION TO FOLLOWERS

At Navy, midshipmen quickly learn that followers rise to the level of the leader's expectations. When a leader successfully communicates a vision and expectation of a follower as performing well above his or her current level, the follower's performance often changes accordingly. When we respect a leader, all of us want to measure up—especially when this leader holds us in high regard and believes we can accomplish things previously unimagined.

So how does a leader create and transmit a vision for the follower? Here are some guidelines:

• Learn about your followers; spend adequate time interacting with them.

- Study their primary talents, their aspirations, and their current weaknesses.
- Articulate a positive and ambitious view of the follower; communicate a vision that motivates, but avoid unfair or unattainable expectations.
- Find ways to consistently communicate this vision to your follower.

Excellent visioning is a bit like "going long" in football. In order for a quarterback to successfully complete a long pass, the ball must be delivered just beyond the receiver—perhaps right around the finger tips so that the receiver must reach and extend to make the grab. As every quarterback learns, tossing the ball too long makes the play impossible and disheartens the receiver. Tossing the ball short not only sabotages the play, it creates the real risk of a turnover. Your followers need you to deliver the ball out front, but make it catchable.

When it comes time to deliver a vision, the leader might introduce a vision with affirming and inspirational openings such as: "I see you as...," "I expect that you could...," "Considering your talents, you really should...." In conveying a vision to the follower, the leader is part mentor, part coach, part surrogate parent, and part motivational speaker.

You may be wondering how in the world you could ever really "vision" for all of your subordinates: how you could ever find the time to get to know followers, discern their gifts, and communicate a personalized vision that challenges and encourages them at deep levels. Sometimes you can't. The CO of an aircraft carrier will be lucky to know all his or her department heads well, let alone all the officers, and forget about the thousands of enlisted sailors. But this CO can still create a climate of visioning that starts in the commanding officer's cabin and emanates throughout the command. In these circumstances, offer excellent visions and images of what your immediate followers can become, and make it clear that you expect them to know their own people well.

I (GPH) mentioned earlier how I tried to learn all of the names of the people in my squadron and how much effort it took. What helped me accomplish this was simply getting out of my office every day. I decided I would spend no more than half my day in the office with paperwork. The rest of the time, I would walk around the hangar getting to know my people. I would drop in on meetings, work spaces, and once even went out to one of my airplanes on the flight line that was having a window replaced and watched as they put it in. They didn't see me as a nosey CO when I explained to them that I had always wondered how they replaced a window and would they mind if I observed?

VISIONING FOR FOLLOWERS AT USNA

At USNA, midshipmen receive both formal and informal visions of what we believe they will become and what we expect they can achieve. In fact, the entire midshipmen experience is designed to prepare them for commissioning as Naval and Marine Corps officers. Colonel John Allen, commandant of midshipmen, said this of the commission in his statement of leadership intent:

> There is no greater demonstration of the trust of the Republic than its expression and bestowal of an officer's commission. The commission itself is sworn before God in a manner exactly as our forbears swore to place their blades in the service of high moral principle. Today, the oath of office, the essence of commission, elicits from each officer a solemn promise of commitment to uphold a set of principles enshrined in the Constitution of the United States of America. It is a total commitment.

This is a weighty vision. Telling midshipmen that they are worthy of commissioning is a powerful thing. Even more powerful is taking the Oath of Office and knowing the awesome responsibilities it encompasses. Midshipmen act in accordance with this vision. They are universally men and women of honor. They take the responsibility of service to the country seriously and they believe they have the know-how and the courage to prevail in any conflict.

The USNA experience is full of visioning. Shortly after arriving at the Academy, small groups of midshipmen are quietly escorted down some granite steps, below the Naval Academy Chapel, and into the crypt of John Paul Jones, the father of the American Navy. After leading the Continental Navy to victory in the American Revolution, Jones died in Paris in 1792. His remains were returned to the United States and laid to rest in 1913. The crypt itself is breathtaking. A 21-ton ornate marble sarcophagus occupies the center of the room. Inscribed in brass letters at the base of the tomb are the names of each Continental ships commanded by Jones during the Revolution. Important artifacts from Jones's life and naval commands adorn the walls surrounding the tomb. A silent but vigilant Marine Corps or Navy honor guard stands watch over the crypt at all times. The atmosphere is reverent and ancient. Many of Jones's famous proclamations are enshrined there (e.g., "I have not yet begun to fight," and "I intend to go in harm's way"). This is the first formal recognition plebes experience and they realize they have entered into an organization steeped in tradition, honor, and courage.

SOMETIMES, JUST A WORD WILL DO

Keep in mind that visioning effectively need not require a lengthy treatise, individual appointments, or personal counseling. Sometimes a follower is deeply moved and highly motivated by just the right word or sentence. I (WBJ) recall hearing a successful businessman and speaker describe a painful and socially isolated junior high school experience. Low in self-esteem and unable to fit in with any group, this man, like the young seaman from the start of this chapter, saw himself as a complete zero—entirely devoid of merit or talent. This all changed dramatically in a single afternoon; it changed with a single word.

During one particularly humiliating gym class, this boy had ripped the seams of his jeans open bouncing on the trampoline. Teased mercilessly by his peers, he skulked off to the nearest stairwell the moment the bell rang. His observant gym teacher caught up with him and said, "Hey, I wanted to tell you I was watching you on the trampoline today. You're very agile." That was it. Agile.

The man recalled that as a gangly, self-conscious 12-year-old, he had no idea what agile meant, but he knew it was good. He looked the word up later that evening. He recalled this as the defining moment of his junior high school career, and to some extent, his young life. From that day forward, he began to see himself as *agile*: characterized by quickness, lightness, and ease of movement; nimble. Interestingly, this young man never questioned the veracity of the gym teacher's assessment. He never doubted for a moment that he must indeed be agile. His confidence soared; he became more involved in athletic endeavors; and he began to come alive socially. Sometimes a powerful vision is also a simple one.

Although Naval and Marine Corps officers are not psychotherapists, their capacity for helping followers to positive and inspiring self-visions is often profoundly healthy and even curative. This is especially true in the case of the *inhibited follower* or the follower who is so discouraged about himself or herself, that potential is muted and unrealized. Some followers report for "duty" entirely demoralized. Others are passively accepting of a very stifling view of who they are and who they can become.

Too often, the "story" they have listened to—the story about who they are and what the future holds for them—has stunted their growth. The original storyteller may have been a short-sighted parent, but now the follower is repeating the story to himself or herself. The follower needs someone credible to challenge the truth in this tale and make it a better match with reality. Sometimes this requires repeated painting of a corrected vision. At other times, a simple word will do the trick. Never underestimate the power of a commanding officer's words when he or she says to a follower: "Excellent work," "I'm impressed with you," "You're a top-notch officer," or perhaps even, "You're very agile."

Remember that followers will rise to achieve the command or organizational vision you create, but only if you simultaneously offer them a vision of themselves as capable and ready to roll. Consider the words of a retired Navy admiral. "My mentor convinced me of my worth and capability—that I was good; that I could be better; that I could be the best." President Carter experienced a similar situation when he went to his interview with Admiral Rickover as a midshipman trying to get into the Navy's nuclear power program.

> When he asked me how I stood in my Naval Academy class, I swelled with pride as I answered, "Sir, I stood 59th in my class of 820." I sat back to wait for his congratulations, which never came. Instead he asked me, "Did you always do your best?" To which I had to say honestly, "No, Sir, I didn't always do my best." He asked me one final question that I have never been able to forget or answer. He said, "Why not?" I later entitled my first book *Why Not the Best?*

CREATING A UNIT VISION

The final level of visioning required for effective leadership is the command or unit vision. Here you will be challenged to create a corporate picture—

an overarching image of what the entire team can get done. An excellent unit vision will be both inspiring and directive; this big picture offers direction to subsequent decisions and activities while allowing individuals and smaller teams enough space for creativity and innovation in achieving the big goal.

An excellent corporate vision will also be simple, concrete, and inspiring; more complex strategies for achieving it will follow, but the vision itself should capture something essential about why the unit is worthwhile, what it does, and perhaps even what it values most. So Captain Abrashoff worked with his crew to develop the vision of becoming "the best damn ship in the Navy." Other military organizations have created corporate visions tailored to their unique jobs and commitments:

- The most successful fighting force anywhere, we project power throughout the world and safeguard freedom on behalf of the American people.
- The most successful rescue squadron in the fleet, we leave no one behind.
- Answering the call 24/7.
- Bringing the world's best medical care to the fleet.
- Or my (GPH) squadron's (The War Eagles) not so eloquent vision—"If you ain't an Eagle, you ain't [crap]!"

Although there is no formula for creating a vision for your team, there are a few important components. First, try to involve the main stakeholders in formulating the vision. A submarine skipper who decides his sub will be the most squared-away and ever-ready sub in the fleet will have little success without buy-in from his officers and chiefs. In fact, if this vision is seen as serving the CO but not the crew, it may be sabotaged at every turn.

Second, make sure the vision plays to the strengths of both the individual followers and the leader. Third, the vision has got to inspire and create a sense of urgent meaning and personal importance among the crew. In our departmental home at USNA, the Leadership, Ethics, and Law Department, we hold a clear vision of ourselves as creating officers for the Navy and Marine Corps; officers who can not only withstand the demands of leading in combat, but who can thrive in this arduous and potentially life-threatening environment.

Fourth, an ideal vision is concrete enough to lead to attainable and tangible results. The vision's outcomes must be observable. It is one thing to say, "We're the best damn ship in the Navy." It's another thing to show proof that this vision has been realized. Finally, remember that the CO had damn well better put the vision into practice himself or herself in both personal and public behavior. No command vision will succeed without the authentic commitment of the leader. The CO had better be a true believer and willing to go all the way with the crew.

If you think the task of fashioning a vision is too hard, or your organization is too large, think again. The Marine Corps had to rediscover itself in the 1920s. Deployed primarily as guards on Naval vessels for most of its entire history, the Marines needed a new vision and a new mission. So, after World War I, the Marines opened a school in Quantico with the foresight that a war with Japan was quite possible in the years to come. Fighting such a war would entail launching amphibious assaults on numerous islands spread far across the vast Pacific Ocean.

Lieutenant Colonel "Pete" Ellis developed a detailed, and probably the most famous, doctrine in Marine Corps history, describing what such a war would entail. He accurately predicted almost every move the Marines and the Navy would have to undertake to win the war against Japan. He also described in great detail the roles that new weapons such as the submarine, the aircraft carrier, and the long-range bombers would have to undertake. WWII would prove his vision correct. The Marines, using Lieutenant Colonel Ellis's vision, redefined itself to meet the needs of the time. The Marines refused to be content and mark time. That is what vision achieves. An organization cannot be stagnant and rely on inertia or it will fail to exist.

THE GOUGE

Excellent leaders are excellent visioners. They create effective and meaningful visions of self-as-leader, followers, and the command as a unit. We think the job of visioning is best described in our second-class leadership textbook. In it we tell midshipmen, "The essential qualities of a successful vision should be simple and idealistic and not a complex plan. It should appeal to the values, hopes, and ideals of an organization's members. The vision should be challenging but grounded in the present reality. The vision should address what is important for the organization and how people should be treated. Finally, a successful vision should be simple enough to be communicated clearly in five minutes or less."

6

INOCULATE
FOR STRESS

On December 9, 1999, a U.S. Marine Corps Force Reconnaissance platoon from Camp Pendleton, California, was tasked to perform a Vessel Boarding Search and Seizure (VBSS) exercise on the USNS *Pecos*. The platoon's leader was marine Captain Eric Kapitulik, USNA class of 1995. Entering his third year as platoon commander, Captain Kapitulik was particularly proud of his 20-man unit. They had become a top-force reconnaissance platoon. The VBSS was to be their final certification before the start of a lengthy deployment to the Persian Gulf region.

THE ASSAULT TEAM

The practice assault team was comprised of two CH-46 helicopters assigned to Marine Medium Helicopter Squadron 166. Captain Kapitulik split the platoon into two elements. The first was led by Kapitulik and the second by his platoon sergeant. The exercise was a simulation of boarding a foreign vessel and called for the platoon to disembark on the fantail of the USNS *Pecos*. Timing was a key element for a successful assault.

At 0600 on board the *USS Bon Homme Richard*, Captain Kapitulik received a warning order to gear up for the VBSS mission. The platoon immediately began preparation for the assault and spent the next four hours checking their gear and rehearsing the assault sequence. At approximately 1000, Kapitulik and his intelligence team briefed the mission to the Marine Expeditionary Unit (MEU) commanding officer. A MEU is deployed on Navy amphibious ships and can carry out almost any type of operation, ranging from short-duration raids on an enemy shore to providing humanitarian assistance after a natural disaster. A MEU consists of approximately 2000 marines and usually has an air component that is also attached to help complete any assigned mission.

At 1230 the Force Recon platoon launched from the USS *Bon Homme Richard*. Captain Kapitulik and nine of his marines were on the first helicopter while the remaining members of the platoon launched immediately afterward on the second helicopter. At approximately 1255, the lead helicopter began the initial approach to the USNS *Pecos*. The platoon initiated its usual pre-assault procedures.

At 1300 the pilots gave the platoon a "five minute" call. Each team member began checking his gear, adjusting goggles, and securing equipment. All marines had anywhere from 50 to 70 pounds of gear on them: heavy body armor, helmet, pistol, carbines, ammo, and breaching equipment. Kapitulik was additionally weighed down with the platoon's satellite communications radio along with his other gear. At one minute out, the pilots gave the call for the platoon to unbuckle. At 30 seconds out, Kapitulik gave his marines the order to stand up and position themselves around the "hellhole" where the Helicopter Rope Suspension Training (HRST) master would deploy the fast rope. As soon as the pilots told the HRST to kick the rope out, Captain Kapitulik and his platoon would expeditiously exit the helicopter, slide down the rope, and begin their assault. But something went horribly wrong that afternoon.

THE ACCIDENT

As the pilot of Kapitulik's helicopter began his descent to the deck of the *Pecos*, the port landing gear became fouled in the netting surrounding the stern of the ship. The pilot could not extricate the helicopter from the net, and in a matter of seconds, it became unstable, rolled on its back, fell away from the ship, and hit the surface of the ocean.

Captain Kapitulik's immediate thoughts as the helicopter became fouled in the ship's net were that it was not stabilizing and something was obviously going very wrong. He instantly shouted to his marines, "Hold on, we're going in." Privately, he thought that they were never going to get out carrying all that extra gear. As the helicopter flipped and plunged inverted into the water, he took a deep breath of air. He was immediately knocked unconscious. Fortunately, he came to just as water began to rise over his head.

With the helicopter inverted, there was no easily recognizable frame of reference. Totally disoriented, Captain Kapitulik could not see anything. It was pitch black. To make matters worse, he had little oxygen. The force of the impact had knocked his breath away. He had been thrown across the back of the helicopter and 70 pounds of gear were dragging him down with the sinking helicopter. As he tried to find a way to exit the helicopter, his gear kept hanging up and he was running desperately short on air. Suddenly, he saw a flicker of light and began pulling himself toward it. At the aft end of the helicopter, the clamshell had opened and Kapitulik was able to squeeze through the opening and begin pulling up toward the surface. As he broke the water's surface, he saw smoke flares had been tossed into the water to mark the crash site. A small boat unit (SBU), using rigid inflatable boats with Navy SEALs on board, was also participating in the VBSS and had positioned itself directly aft of the USNS *Pecos*. Seeing the helicopter crash, the unit responded immediately and began retrieving the survivors. Although it had seemed like a lifetime to Captain Kapitulik, the helicopter had taken only 5 to 8 seconds to sink after hitting the water.

In all, six marines and one sailor died in the crash. Five of the marines were from Kapitulik's platoon. By the time they escaped the helicopter, several survivors reported that they were 20 feet or more below the surface. Negatively buoyant due to their heavy equipment, the marines had to struggle desperately to surface. Like Captain Kapitulik, they were all out of breath by the time they broke the surface of the water.

A PLATOON COMMANDER'S REACTIONS

After Kapitulik was recovered from the water, he began to look around frantically, hoping that his marines would all be coming up out of the helicopter. Soon, however, he began to realize that not all had made it. He began to grieve for his marines. In shock, and with so much adrenaline flowing, he did not recognize a compound fracture in one of his own legs. In fact, he moved around the deck of the ship for some time attempting to locate his marines before the pain set in and the medics began attending to his fracture. All of the survivors were airlifted to the nearest ship with a medical facility. The survivors spoke little then. They were shocked and dazed.

The following morning, Captain Kapitulik participated in a short memorial service on the flight deck of the USS *Bon Homme Richard*. Although this was a somber occasion like none other in his lifetime, he delivered a brief reading—believing his men should see him pay homage to their lost comrades. Returning to Camp Pendleton the next day, Captain Kapitulik and his remaining platoon were met by the wives and girlfriends of the company, including one of the widows.

During the following days and weeks, Captain Kapitulik underwent some very traumatizing moments. First there were the formal calls on the families of his lost marines. His was a typically tight Marine Corps unit. Having been a true friend to his marines and their families before the accident, he felt bound to go to each widow and explain what had happened. He later recalled this as one of the most difficult tasks he had ever undertaken. To his relief, he found no animosity from the widows that he had lived and their husbands had not.

CLIMBING BACK IN THE SADDLE

Because the company's deployment schedule had not changed, Captain Kapitulik had to immediately begin reorganizing the platoon. Five members of the company quickly volunteered to join his platoon. Reforming the platoon into a close-knit fighting force was not easy. There were lingering memories, anxieties, and the obstacles associated with bringing new members into a team that had learned to move together like clockwork. Perhaps the most traumatic event, however, was preparing to complete the VBSS assault exercise again. In order to be combat ready, the platoon would be required to successfully complete the assault exercise. So, three weeks after the accident, Captain Kapitulik, still in a full leg cast, found himself climbing back on a helicopter with his platoon. Though much discouraged from going along on the exercise by his commanding officer, the captain felt it essential that his men not go without him. That day, the apprehension inside the helicopter was palpable.

THE AFTERMATH

In the days and months following the crash, Captain Kapitulik suffered many of the classic symptoms of trauma. These included nightmares and daytime thoughts of the crash. In his nightmares, he was back in the helicopter with water rising around his face. While swimming for exercise, he often became anxious and felt he wasn't getting enough air. He became edgy, irritated, and prone to uncharacteristic outbursts. Things actually changed for the better when his platoon finally deployed to the Gulf. After all they had been through, it was a relief for him and his marines to know they were "still in the fight." On the other hand, he seldom went long without thinking about his lost marines, their widows, and their five fatherless children.

This tragic accident and its aftermath have reinforced many of the leadership principles Captain Kapitulik learned as a midshipman at USNA. The experience has caused him to zero in on what he believes to be most important for leading a Force Reconnaissance Platoon. First, he keeps extremely fit physically. He runs and swims constantly and believes that those who survived did so only because they were intensely committed to an aggressive regimen of stamina and strength training. Second, he believes a leader should do everything his or her troops do. Never expect subordinates to do a task you are not willing to do yourself. Finally, he says, "Be compassionate, but do not let grief overcome you." In the period following the accident, his troops expected compassion from him and he gave it to them. He extended this same compassion to their wives and widows. But it was also his job to remind his men that life goes on. Unwilling to stay mired in grief or anxiety, he required his men to get moving—to follow him back into the helicopter and back into action.

WHY LEADERS MUST PREPARE FOR STRESS

The regulations of the Navy require you to pass through a severe ordeal before you can be promoted.

(WORDS OF THE NAVAL ACADEMY'S FIRST SUPERINTENDENT, COMMANDER FRANKLIN BUCHANAN, ON THE OCCASION OF WELCOMING THE FIRST MIDSHIPMEN TO USNA IN 1845)

Stress happens. And it happens quite often for men and women who spend their lives leading (or preparing to lead) in combat. Although there are many forms and manifestations of stress, most agree that it is an unpleasant state of arousal that occurs when we perceive that an event threatens our capacity to cope effectively. Most leaders understand that stress is inevitable. At times it can spur good coping and even enhanced performance. When chronic or overwhelming, however, stress is associated with a host of physical and emotional problems. We know, for example, that sustained or poorly managed stress is connected to psychosomatic ail ments (e.g., ulcers, headaches, cardiovascular difficulties) and psychiatric disturbances (e.g., depression, anxiety, substance abuse).

For the leader, stress comes in three primary flavors—catastrophes, major life events, and microstressors. Combat leaders had better be able to manage all three. Catastrophes include the unpredictable and sometimes traumatic incidents that devastate a unit. They wreak destruction and sometimes death. They can leave a team in disarray and psychological shock. Captain Kapitulik knows about leading through catastrophe. So do hundreds of managers, police officers, and firefighters who led their people on the front lines of the September 11 attacks. When members of a unit are faced with hostile attack, sudden tragedy, or a bitter defeat, the leader had better be able to keep corporate stupor and anxiety contained.

LEADING THROUGH CATASTROPHE

When leaders are ineffective following a catastrophe, people stand a greater risk of developing chronic post-trauma syndromes. Decades of research on trauma shows that incidence of post-traumatic stress disorder (PTSD) is drastically reduced when members of a traumatized unit are quickly reintegrated, when leaders get members to give voice to their experience of the traumatic event, and when the team can quickly return to the "front lines."

During the first world wars, American psychiatrists and psychologists discovered the folly of pulling battle-fatigued soldiers back from the front lines and putting them in medical centers. Treating shocked soldiers like patients heightened rates of disturbance and lowered the probability that they would ever return to combat. Here is the bottom line: When catastrophe strikes, acknowledge it, bury your dead, let your team talk about the experience, and then pick up your weapons and get back in the fight.

During my (GPH) second squad tour in Hawaii, my squadron and three others were participating in a major Anti-Submarine Warfare training exercise against a U.S. submarine off the islands. About halfway through the exercise, on a very dark night, a P-3 from one of the other squadrons flew into a mountain top on the island of Kauai. It hit just 10 feet from the top of the ridge line. Fourteen crewmembers were killed. It was a great shock to the entire base. My commanding officer gave us a two-day stand-down from flying (one of the pilots killed was the brother of a pilot in my squadron), but on the third day, he made every crewmember in the squadron (approximately 150 officers and sailors) get back in the air. We all completed a three-hour refamiliarization flight. The CO understood that in aviation accidents happen. But that doesn't mean we shut down and stop flying. In fact, you'd better get back in the air fast, work out any lingering trepidation, and put the crash behind you. If you can't do this, you've taken yourself out of action.

When my (GPH) son Brendon was deployed on the USS *John C. Stennis*, a nuclear aircraft carrier, an F-14 crew was catapulted off the carrier one morning and they lost power to both engines. As the plane was heading for the ocean's surface, both crewmembers ejected, were picked up by a helicopter, and brought back to the ship. A flight surgeon looked them over, deemed them fit to return to duty, and their commanding officer put them on another F-14 that same afternoon. Stress comes with the job in the Navy and Marine Corps, whether you're in an airplane, on board a surface ship, under the water in a submarine, or on the front lines in Fallujah. Seasoned officers have seen plenty of catastrophe; they learn to keep moving and leading in the aftermath.

LEADING THROUGH NONCATASTROPHIC STRESS

Even when catastrophe is avoided, leaders must contend with major life events—significant life changes that require important adjustment and adaptation. For midshipmen, such events begin with leaving home and surviving plebe summer. They continue as the plebe begins the rigors of academia at USNA, learns to survive on little sleep, and copes with major new responsibilities waiting each time he or she advances to the next rank in the midshipman class system. It is crucial that future Naval leaders learn to cope with these life events; they will be continuous throughout an officer's career.

So too will microstressors, or the seemingly constant sources of stress that can eventually tear down and overwhelm one's immune system and ability to cope. Common microstressors include crowding, noise, inadequate supplies of resources, relational problems, and chronic rushing to meet time demands. Each summer, every new plebe class develops what Academy doctors call the "Plebe Hack." It is a mild but very irritating cough. Plebes don't have colds and they're not sick but Plebe Hack runs rampant throughout the summer.

INOCULATION AT USNA

So how do we go about inoculating midshipmen against major life events and microstressors? We expose them to doses of each so that they can begin formulating effective coping strategies. In fact, nearly every activity on the campus at USNA might be considered a sort of inoculatory strategy. Rear Admiral Alfred Metsger (class of 1931) put it this way:

> The discipline, the initiation activities, are essential in preparing naval officers for their destiny. If a young person loses his stability and sense of humor in this process, he is not the person to be trusted in command of our young in storm or battle.

Rear Admiral Metsger has nicely articulated the reason USNA is so focused on inoculating leaders for stress. The reasoning goes this way: The best way to heighten your capacity for resisting and adapting to negative events is to expose you to consistent doses of stress—punctuated by periods of even more intense stress.

Consider a day in the life of a plebe. Waking-up hits with a bang (this is literally the case in plebe summer when the startling sound of a metal bell throughout Bancroft Hall yanks plebes from a deep sleep) around 0600. During the academic year it's usually earlier because there are more "rates" a plebe must learn. Plebes must then scramble to shower, dress, and memorize the day's entire menu, uniform of the day, scheduled events, and officers-of-the-watch and be familiar with three current events articles from the *Washington Post* or *Baltimore Sun*. They also must be familiar with an article from the sports pages, especially if it contains one about Navy. All of this information must then be delivered in the form of a "chow call" or a staccato shout down the corridor at about 0620 as a means of both waking up and informing the upperclass mids of the coming formation and meal.

Next, the midshipman must scramble to pull together material for the entire day's classes and attend formation in the company where he or she will stand at attention while crucial information for the day is passed on by the company commander. The plebe must then "chop" (run down the center of the corridors in Bancroft Hall and turn each corner squarely while yelling "go Navy, beat Army") and then scramble down the stairway (ladders in Navy jargon) en route to breakfast. At meals, plebes will not speak unless spoken to and they have to eat their meals while "bracing up." In a "braced-up" posture, plebes stand or sit on their chairs rigidly at attention with their chins pulled as far back as possible into their necks while keeping their heads straight. Not only do plebes have to "brace up" at meals but also any time they are not in their rooms or talking to an upperclassman or officer. Additionally, while "braced-up" at meals, plebes must keep their "eyes in the boat," meaning they must continually look straight ahead. If all of that doesn't make their meal miserable, plebes must also sit on only the first three inches of their chairs while eating their meal in the "braced-up" position. Meals are not the most delightful times for plebes.

He or she will attend at least six or seven rigorous classes (typically including engineering, calculus, chemistry, and leadership or navigation). At noon there will be a formation of the entire brigade and a formal procession to lunch. Immediately following the final class of the afternoon, the plebe will proceed to at least two hours of intramural or varsity athletics. Following the evening meal, the plebe will be involved in extracurricular activities including volunteer organizations, cleaning and preparing rooms and uniforms for inspections, and tackling the huge volume of homework typically assigned during the day. Companies may have additional activities scheduled and there are often compulsory lectures or required research activities in the evening. By midnight (with permission to stay up beyond the 2300 taps), the exhausted plebe must have lights out. He or she will probably get five to six hours of sleep before the ritual begins again.

Although this is the prototypical schedule for a plebe at USNA, this description fails to capture fully the moment-to-moment stress most plebes experience around campus. Because the entire Brigade of midshipmen is responsible for "training" plebes, moments when a plebe is not being scrutinized, reprimanded, or required to repeat a performance in some area are rare. Consider the tradition of the "come around" at USNA. Any apparent violation of protocol by a plebe (e.g., failing to chop thoroughly on stairs or accidentally glancing sideways during a meal) can result in the plebe's being ordered to "come around" or report to the room of an upperclassman for a session designed to chastise and "train." Zino describes the come around this way:

> This session consists of the plebe being drilled to demonstrate his rote memorization ability as he recites passages, statistics, and historical minutia from his handbook of naval trivia known as "reef points." These sessions also test his general knowledge of academics, sports, current events, and other tidbits of information (the elevation of Mount Everest, the number of window panes in the Naval Academy Chapel, the number of cobblestones in Tecumseh Court, etc.).... All in all, the come around gives the plebes an opportunity to prove to themselves and to others their mental and physical toughness.

Inoculation demands exposure to the very stimuli that might overwhelm or even kill the unprepared organism. At Navy, leaders must be inoculated to the kind of chronic stress associated with leading a unit through arduous and unpredictable military deployments. So midshipmen learn to handle heavy demands on their time and performance. They acquire adaptive responses to failure and creative approaches to solving the many conflicting demands impinging upon them daily.

A SENATOR'S RECOLLECTION OF PLEBE INOCULATION

Senator John McCain's experience of plebe year at Navy is deftly recorded in his excellent memoir, *Faith of My Fathers*. We offer an extended quote from McCain's book here to highlight a phenomenon we find common among USNA alumni. Although a midshipman weathers the trials and tribulations of plebe year inoculation, he or she is unlikely to report much appreciation for the experience. But later, in the fleet, these same men and women often experience insight about the purpose and value of preparation for managing adversity. Sometimes the insight comes in the form of gradually dawning awareness. Other times the insight strikes like a lightening bolt—perhaps when the officer gets a first taste of combat or must manage the aftermath of a horrific training accident on the deck of carrier. In either case, Senator McCain's words highlight the phenomenon nicely:

Now, more than 40 years after my graduation from the Naval Academy, I understand the premise that supported the harsh treatment of plebes. I may have even grasped it at the time I experienced it, but was simply reluctant to accept its consequences personally. Service academies are not just colleges with a uniform dress code. Their purpose is to prepare you for one profession alone, and that profession's ultimate aspiration is a combat command. The Academy experience is intended to determine whether you are fit for such work, and if you are, to mold your natural ability into the attributes of a capable officer. If you aren't, the Academy wants to discover your ineptitude as quickly as possible. Their period of discovery is your plebe year, when you are subjected to as much stress as the law and a civilized society will allow.

Of course, nothing in peacetime can replicate the dire experiences of war. But the Academy gives it a hell of a try. The workload imposed on you by instructors is daunting but by itself is probably not enough to break all but the least determined plebe. It is the physical and mental hazing by upperclassmen that makes the strain of plebe year so excruciating.

It was a trying time. That was the point, of course. Though I may now understand the purpose of that punishing year, even grant the necessity of learning to tolerate the barely tolerable, I nevertheless hated every minute of it. And I resented everyone who inflicted it on me. I dislike even the memory of it. But, like most graduates of the Academy, my hate for the experience does not constitute regret. It rests in memory, paradoxically, with my appreciation, gratitude really, for the privilege of surviving it, and for the honor of that accomplishment. At moments of great stress, your senses are at their most acute; your mind works at a greatly accelerated pace. That's the purpose, I take it, of plebe year—not simply to test your endurance, but to show that you can function exceptionally well, as a leader must function, in concentrated misery.

STRESS AND THE ART OF ACCURATE APPRAISAL

All leaders face stressful circumstances. Excellent leaders understand that appraising a situation as manageable is half the battle. At USNA, midshipmen receive explicit training in event appraisal. Stress researchers Lazarus and Folkman have identified two distinct phases in this process. At the *primary appraisal* phase, leaders must decide whether an event is a direct threat (liable to harm or damage) or merely a challenge (although difficult or unpleasant, the event may yield some gain). When we determine that a stressful event constitutes a threat, our sympathetic nervous system kicks into gear—mobilizing us to fight or run like crazy. Physiological signs of this threat response include muscle tension, heightened blood pressure, hyperalertness, and inhibited sleep. Of course, maintaining this state for an extended period is exhausting and eventually dangerous (e.g., long-term fatigue and lowered immune system functioning).

Combat leaders must accurately interpret real threats and respond accordingly. Failure to do so will result in death for the leader and the entire unit. But most stressful situations do not qualify as dire threats. Most are challenges. Appraising a situation as a challenge will typically produce useful stimulation and mobilization without overwhelming anxiety and dysfunctional adrenaline. Midshipmen learn that, in fact, there are very few real threats in life. They learn to perceive most events accurately as challenges. And doing so prepares them for adaptive and creative responses.

I (GPH) remember going through flight school and facing the numerous water qualification challenges required of us before we even entered an aircraft. One that stands out is the "Dilbert Dunker." You may have seen it in the movie *An Officer and a Gentleman.* A simulated cockpit has been adapted to ride on two rails into the water. You start about seven or eight feet above the water, are strapped into the cockpit as you would be in an aircraft, and are then launched. As the cockpit shoots down the rails and into the water, it inverts so that once you enter the water you are upside down. Many students become quickly disoriented. After you settle in the water, you then have to release the restraining harness, exit the upside-down cockpit, and swim to the surface. It sounds simple, but as you stand in line watching the others go before you and see some of them not making it, you become extremely apprehensive. The stress is palpable and the challenge is very real.

ACCURATELY APPRAISING CAPACITY TO COPE

The second phase in the appraisal process, called *secondary appraisal*, involves an estimation of one's capacity to respond effectively to the situation. Is the situation hopeless? Do I have what it takes to fix or correct the problem? Will I be able to make a difference? It might reasonably be said that four years of training at USNA is directed firmly at this stage of the stress-appraisal process. We want leaders who believe they can act effectively to direct change without becoming overwhelmed. Repeated exposure to stressful events effectively raises their threshold for feeling overwhelmed. The result is a leader who interprets most events as challenges and responds with self-assurance and optimism.

Lazarus and Folkman summarize a range of research showing that when we interpret an event as challenging versus overwhelming, we engage in what they term *problem-focused* coping. Problem-focused coping involves acting calmly, directly, and proactively to tackle the situation and improve it. Because we perceive ourselves as capable of handling the problem, we are mentally freed to act without anxiety or hopelessness.

Imagine yourself as the captain of the USS *Cole* the day a small boat full of explosives detonated against its hull in a terrorist attack. Would you be capable of engaging in problem-focused coping on the spot? In order to save the ship, and possibly more lives, it is essential that you refuse to panic, quickly gather salient information about the extent of damage and any remaining threat, and react with protective measures designed to control damage and aid the wounded.

PROBLEM- (VERSUS EMOTION-) FOCUSED COPING

In the military and in life, we need problem-focused leaders at the helm. The alternative is *emotion-focused* coping. Emotion-focused coping on a warship or in the chairman's office can be deadly. We engage in emotional coping when we identify a situation as impossible, unmanageable, or beyond repair. Emotion-focused coping may involve panic, hysteric reaction, or, worse, hopelessness.

Emotion-focused coping is similar to what psychologist Martin Seligman refers to as *learned helplessness*. Consider one of the earliest demonstrations of this phenomenon in the laboratory. An unsuspecting rat is dropped into a bucket of water. Although the rat cannot escape, it engages in frantic swimming and ardent attempts to climb the smooth sides of the bucket to safety. After about 20 minutes of intense effort, the rat, now exhausted, drowns. Next, an identical rat is held in the researcher's firm gloved hands for several minutes while the rat struggles to get away. After several minutes, the rat capitulates and stops struggling. It is then dropped into the same bucket of water. It drowns within minutes.

Why? Learned helplessness or emotion-focused coping caused the second rat to decide that its efforts were fruitless. It simply gave up. Seligman later extended this research to dogs. Many dogs that received unpleasant shocks from the floor of a cage eventually gave up trying to escape and lay upon the floor passively receiving them with small whimpers. Later, when the cage was modified so that the dog could easily step out of the cage and into an adjoining cage with no electric shocks, the dog made no effort to do so. Again, these dogs had developed a syndrome of helplessness.

Why is this learned helplessness idea so critical to leadership? When a ship's crew ends up in the water or when a squad of marines is taken prisoner, one of the strongest predictors of survival is mental inoculation to stress and trauma. The question is this: Can the leader mobilize his or her people psychologically to remain problem- versus emotion-focused? Will the leader consistently appraise the situation as a challenge to be managed, and will the leader refuse to engage in hopeless or panicked behavior?

As in the case of intellect, character, and personality, it helps to stack the deck when it comes to resilience to stress. At USNA, we tend to admit future leaders with a performance record suggesting *hardiness*. Hardiness is a personal trait that research shows helps to moderate reactions to stress. Hardy leaders are prone to believing in not only the possibility, but also the high probability of a positive outcome. They act with optimism and often report milder responses to loss or stress. Hardiness predicts confidence in the leader role, better health (including immune system functioning), and greater resilience when catastrophe strikes or stressors mount. At USNA, the majority of our students report for duty with higher than average levels of hardiness. We work hard to strengthen this trait.

LEADING THROUGH SLEEP DEPRIVATION

We live in a culture of inadequate sleep. CEOs and other high-level managers often get to these positions at least partially as a direct result of Type-A workaholism—including a pattern of late-night and early-morning work that cuts into an otherwise normal period of rest. Although each of us varies in our requirement for sleep, most of us require between seven and eight hours of sleep daily for maximal functioning. As the number declines, research documents a range of sleep-deprivation symptoms including: reduced attention, memory difficulties, delayed reaction time, irritability, errors in judgment, unpredictability, and decision-making impairment. Sleep-deprived leaders become less effective, and, in certain situations (e.g., driving a ship, running a nuclear power plant, flying a plane), they become downright dangerous.

During my (GPH) first tour, my squadron was deployed to the Azores, in the middle of the North Atlantic. We had been prosecuting a submarine for almost a week and my crew was on its fourth or fifth mission flying in the middle of the night. P-3 flights last about 10 hours, but we also have a 3-hour pre-flight to get the plane ready to launch, and usually a 2-hour debrief after we land. So that night, in the middle of the dark Atlantic, the crew was pretty tired. I was in the back of the plane when I heard the tactical coordinator (Tacco), the officer who runs the tracking of the submarine, call the cockpit. No one answered. I heard him call a second and a third time with no answer. So, I went forward to the cockpit and looked through the drapes, which were closed to keep the cockpit dark, and saw both my pilots and the flight engineer asleep. The plane was flying in circles on automatic pilot.

Needless to say, I raised my voice in frustration (and horror) and roused the sleeping cockpit. A cascade of choice words followed, and when I left the cockpit I told the Tacco to call them every two minutes to make sure they stayed awake. After about 15 minutes, they got the message and asked that they not be called so frequently. I never forgot it, nor did they.

One of the toughest things for midshipmen at USNA to learn is how to "get it all done" in a day and still leave time for sleep. This may be one of the hardest lessons of plebe year. A midshipman, and we would say other leaders, must answer the following questions: (*a*) How much sleep do I *need* per night? (*b*) What are the signs of sleep deprivation in my behavioral and emotional functioning? (*c*) How long does it take me to recover from a poor night's sleep? (*d*) How does lack of sleep impact my leadership style and effectiveness? Although leaders may be tempted to believe they are unique in their capacity to do without adequate sleep for extended periods (some even become boastful and arrogant in this regard), the research is in. Ongoing sleep deprivation results in lowered cognitive and physical reaction times, mental confusion and error-proneness, and negative emotional symptoms. If severe, sleep deprivation can result in hallucinations and delusions. In my (GPH) classes, I always used the P-3 story to emphasize the importance of getting a good night's sleep in the fleet and as midshipmen, even though they have a lot to accomplish every day.

Although it would be lovely if military leaders could always be assured adequate opportunity for sleep, this is simply not reality. Therefore, future leaders at Navy are inoculated for sleep deprivation. They are not only required to acclimate to periods of decreased sleep, but we expect them to learn to balance their responsibilities such that they can get sleep and respond to endless demands on their time. Without a doubt, plebe year is the hardest in this regard.

After some initial experience with severe sleep deprivation, most midshipmen learn to strike a balance that allows for reasonable sleep—even in the context of seemingly impossible demands upon their time. They really seem to manage it better as they become upperclassmen. They appreciate the fact that sleep is restorative in both a physical and psychological sense. They begin to understand the paradox that stealing from sleep time to get ahead often results in diminished performance and less attention to detail.

Of course, there are times when sleep deprivation is an inevitable part of leading. We refer to combat situations or other high-tempo military operations. Sometimes, sleep deprivation is not a choice but a necessity. On the battlefield, it is not uncommon to go days with little rest. Both of my

(GPH) sons, when entering Iraq, went more than 48 hours without sleep just to get to their destinations safely. In these contexts, effective leaders learn a variety of strategies for maintaining a reasonably high level of performance. These include beginning a period of combat well-rested, use of caffeine for brief bursts of alertness, and napping. Research on military personnel shows that even one 30-minute nap can stave off some of the worst brain-based symptoms of sleep deprivation. Just remember that this is a short-term fix and that the effects of deprivation will eventually catch up to you.

INOCULATE FOR SEVERE STRESS

Near the end of the plebe year at USNA, the plebe class begins to stir with anticipation. The first year of classes has been weathered, plebes have survived the relentless stress of drilling and training from the upper classes, and the Herndon climb and the end of the plebe year is squarely in sight. But not so fast. First, there is a little matter known simply as *sea trials*. Sea trials is one very long day of nearly constant physical and psychological challenge. Visualize the most grueling obstacle course you can imagine and then contemplate running it all day long without end. Imagine starting your day with a swim in the mud and continuing through the entire day with a thick mud coating underneath your soaked battle gear.

During sea trials you will run, you will race, you will sprint up hills, and you will swim in the salty brine of the Chesapeake Bay. You will carry heavy objects over your head, run in formation, and, if the weather is right, sweat profusely in the Annapolis spring humidity. By the end of your sea trial experience, you will have difficulty walking, let alone running. You will be utterly depleted. Most important, you will have learned something crucial about yourself. You can take more than you thought you could. During the day, you will have come (often more than once) to some wall of exhaustion and then moved beyond it. This insight will serve you well as a leader in combat: You can always go farther than you think you can.

Of course, this inoculation continues for leaders in the Navy and Marine Corps when they enter the fleet. Perhaps the best example of this is SERE (Survival, Evasion, Resistance, and Escape) school. I (GPH) attended SERE school when I was a lieutenant commander. (This was not good because I was the second senior officer in our class. The more senior you are, the more you are singled out from the rest of the class for extra attention). It was the most grueling training I have ever experienced. It is the one Navy certificate of completion that I took home and locked in my safe because I never wanted to do it again. I wasn't going to lose that damn certificate!

Air crewmen, Special Forces members, and some Intelligence officers, must complete this mandatory course at one of two SERE training centers run by the Navy. During this training, you learn to survive and evade capture, simulating that you were shot down or lost in enemy territory. The initial phase is spent using survival strategies. You simulate being shot down and have to exist with what you have on your back and what you can find to eat. We spent a couple of days in the desert and then were moved to more mountainous terrain. During the five or so days in the survival phase, my group of 54 "survivors" was able to catch one small rabbit to share. We made rabbit stew, which was rather tasty, but we were all still extremely hungry. After five days, we were exhausted, starved, and mentally at a low point. When the instructors got us to that point, we entered the next phase, which is the evasion phase.

We were given a two-hour period to traverse a large remote area and evade the instructors to the best of our ability. Of course they were riding around in humvees and other vehicles and had a distinct advantage of maneuverability, especially because we were so tired and hungry. Of course, in the end, everyone gets captured. Next, we all entered the POW compound. Once captured, we were taught to endure and resist as prisoners-of-war. The POW camp is very realistic, or as realistic as they can make it without actual torture.

During a period of several days, we were exposed to many of the features of extreme deprivation and mistreatment common in previous prisoner-of-war situations for American service personnel. As days in the captivity segment of SERE went by, we were sleep deprived, food deprived, and constantly harassed and physically challenged. Some very tough officers and enlisted personnel were reduced to tears. Many of them gave up "secrets" during this exercise and were later shocked at the limits of their own ability to endure extreme stress. SERE school and experiences like it are designed to inoculate combatants to the worst effects of extreme duress and deprivation. Such inoculating experiences help create what some military psychologists have described as the "bulletproof mind."

Although most leaders will never lead in combat, and most will never lead in situations of dire personal threat or extreme deprivation, we think it wise for leaders to be prepared for the worst they could face in the leader role. Are you ready to manage your people through a natural disaster? What about a horrific accident? How will you handle an economic crash that places your company's very existence in jeopardy? Excellent leaders must be inoculated for the worst-case scenario.

THE GOUGE

Let's face it, stress is an omnipresent and pervasive fact of life for leaders. In the frantic life of a CEO or combat leader, there is simply no way around stress. Although stress can't be prevented, it can be minimized and adapted to. It's what you do with stress that counts.

Framing circumstances as challenges, remaining problem-focused, practicing relaxation, and keeping fit are all important components of adapting well. Captain Kapitulik has handled stress from the helicopter crash by becoming a triathlete. He has competed in several triathlons to raise money for the children of those men killed in the crash. At last count the total amount he has helped raise is over $60,000.

In dire situations, leaders must step forward, maintain focus, and bring followers back safely. Always, the leader must revise goals, define common objectives, and offer solutions to deal with the sources of stress and conflict. At other times, leaders must realize that they may be the source of stress for their followers. Hasty decisions, unrealistic timelines, and undue pressure will not get you or your team to your desired goals.

At Navy, we deliberately inoculate future war fighters for intense stress. When midshipmen experience unrelenting demands here at the Academy, they will be prepared for it in the fleet. We need officers like Captain Kapitulik and the commanding officer of the USS *Cole*; we need officers who can take the worst and keep on leading.

7

SHIPMATES FIRST

*Sign on and sail with me. The stature of our homeland is
no more than the measure of ourselves. Our job is to keep
her free. Our will is to keep the torch of freedom burning
for all. To this solemn purpose we call on the young, the
brave and the strong, and the free. Heed my call. Come to
the sea. Come sail with me.*

JOHN PAUL JONES

For many years, midshipmen walking the corridors of Luce Hall would
look upon a seemingly endless line of plaques devoted to USNA graduates who had been awarded the Medal of Honor. Each plaque offered a
photo of the honoree and a short citation recounting the officer's heroic
actions in combat—typically some selfless behavior in the face of unreasonable odds. Most of the young faces peering out from these plaques were
those of young men who had been killed in the context of performing this
heroic feat. Many had given their lives in WWI or WWII, others in wars
dating back to the mid-1800s. Of course, the Korean and Vietnam conflicts produced many additional Medal of Honor recipients from among
the Academy's alumni.

When one paused and actually read these important citations, a salient theme quickly emerged; in addition to demonstrating unusual bravery, these men and women had often made the ultimate sacrifice in the context of taking care of others. As officers and leaders in the Navy or Marines, they had come under hostile fire or accepted a mission involving tremendous risk. When things were bleak and options diminishing, these officers had made a decision—typically a very rapid decision—to place themselves between the enemy and their comrades, to stay with a stranded or wounded man in spite of advancing forces, or to make a suicidal charge as a means of neutralizing a position of grave threat to the rest of the unit. Although there is no way to interview most of these recipients today, we suspect that if asked about the motivation behind their behavior in action, many of them would tell you they were just watching out for their shipmates.

SHIP, SHIPMATE, SELF

Ship, shipmate, self. This is one of the most important phrases new midshipmen learn as soon as they put on the uniform at the Naval Academy. It sets the tone, not only for their years at the Academy, but also for their entire career, and many would say for the rest of their lives. For sailors in the Navy, it is not about self. First, foremost, and always, it is about the ship, squadron, submarine, or Marine unit. Protecting the ship and completing the mission must always be foremost in every sailor's or marine's mind. Nothing is more important; no duty is more sacred.

Next in importance come one's fellow shipmates, those important people they will serve with and sail with into "harm's way." In fact, when it comes to importance, the safety and survival of shipmates comes only after the safety and survival of the ship and the completion of its mission. A sailor must depend on his or her shipmates; one's own life must be placed in their hands. When ship and shipmate are taken care of, the midshipmen learn that then, and only then, can they consider self.

My (GPH) Marine son, Brendon, was attached to a unit in Yuma, Arizona, but when the Iraq war started, he and three of his enlisted men were assigned to the 1st Marine Expeditionary Force. Once they crossed the Iraqi border, 1 MEF was in the thick of the fighting. Brendon and his troops had advanced to just outside of Baghdad when his general told Brendon he was sending him back to another unit that required his expertise. He is an intelligence officer and the Marines in the rear were having trouble using a new system that he had helped develop in Yuma. Brendon requested that his marines accompany him because he did not want to leave them behind. The general said, "No"—that only Brendon was being transferred. Brendon told the general that if that were the case, he would stay with his men. The general ordered him back anyway (the mission was what mattered) but a short time later, Brendon was able to work it out and get his men assigned back to him. That's what shipmates do for one another.

At USNA, *shipmate* is one of the first terms memorized by new plebes. It is also among the most enduring concepts our graduates hold on to in their lives and service after the Academy. At Navy, a shipmate is another midshipman, someone who has taken the same oath, suffered through many of the same ordeals, and someone to whom each midshipman now owes an abiding trust and allegiance. As one midshipman put it:

> The Academy defines brotherhood and family by more than Greek letters, and, if you let it, will be the tie that binds you with the strongest values of the United States.

There is an unconditional quality to the shipmate concept. If you are my shipmate, I stick up for you through thick and thin, not because of your performance, but because of your station. Wearing the uniform entitles you to this service from me. There is personal honor at stake here. If we are shipmates, you and I have an implicit agreement for mutual care and protection. I expect you to watch out for my interests and I will always do the same for you. Following through with this contract—especially when nobody is watching—is a matter of integrity. This contract doesn't end once you leave the ship.

The abiding commitment to take care of one's shipmates is manifested in many ways, but no situation will call forth the shipmate bond more quickly than conflict. When a midshipman gets into a bind "out on the town" or elsewhere in public, he or she can count on shipmates to close ranks and render whatever assistance or service is required to get him or her out of harm's way and safely back to base. One midshipman put it this way:

The best part of the Naval Academy is teamwork. You are not alone ever; someone will always be looking out for you.

Being a shipmate is about loyalty. Whatever petty squabbles we may have in our daily lives, all of it goes by the wayside the minute you really need my help. Social psychologists might refer to this behavior as the principle of reciprocity. A sense of reciprocity is a strong emotional conviction that we must repay whatever has been given to us. As a midshipman, and later as a Naval officer, I am likely to feel indebted to my shipmates for their service, kindness, loyalty, commitment, and trust. In fact, I am likely to feel indebted even without any grand demonstration of heroic sacrifice on my behalf. I assume that you are ready to sacrifice on my behalf when the time comes. I bank on it.

Here at the Academy, a corollary to shipmate loyalty is classmate loyalty. Being loyal to your classmates is learned very early in plebe summer. I (GPH) remember that during plebe summer my company was jogging around Farragut Field. We were all in a single line and, while circling the field, the last midshipman in line had to fall out, run past the other midshipmen, and fall in at the head of the line. As soon as he fell in, the midshipman at the end of the line would begin again. When my turn came, I passed the rest of my classmates and fell into the front of the line about eight feet in front of the column. Well, my second class (upperclass squad leader) started screaming and yelling and calling me all sorts of things because I had "bilged my classmates" (we'll explain shortly) by showing off and placing myself that far ahead of the rest of the group. As punishment for not being loyal to my classmates, I had to run ahead of the group, circle the entire field (it's a good mile if not more), and try to catch up with the company, then ask permission to rejoin the classmates I had "bilged." I never repeated that mistake again.

NEVER BILGE A SHIPMATE

Not only is an academy midshipmen bound to keep track of his or her shipmates, there is also a clear prohibition against doing anything to take advantage of, get one over on, or bring a shipmate to the attention of superiors in a negative way. Such behavior would be considered "bilging a shipmate," and it is ardently avoided. One can also bilge a shipmate by neglecting to provide important information or by failing to help a shipmate correct an obvious problem (shirt untucked, shoes poorly shined, or a presentation incorrectly prepared) before it comes to the attention of an officer or upperclassman. John McCain wrote about his experience with not bilging a classmate:

> The most sacrosanct principle governing a midshipman's behavior was the unwritten rule to "never bilge a classmate," which required midshipmen to overlook a violation of the rules by a fellow midshipman short of honor code violations. In September of my last year, my roommates and I, along with four roommates in the next room and two other midshipmen on our deck, chipped in to buy a television. In those days, Academy regulations enjoined midshipmen from keeping electrical appliances of any kind in their rooms. Even hot plates were considered contraband. Mindful of, but undeterred by the regulation, our small syndicate had decided we would risk the wrath of our superiors for the pleasure of watching the Friday night fights on our television. We kept the set hidden in the crawl space in our room, located behind a wooden panel. The panel could be easily removed by hand, and we would bring the set out to watch the fights on Friday, "Maverick" on Sunday, and other popular television programs of the time. My pal, Chuck Larsen, whose exemplary scholastic record and obvious aptitude for command had won him the highest office a midshipman could hold, Brigade Commander, was serving as midshipman-of-the-watch one night. Academy officials would have been disappointed to discover their prized midshipman among those gathered around the television in my room to watch a boxing match, shirking the duties of his office to enjoy a few minutes of illicit fun with some of the more "disreputable" midshipmen at the Academy. In the middle of our viewing, the mate of the deck rapped on my door to warn us that the officer of the watch was approaching. We quickly returned the television set to its hiding place and stuffed the midshipman of the watch (Larsen), dressed in his formal blue uniform and wearing his sword, along with his startled plebe mate, into my closet. The rest of us opened up textbooks and earnestly affected the appearance of dutiful midshipmen gathered in a study group. Fortunately, the officer never

bothered to enter our room. Had he done so, our atypical studiousness surely would have aroused his suspicion.

Of course, John McCain went on to become a U.S. senator but admits that he wasn't very good at following most of the Academy rules. Chuck Larsen became a four-star admiral, served as commander-in-chief, Pacific, and served twice as superintendent of the Academy, the only naval officer ever to have done so.

There is only one exception to this time-honored requirement to protect one's shipmates: violations of the honor code. We have already described the midshipman honor system. Although no midshipman is eager to report a peer for a problem of honor, midshipmen are nonetheless the most stringent members of the USNA community when it comes to accountability to this code. In a profound way, this is also a crucial part of being a shipmate; you can count on me to hold you accountable, just as you can expect absolute integrity from me.

SHIPMATE AS LEADER

So why is the shipmate concept so essential to leadership? Too often, leaders in organizations try to go it alone. They use the John Wayne strategy—deluding themselves into believing that a one-man (or one-woman) show will get results. It never works. Imagine an aircraft carrier CO trying to get results from 5000 to 6000 subordinates with a detached self-promoting approach. No way. You want to take me to sea for six months, ask me to work long hours in unpleasant circumstances, and put my life on the line each day flying or supporting dangerous missions? If so, you'd better make damn sure I believe in you or, more important, that I believe in your commitment to me. You'd better make sure you've earned the right to be called shipmate.

When a leader views his or her followers as precious resources to be served and protected, followers pick up on this attitude quickly. And nothing will inspire deep and unrelenting loyalty as quickly as a leader whose quest is to take care of his or her people in the context of achieving a mission. Sadly, too many leaders in other environments overlook the simple truth that responding to followers as "mates" versus subordinates can make all the difference. Sometimes, it's the simple things that leave a lasting impression.

LEADING BY SACRIFICE

One of the interesting facts about real leadership is that it usually costs. In fact, the most successful leaders are those who see themselves as serving their followers. Anything else is self-aggrandizing, and it's destined to become transparent.

When Robert Greenleaf introduced the term *servant-leadership*, he described a phenomenon deeply familiar to military officers. Servant leadership is defined as a natural inclination to serve others first. This serving leader is primarily concerned with the needs and best interests of his or her followers. This motivation for leading cannot really be taught. There is something intrinsic and internal about the capacity for serving others. Servant leadership can be nurtured and inspired though. Following someone who serves in this way often makes a profound impact upon one's own sense of the meaning of leadership. Stephen Covey has also highlighted the fact that real leaders are service-oriented:

> Those striving to be principle-centered see life as a mission, not as a career. Their nurturing sources have armed and prepared them for service. In effect, every morning they "yoke up" and put on the harness of service, thinking of others…. I emphasize this principle of service or yoking up because I have come to believe that effort to become principle-centered without a load to carry simply will not succeed. We may attempt to do it as a kind of intellectual or moral exercise, but if we don't have a sense of responsibility, of service, of contribution, something we need to pull or push, it becomes a futile endeavor.

One of the lessons learned early on by midshipmen and followers in any context is that service-oriented leaders typically lead quietly and without expectation of recognition and reward. Contrast this style with the flamboyant self-promoting leader who views the leader role as a stepping stone to increased power and prestige. At USNA, midshipmen who rise to positions of command within the brigade of midshipmen are called "stripers." Stripers have typically been recognized by both peers and company officers as effective when it comes to getting subordinates to follow their lead, and selfless when it comes to their own time and resources. We think these things often go together. Selfless leadership engenders reciprocity. We want to serve and to please a leader who cares about us and who makes leadership decisions with our interests sincerely in view.

Perhaps the best reminder of servant leadership at Navy is the annual presentation of the Draper L. Kauffman leadership excellence award. The Kauffman award recognizes a first-class midshipman who has distinguished himself or herself among the entire graduating class as a remarkable example of volunteerism, service without expectation of reward or recognition, and resolute focus on mission accomplishment. Recipients of this award each year are truly exceptional young leaders—not simply because they have excellent grades, inspiring military bearing, and solid athletic performance. They have all of these attributes, but they have more.

Kauffman awardees have a long track record of going out of their way to serve their shipmates. They go out of their way to tutor shipmates struggling with arduous engineering courses; they hold their own EI (extra instruction) sessions for peers; review drafts of their papers; and constantly encourage them to hang tough. They volunteer to organize extra "inspirational" physical training for midshipmen peers who have trouble meeting the fitness or weight standards at USNA, and they constantly arrange to lead shipmates on volunteer missions for community outreach. And here is the most fascinating thing about the annual Kauffman award: The midshipman selected each year is often genuinely shocked to receive it. We think this is striking. The midshipmen leader most likely to be viewed by his or her followers as inspirational and selfless is also among the least likely to ever think about or anticipate how his or her sacrifice will ultimately pay off. It is a delight to observe their humble reception of this richly deserved award.

LEADERSHIP AS OBLIGATION AND OPPORTUNITY

All of us have heard the phrase, "The Captain goes down with the ship." This is an interesting idea. Although it has become an overused cliché in modern culture, it carries an underlying message—a sober message for leaders. Leadership is first and foremost an obligation. Although it is an obligation freely accepted, it would be a mistake to deny the fact that increasing leadership brings increasing responsibility.

It is interesting to observe USNA midshipmen advance in class rank during their four years. As a plebe, it is easy to focus on the privileges and perks enjoyed by upperclassmen (additional time away from the yard, later curfews, and fewer required activities each day). Yet, as these plebes advance, they come to appreciate the additional responsibilities that accrue to upperclassmen. These include responsibilities for correctly training plebes, ensuring that the commandant's and superintendent's orders are carried out by the entire brigade of midshipmen, and taking care of subordinate shipmates such that they enjoy success and avoid negative attention around the yard. Midshipmen come to appreciate the fact that their followers' appearance and performance are direct reflections of their leadership. They may also learn the hard way that when the worst happens in your company, the buck stops with the senior midshipmen leaders. One graduate recently wrote this:

> I served as first battalion commander for the fall semester of my first class year. On the day the brigade returned for the academic year, I was responsible for reporting the muster reports for the battalion. A couple of companies were late reporting to me. When the officer of the watch asked me to account for First Battalion, I explained the situation and indicated I was having difficulty obtaining information from two of my companies. The officer of the watch then proceeded in no uncertain terms to remind me of the five basic responses, one of which was "No excuse, Sir!" His rebuke stung, but he made a good point. I should stick up for my subordinates, taking the heat and shielding them, even if it's not my fault. To do otherwise squanders an opportunity given to me to show my subordinates that I care for them enough to put myself in "harm's way" for my troops.

Although it is a fact that Navy and Marine leaders do go down with their ships when things go south, and although it is true that the excellent leaders fully expect the buck to stop at their doorstep every time, truly exceptional leaders see even this level of obligation as an opportunity. One week after taking over as commanding officer of my (GPH) squadron, an instructor pilot had a young pilot out in the pattern doing "touch and go's." This meant that they were going round and round in the flight pattern practicing takeoffs and landings. I got a call in my office from the flight line telling me to come out to the runway right away, but not explaining why my presence was required. Walking out of the administration building and looking out on the runway, I could see why. Tire debris littered the runway and the plane was sitting at an awkward angle. It seems that the young pilot, when he touched down, had accidentally hit the brakes. On a P-3, we use reverse thrust to stop an aircraft and only in dire straits would we use the brakes. Using the brakes caused all of the plane's tires to blow out.

Looking at the all the debris and my plane with five flat tires, I could only imagine what my boss was going to say to me after only one week in command, when I placed the call back to our home base informing him of the incident. The only thing I thought to myself was, "Well, at least I had a week in command." The only thing he said to me was, "Don't ever let that pilot touch the brakes again!" I was extremely grateful for the opportunity to continue to serve and I made sure everyone in the squadron knew what happened when you used brakes on a P-3 trying to land.

As a midshipmen leader at USNA, keep in mind that you are leading some of the brightest young men and women in the country. They are smart, loyal, dedicated, and sincere. Add to this the fact that the country's citizens are counting on you to take care of these valuable national resources, and it is easy to see why leaders at Navy feel honored to lead. It is a profound opportunity. In our experience, leaders move from good to great at the same rate at which they begin to see their leadership duties less in terms of onerous obligation and more in terms of sacred duty and remarkable opportunity.

For generations, shipmates the world over have ended tours of duty with the words, "It has been a pleasure to serve with you." This is very important. Not only are leaders serving their subordinates (by agreeing to be the one to go down with the ship if needed), they are simultaneously serving alongside their subordinates. Although the leader may be a four-star admiral and the follower a seaman, both understand that, on some level at least, they are standing side-by-side looking ahead at a superordinate mission (defending the country from enemies foreign and domestic).

THE GOUGE

Here is the bottom line: Being a shipmate and having shipmates is something sacred. The bonds between shipmates are the glue that holds the organization together; they create an emotional charge that endows commitment to the Navy with meaning. Shipmates look out for one another, take care of one another, and in some cases will give their lives for one another. Being a shipmate is a two-way street. It doesn't matter what your rank is or whether you're the commanding officer or a seaman on the flight deck. You are all in it together and that makes it something special. Whether a ship, plane, or submarine founders or triumphs in combat, every member of that crew will share the same fate.

Leaders have an obligation to their shipmates. Excellent leaders see themselves as servants of their people. Part of serving through leadership is acceptance of the obligation to sacrifice for others. This is the burden of command and throughout the history of military leadership it has at times been a terrible burden. Nonetheless, the most mature and successful leaders manage to reframe this obligation as opportunity. The demands don't change but the leader's assessment of those demands does. In the end, the finest leaders anywhere mean it when they say, "It has been a pleasure to serve with you."

8

SUCCESS IS
IN THE DRILL

On the morning of July 29, 1967, the crew of the USS *Forrestal* was going about their business as usual. Stationed several miles off the coast of North Vietnam on Yankee Station, the carrier's pilots were getting ready to conduct daily combat operations over that country. The first of the Navy's "supercarriers," the *Forrestal* was an 80,000-ton ship capable of carrying 5000 officers and enlisted men and launching more than a hundred fighters and bombers. After four consecutive days of bombing missions in the humid waters of the Gulf of Tonkin, the *Forrestal* crew was just hitting its combat operations tempo when catastrophe struck.

At around 10:50 a.m., just as the ship's crew was preparing to launch the day's second wave of bombers, a zuni rocket accidentally fired from an F-4 Phantom into a parked and armed A-4 Skyhawk (John McCain's aircraft). The rocket ruptured the Skyhawk's fuel tank and caused a 1000-pound bomb to drop from the Skyhawk onto the deck of the *Forrestal*.

Highly volatile jet fuel—JP-5—leaked across the deck and ignited, surrounding and effectively "cooking" the giant bomb as the shocked crew members began scrambling to quarters and preparing firefighting equipment. Within a minute, the 1000-pound bomb exploded and sent a thunderous shock wave across the deck. At this point, crewmen later noted that "all hell broke lose." Numerous jet aircraft, all fully loaded with highly flammable fuel, rockets, and bombs, were engulfed in a gargantuan wall of flame. More bombs and rockets exploded, at times blasting large holes in the deck of the ship, killing crewmembers and blowing several of them right over the side of the ship. Many brave sailors rushed toward the flames with fire-fighting equipment and were killed as bombs exploded. The deck of the *Forrestal* rapidly became an inferno through which chunks of shrapnel flew hundreds of feet into the air at high velocity. The loss of life in the fist several minutes of the conflagration was horrendous. As jet fuel poured through large craters in the flight deck, fires ignited in compartments below decks.

Deep in the ship, smoke and fire filled many compartments and further explosions occurred as fuel and oxygen tanks ignited. There were many acts of heroism that day as ordinary seamen and junior officers remained at their posts in spite of heavy smoke and clear danger in order to usher sleeping, disoriented, or wounded shipmates to safety. Damage control and fire-fighting crews followed protocol and, despite many injuries and some loss of life, they began to turn the tide of the battle and slowly contain the fire. Volatile ordinance was jettisoned overboard; witnesses later reported small sailors carrying bombs weighing over 200 pounds to the side of the ship and dropping them overboard. Procedures for stabilizing and evacuating wounded and burned sailors were followed and these were successfully transitioned to waiting support ships.

For the next 13 hours, the crew of the *Forrestal* battled the fire relentlessly. Although some of the firefighting equipment had been disabled in the fires and explosions, the crew used all available means to extinguish the flames. Many of them worked frantically to jettison bombs, rockets, and ammunition overboard before it could ignite. As the flames were controlled and the fire contained, many of the crew had to turn their attention to the dead and injured among them. In all, this tragic accident left 132 dead, 2 missing and believed dead, and 62 seriously injured. Recovering the burned bodies of shipmates was an astoundingly gruesome task.

Considering the fact that the *Forrestal* sustained more than a dozen major explosions from 1000- and 500-pound bombs, as well as numerous explosions of aircraft, fuel tanks, and missiles, it is remarkable that the ship survived at all. No carrier before or since has sustained this kind of catastrophic impact and remained intact. Twenty-six aircraft were entirely destroyed or jettisoned overboard and another 31 were damaged. Much of the credit for the fact that the carrier was quickly repaired and returned to duty must be directed to the men who performed magnificently under the most dangerous and life-threatening conditions.

So what was the difference between sinking and staying alive to fight another day? How did the *Forrestal* crew manage to prevent the demise of a ship that was literally being blown to bits and burning from top to bottom? Certainly bravery and heroism played a part in the *Forrestal* story. One might also argue that luck or circumstances such as fair weather and some fire-fighting support from nearby ships helped. They may have.

But we see something else in the *Forrestal*'s survival; we see the outcome of constant training, drilling, and preparing for adversity. We call this "drilling for success" and it is a cornerstone of life in the Navy and Marine Corps. It is also a core lesson at the Naval Academy. Distilled to its most basic form, the lesson would go something like this: If you want to respond effectively in combat, and if you want to maximize your chances of survival when the worst of circumstances strike, you'd better prepare so thoroughly and so consistently that the actions required to achieve these goals are automatic and reflexive. Success comes from over-learning.

DRILLING AS A WAY OF LIFE

Practice makes perfect, or almost perfect. When fire breaks out on deck or when the bullets start flying, it's too late to determine how to respond. A leader and his or her people had better already know how to respond—to *every* eventuality. Ask any midshipmen at USNA about drilling and you'll get an ear full. Most often you'll hear about endless hours of marching in tightly synchronized formation as the entire brigade of midshipmen (over 4000 strong) marches to the drill field, marches into position company by company, and then stands at attention while the various company commanders report to the brigade commander on the status and readiness of the members of each company. The brigade will intermittently come to attention, stand at parade rest, respond to various orders, and execute a number of well-choreographed movements and maneuvers with rifles and flags.

Although drilling may appear quaint but frankly pointless to the outside observer, its historical and contemporary importance are never lost on USNA leaders. Historically, the formal pass-and-review parade was a prelude to battle. Prior to leading their troops into combat, admirals and generals would observe them "forming up" or preparing to march onto the battlefield. This was a sober occasion and it was essential that each company and battalion officer give an accurate reporting of his or her subordinates' presence and readiness for the fight. Today, it is equally imperative that midshipmen learn to approach preparation and training with sober and deliberate attention to detail. When the battle comes, the rationale for all the repetition will become clear.

Looking back on that experience, every midshipman fondly recalls how awkward and uncoordinated they were when they began drilling, or how amusing it was for upperclassmen to watch plebes almost knock themselves unconscious as rifle butts hit many a plebe head. Yet, after many hours on the drill field and by the end of their six-week indoctrination, they are usually quite proud of their new-found synchronicity. They appear to be very professional military men and women. What was awkward has become smooth and automatic.

Midshipmen often describe drilling with a sense of weariness in their voices. The reason is simple. They do it all the time. Forming up, marching, and executing parade orders become nearly unconscious activities. In fact, many of them find it humorous that when they are on liberty in Annapolis, as they walk along together, they unconsciously "march" through town in step. Many of the component parts are reflexive and instantaneous by the time a midshipman leaves USNA. From the moment midshipmen check on board at USNA they drill. And they drill in all conditions. Rain, snow, mud, intense humidity, and blistering heat will all become part of the midshipmen's recollection of drilling.

I (GPH) remember that, during my second class year at the color parade, a fellow midshipman in my company passed out due to heat exhaustion and fell on the bayonet of the midshipman next to him. Back then, we still had to wear the heavy wool dress uniform that doubled over in the front. Fortunately, it provided enough padding to save the midshipman from any major injury and he suffered only a minor cut. Another thing midshipmen learn quickly during drill is not to "lock-your-knees" while standing at attention. This is a quick way to cut off circulation and more than a few midshipmen have discovered the hard way that locked knees will put you out of commission on the parade field.

SOMEDAY, THE DRILLING WILL MAKE SENSE

Beyond drilling for parades, midshipmen's lives are nearly dominated by routine, repetition, and memorization—especially during the plebe year. Chopping, marching, drilling for parades, memorizing reams of apparently worthless information are all part of a larger design: make these future officers into men and women with the ability to memorize information, attend to details, follow orders instantaneously, adhere to custom and protocol, and understand the virtue of over-learning vital mission-related information and skills. By over-learning we mean going over material or practicing protocols so many times that the material or activity can be repeated or carried out instantly and automatically—without taking time to reconsider the material or seek guidance regarding how to respond. One graduate put it this way:

> During plebe summer, we had a talk by one of the Marine company officers. He was describing his combat experience in Vietnam in which he was flying his jet on a mission over the North. He described in detail the antiaircraft flak exploding all around his aircraft while trying to handle an in-flight emergency. His words, which I never forgot and often thought of during the most difficult moments of plebe year were, "With all of this going on, I thought to myself, you know, I've had tougher plebe come-arounds than this!" I believe this inspirational quote illustrates the confidence in oneself that a trying experience like plebe year can instill in future Naval and Marine Corps officers. It worked for me.

DRILLING JUST MIGHT SAVE YOUR LIFE

So what's the big deal about drilling? And how does the value of drilling at USNA translate to the fleet and to life as a leader beyond the Navy? The answer is as clear to us as it must have been to the survivors of the USS *For-restal* fire. When a crew constantly prepares for combat and adversity, they'll be ready when the time to confront these challenges arrives. And it nearly always arrives.

Let us give you another good example. When I (GPH) was in Hawaii, one of our sister squadrons had an incident that every P-3 crew dreads—a propeller over-speed. Although the propellers normally run at 100 percent rpm, infrequently a propeller will over-speed—reaching revolutions over 100 percent. Pilots practice what to do in this situation over and over again. It is quite frightening because the sound of the propeller increases significantly, the plane starts to shake, and the wing will vibrate violently if the propeller is not shut down (feathered) immediately.

The P-3 crew was near Johnson Island, southwest of Hawaii, when their propeller began to over-speed. Although the cockpit went through the normal emergency procedures to feather the propeller, and, when that didn't work, to shut the engine down, nothing happened. The crew immediately began methodical preparations for two likely emergency procedures—parachuting out of the plane or ditching the aircraft at sea. Remarkably, no one panicked.

As the crew turned toward Hawaii (unfortunately, the airfield at Johnson Island was not adequate for a P-3 to land), everyone continued detailed preparations for the worst. The propeller began to vibrate more violently. The radioman made contact with Hawaii and the squadron and informed them of their situation. Pilots from the squadron got on the radio and tried to offer suggestions, but nothing helped. The crew continued their efforts to get the propeller feathered but by this point the propeller was beginning to come off the engine. Parachuting out of the airplane again became a distinct possibility, but the mission commander did not want to scatter the crew over a significant area of water. If they parachuted, would they be able to locate everyone and get them into the liferafts the P-3 carried? Probably not. So the crew descended to a low altitude and prepared to ditch the airplane at sea, all the while continuing to try to get either the prop or the engine to shut down.

Somehow, the propeller stayed intact. Hawaii finally came into sight and the crew began their approach to the runway. As they crossed the edge of the runway, the propeller finally departed the airplane but the crew was able to control the P-3 for the final touchdown and stop the aircraft safely. What began as a routine mission became a nightmare. We think it safe to say that all traumatic and catastrophic events begin as routine missions. The important lesson here is that the crew's level of preparation and training paid dividends. Though they could not get the propeller to shut down, no one panicked. The crew made preparations for worst-case eventualities. Although ditching at sea or parachuting out of the aircraft are risky measures, each procedure had been drilled hundreds of times. Constant drilling helped this crew handle a very bad situation professionally and without panic. Drilling may have saved their lives.

Consider life on board a submarine. Nearly every eventuality could be a threat to the crew's survival. Contact with submerged objects, fires, depletion of oxygen, leaks in the sub's hull, or failure of vital navigation, cooling, or propulsion systems all create significant danger when the crew is several hundred feet under the surface of the ocean.

I (WBJ) was fortunate enough to have a short underway deployment on one of our country's fast-attack submarines. Although I was surprised by many facets of life on a nuclear submarine (cramped living quarters, narrow passageways, the odd sensation of sleeping while the submarine turned at strange angles—often nearly ejecting me from my rack), nothing surprised me more than the nearly constant cacophony of alarms and overhead announcements signaling emergency drills. There were fire drills, drills involving a nuclear incident, damage-control drills designed to stop incoming water in the event of a hull rupture and get the sub to the surface as quickly as possible, and, of course, there were drills designed to simulate enemy attack, a mine in the water, and other combat-related scenarios requiring the entire sub's crew to scramble to general quarters. Always, the sub's crew took the drill as seriously as though the sub were actually ablaze or sinking fast. Emergency gear was donned, water hoses raced through passage ways as crewmen yelled "Make a hole" and shipmates pressed themselves tightly against bulkheads to allow damage-control or fire-fighting crews to race through.

Always, the captain of the sub was watching. He timed and evaluated the crew's performance during each drill. He was looking for efficiency, accuracy, and effectiveness. The question in his mind was this: If this were the real thing, would we all survive? Would we save the sub? Would we kill the enemy or would he kill us?

Although the United States enjoys a remarkable record of safety and success in its submarine fleet, subs, like ships and planes, have occasionally been lost. Sometimes the circumstances were unavoidable or unpredictable. At other times, human error or poor adherence to protocol can be blamed. This is why a military leader drills troops. When the lights go out, the sub is drifting toward the bottom, and crucial systems are failing, it's time for the crew to act. Make sure they know exactly what to do and how to do it. But more than that, make sure they've practiced it so often and under so many different circumstances that they can do it in pitch black conditions while breathing smoke and wading through water. This is not the time to crack open the training manual. These people had better be trained. Your success as a leader and their lives depend on it. Batallion Commander Hal Moore described it this way in *We Were Soldiers Once...and Young:*

> During the 14 months before we sailed for Vietnam, we spent most of our time in the field, practicing assault landings from helicopters, and the incredibly complex coordination of artillery, tactical air support, and aerial rocket artillery with the all-important flow of helicopters into and out of the battle zone. Commanders had to learn to see terrain differently, to add a constant scan for landing zones (LZs) and pick-up zones (PZs) to all the other features they had to keep in mind. We practiced rapid loading and unloading of men and materiel to reduce the helicopter's window of vulnerability. Total flexibility was the watchword in planning and attitude. There was one bit of sobering reality that I insisted be introduced at every level in this training. We would declare a platoon leader dead and let his sergeant take over and carry out the mission. Or declare a sergeant dead and have one of his PFCs take over running the squad. We were training for war, and leaders are killed in battle. I wanted every man trained for and capable of taking over the job of the man above him.

PRACTICE PLUS CREATIVITY EQUALS SURVIVAL

When it comes right down to it, practice, drilling, and over-learning contribute more to survival in combat than anything else. The object of drilling is to reduce delays in responding and minimize the deleterious effects of human error (often the result of poor preparation or inadequate training). Human error is an insidious component of most mishaps—both in the military and in the civilian sector. Consider the case of military aircraft accidents. In 1996, the government's General Accounting Office (GAO) reviewed military aircraft accidents involving fatalities or severe aircraft damage. The GAO discovered that military aircraft were involved in 3828 mishaps between 1975 and 1995 resulting in 3810 fatalities and 3483 destroyed aircraft. During the most recent fiscal year covered in the report (1994 through 1995), a full 73 percent of the accidents involved human error. So, in the majority of cases, pilots made incorrect calculations, poor decisions, or erroneous maneuvers resulting directly in loss of life or aircraft. The same pattern would be found in mishaps on ships, submarines, or on the battlefield with Marines. When it comes to loss of life and property, human error presents a more potent and consistent threat than any foreign enemy.

So is there a formula for reducing human error and minimizing damage? Although there is no foolproof method for doing this, the ideal formula seems to contain about 90 percent preparation and 10 percent spur-of-the-moment creativity and improvisation. On board a ship, commanding officers have long recognized that surviving damage at sea depends primarily on training. Consider the following excerpt from the Damage Control chapter of the Operations Manual from the USS *Enterprise* (CV-6) during World War II. The *Enterprise* was the most decorated Navy ship of the Second World War and the authors of this 1940s era manual understood that success in bad situations hinged primarily on the right preparation:

> Damage control comprises the entire system of maintaining watertight integrity, controlling stability, repairing damage, providing for defense against gas, and caring for injured personnel. It deals with material, personnel, operations, methods, and organization. The control of damage is dependent, to a great extent, upon the measures taken prior to action to reduce and localize the effects of collision, grounding, or the casualties of battle. The prevention of the spread of fire and gas within the ship by closing all openings and the elimination of flammable material is greatly aided by the care with which the damage control preparation for war and battle is made.

Once damage control procedures are memorized and executed without hesitation or error, a leader must nurture and encourage the development of creativity and on-the-spot improvisation when even the best-laid plans fail to address an emergency. At Navy, we work to help our students blend over-learning with innovation. Rick Zino described an induction day exercise plebes in the class of 1967 had to endure that nurtured this think-on-your-feet mentality:

> Plebes were ordered to stencil their laundry numbers to every piece of clothing they had been issued. Ten minutes before lights out, all 40 plebes in the company were ordered to bring every piece of clothing they had into the corridor and throw them into a big pile. The plebes were then instructed to toss them in the air, mix them up thoroughly so that all 40 plebes' clothing was interspersed, scattered wildly, and could only be reclaimed by laundry numbers. Just then lights out sounded. Each plebe had to take an armful of clothes and remove it from the corridor.

Zino noted that it took weeks for all the plebes to recover their gear during rare moments of free time, using laundry numbers. Those who had failed to follow orders and stencil every piece of their gear lost it. Odd as this exercise may sound, plebes learn from day one to follow orders, to prepare for the unexpected, and to direct great attention to small details. They must also be creative and make the best of a bad situation if they want to survive (or, in this case, get their underwear back).

Midshipmen are taught to appreciate the importance of drilling for every possible scenario to be faced at sea. As leaders, it will be their duty to ensure that their followers are ready for whatever may come. Failure attributed to inadequate preparation is unpardonable. While human error will never be entirely eradicated from military operations, errors rooted in poor attention to detail or lax preparation of subordinates are almost never tolerated.

But even the best-prepared crew can face defeat in light of bad circumstances, terrible luck, or a superior enemy. In these situations, spur of the moment ingenuity, tenacity, and creativity must combine with outstanding training if the job is going to get done and the ship and crew salvaged. There is perhaps no better example of the power of blending drilling with innovation than that displayed by the captain and crew of the USS *Samuel B. Roberts* (FFG-58) on April 14, 1988.

THE MINING OF THE USS *SAMUEL B. ROBERTS* (FFG-58)

The following account was compiled from a lecture given by Captain Paul Rinn, USN (RET) to our leadership classes and is one of the case studies used in our leadership textbook. The afternoon of April 14 started off quiet and quite routine for the crew of the USS *Samuel B. Roberts*. She had been assigned to monitor Iranian and Iraqi hostilities in the Gulf region and to escort Kuwaiti merchant ships safely to and from the Straits of Hormuz.

Although the waters around the Gulf were notorious for hidden mines and sudden attacks from Iranian speedboats, the crew of the *Roberts* was understandably confident in their ability to successfully navigate these dangers while fulfilling their mission. During the previous year, the *Samuel B. Roberts* won the Battle "E" and had earned the highest grades any ship had ever attained in damage control training during her refresher training at Guantanamo Bay just prior to her deployment to the Gulf. The captain and crew had drilled effectively and preformed magnificently. They had every reason to feel confident, perhaps even a bit invincible.

Just after 4:30 in the afternoon, the ship's bow watchman noticed what he thought were dolphins in the water in front of the ship. Only these dolphins weren't moving. Checking his binoculars, he spotted the spikes on these floating objects and immediately notified the bridge. The commanding officer notified all hands that the ship had entered a minefield and sent the crew to general quarters. The ship came to all stop. While the ship maintained a safe distance from the three floating mines, the captain attempted to slowly and carefully "tip-toe" out of the minefield by reversing course and essentially backing the ship out the way it had entered the field. Unfortunately, approximately 21 minutes after spotting the floating mines, the ship struck a submerged mine.

The detonation of the mine's 250 pounds of TNT lifted the ship 10 feet out of the water. The port side, directly below the main engine room, was ripped open resulting in a 22-foot gash. Within 15 seconds, the engine room was flooded while flames shot up the main stack and 150 feet into the air. The ship's propulsion system was entirely disabled and the keel was bent and twisted over to starboard. Fires flashed through several compartments and the gas turbine auxiliary engines were in flames. Engineering's central control station was engulfed in flames and water poured into these sections of the ship as well.

At this point, the crew's intensive training kicked in. Although the diesel engines had shut down, causing the ship to go dark below decks, and although many compartments were filling with water and smoke, the crew immediately initiated firefighting and damage-control procedures and hoses and protective gear were immediately seized and prepared. As dusk fell, sailors, some still in the engineering spaces, risked their lives to rescue their trapped and badly burned chief and other seriously injured shipmates. The chief, who had serious head and back injuries, had been trapped under a deck grating by the flooding of the main engine room. He had barely escaped when sailors working to save him had used a battle lantern to light the way for him to swim 15 feet underwater through mangled equipment.

The well-trained corpsmen set up a triage station on the mess decks and then moved the injured to the helicopter hangar. Ten members of *Robert*'s crew were seriously injured, most of them engineering personnel with second and third degree burns, four of whom would require evacuation to a stateside burn center.

In the first moments after the mine blast, damage control reports began streaming in to the bridge, just as they were supposed to. To the CO, the crew seemed to be doing everything in sequence, exactly as it was trained to respond. This "real thing" event was very similar to the exercise situations the crew had so frequently labored to prepare for, only now there was much more at stake. Having been through this scenario over and over, the crew knew exactly how to respond. Crewmen slapped on OBAs (oxygen breathing apparatuses) with the confidence that can only come from practice. There were no stutter-steps, no false starts, and no hesitations. This was no drill, and yet it was "the" drill. Every man went to his station and executed his part in the plan to save shipmates and ship.

The situation in the engine and machinery rooms below decks was now critical. If flooding and fires continued for long in these spaces, the main bulkhead in these areas of the ship could separate, killing most of the crew instantly. Although the crew had been through the damage-control trainer repeatedly, this damage was worse than anything they'd ever fixed in a drill, and there would be no opportunity to try it again if they didn't get it right the first time. The crew worked endlessly that night attempting to plug leaks with blankets, pillows, and wedges while dewatering with portable eductors and fire pumps.

When the CO toured the damaged areas, he immediately recognized the precarious state of the bulkhead and realized it could give way at any second, killing his crew. At the same time, he felt a tremendous sense of confidence as he watched his men work to stop the flooding in the auxiliary machinery room. They were confident. "We can win this one, Captain!" one sailor said. "We can do it," another echoed. As he surveyed the situation, he made the decision they were going to save the ship. However, he soon discovered a crack running up the center of the bulkhead and completely across the ship. The ship was breaking in half. Meanwhile, partly due to the firefighting efforts going on below decks, the ship was getting heavier as it filled with water and its aft end was sinking dangerously low in the water.

Unsure of how long the ship would hold together, the CO spoke to the crew over the 1MC (ship's intercom). He explained the ship's status, and then said again, "I think we can save the ship, there is no doubt in my mind." Although still in danger of losing the ship, there were no good alternatives to fighting with everything they had to save her. Going into the water meant swimming with poisonous sea snakes and sharks in the dark. *Roberts* was at least 80 miles from anyone, except maybe the Iranians. And worse, any ship coming to their assistance would also have to enter the mine field. No, the men of the *Roberts* would have to find their way out of this predicament alone. Losing the ship or surrendering were not options. The simple objective at that moment was merely to survive until dawn.

Four hours after hitting the mine, a daring investigation by the chief engineer and a BM3 finally pinpointed the source of the fuel oil fire. By midnight conditions were relatively stable with shoring and fire reflash watches set, yet there was still danger of the ship's breaking apart. One of the ship's chiefs showed profound creativity in proposing that steel cables be strung across the cracks in the hull and superstructure, "lashing" the ship together. It was grueling work, but men throughout the ship pitched in, working through the night. By 0300, using auxiliary propellers, the ship was slowly sailing to safety outside the minefield. The entire crew had battled for 10 hours to save the ship against long odds. By 5 a.m., the *Roberts* was again underway with two of its major weapons systems again operational so that she could defend herself.

Sometime later, 31 *Roberts* crewmen received awards for bravery for saving the ship or for injuries sustained. When interviewed, they all said that because of their training and drills, they felt they had done it all before. Their ship's realistic and combat-oriented damage control training had prepared them for the worst. The commander, Joint Task Force Middle East, noted, "They saved a ship that most knowledgeable people would say we probably should have lost. The ship was saved due to innovative and strenuous training, enforced by aggressive command involvement." The men of the USS *Samuel B. Roberts* saved their ship in the face of uncontrolled fires, massive flooding, and probable breakup and sinking.

Is there a moral to the story of the *Roberts* and its crew? We think so and that is why the story is included as a case study in one of the USNA leadership courses. We want men and women who might soon be standing in the shoes of the *Roberts* CO to understand exactly why leaders drill their crews.

In contrast to what observers of a formal USNA parade might think, learning to drill effectively is more than just quaint. Someday soon, all of these future officers will be evaluated on the basis of how effectively they prepare followers for combat. In order to save lives, ships, submarines, and aircraft, these leaders had better take training seriously. If there is a secret here, it would go something like this: Drill, drill, and then drill even more. Ensure that the crew reacts instantly and reflexively to emergent situations. And always encourage and listen to innovative ideas and fresh recommendations about how to get the job done—especially when the sheer magnitude of the challenge requires something novel.

CREATING A CULTURE OF PREPARATION

Although the truth of the matter is that drilling is often arduous, fatiguing, and even boring, the manner in which a leader promotes and delivers "opportunities" to train can make all the difference. We are referring here to the idea of *command culture*—particularly as it applies to creating an environment conducive to positive attitudes about preparing for adversity. Culture includes formal and informal rules and attitudes regarding training. Both previous and current leaders influence the training culture—often most powerfully by the way they themselves act and by what they elect to tolerate.

Consider the manner in which Captain Robert Howe, commanding officer of the USS *Dubuque* (LPD 8) got his crew to actually enjoy all the taxing damage control training while simultaneously getting exceptionally good at it. Like all Navy shipboard personnel, *Dubuque* sailors practice and train constantly in damage control techniques, hands-on training, classes, and one-on-one instruction. But unlike most of his fellow captains, Captain Howe gets his crew fired-up and excited about this training by holding monthly "Damage Control Olympics." The competition features events such as a pipe patching race, the ruptured hose drill, firefighting ensemble dress out, oxygen breathing apparatus relay, peri-jet race, and, of course, the damage control Jeopardy game. This monthly competition pits damage control crews from various parts of the ship against one another as they demonstrate their high levels of proficiency in firefighting, handling medical emergencies, controlling and stopping flooding, and handling the effects of a chemical spill or attack.

Not only have the Olympics helped the *Dubuque* crew to achieve excellent proficiency in all damage control related drills, the crew has responded enthusiastically. The friendly rivalry has helped break up the monotony that can set in when drilling for long hours. This creative approach to training has also helped tighten the bonds between shipmates and enhance overall job satisfaction among sailors.

At USNA, as in the world of business, the most successful leaders are those who manage to get their followers "fired-up" about performing exceptionally well—even when it comes to rote and repetitive tasks such as uniform inspections and parade performance. Inevitably, one finds a charismatic and creative leader at the helm of a successful military unit or civilian company.

ENHANCING FRUSTRATION TOLERANCE

We end this chapter on drilling for success with a comment about the importance of building followers' capacity for enduring frustration and handling discomfort. Successful damage control, firefighting, and combat operations all depend on delaying comfort and rejecting immediate gratification in the service of achieving some higher purpose—namely the survival and success of the entire fighting unit. Nothing will lead to expressions of poor frustration tolerance more quickly than repeated drilling and constant training. Even the best among us get bored, tired, uncomfortable, and irritable. We are tempted to utter phrases such as "I can't stand this," and "This is too much to bear."

Of course, your followers *can* stand it. The question is how do you get them to change their self-talk and heighten their frustration tolerance? Although a CO can invoke creative strategies such as the damage control Olympics, at times we find that nothing short of direct confrontation will suffice. So, when the leader begins to hear that the crew can't "stand" it, "tolerate" it, or "live with" it, it may be time to name this mindset what it is: *frustration intolerance*. Frustration intolerance prevents people from reaching goals. Believing that they can't stand discomfort, they refrain from facing adversity, taking risks, and working harder to maximize productivity—even when they are already tired.

Frustration intolerance could sink ships or sabotage missions if not corrected. In my (GPH) class I used a short clip from the movie, *Run Silent, Run Deep* to impress this point on the midshipmen. At the beginning of the movie, a World War II submarine captain has lost his submarine and most of his crew to a Japanese attack but he survives. Deskbound in Honolulu, he relives the attack over and over again, and on his desk, he uses model ships to replay the attack and devise new tactics in the slim chance he ever gets command again. Sure enough, he gets command of another submarine and on the way to his patrol area, he drills his crew over and over again on loading torpedoes quickly while remaining on the surface. He times them on each drill and repeatedly tells the crew that they are not getting the job done fast enough. Of course the crew thinks the captain is way too demanding. They get demoralized and frustration sets in. They don't know what he wants, but the captain keeps the drills up and their frustration continues. When they finally arrive at their designated patrol area, they attack a convoy that is escorted by a Japanese destroyer. In the middle of the attack, the destroyer bears down on them from dead ahead. This is the point where the captain's constant drilling bears fruit. Rather than submerging and trying to evade the destroyer, the captain sails his submarine head-on into the destroyer on the surface and conducts his attack. He fires his torpedoes down the destroyer's throat, something never before attempted in combat. Of course, the submarine sinks the destroyer and the crew finally realizes why they had to endure all of the constant drilling.

Rather than let low frustration tolerance fester, the wise leader will challenge it with questions such as "Prove to me that you can't stand it; I've never seen anyone die from too much practice"; or "How does it follow that just because you're sick of running this drill you can't get the lead out and run it over and over again until you get it right?" Or "If you can't stand putting on the fire-fighting gear one more time, I guess we need to practice this more until you are unquestionably certain that you *can* stand it." The point in confronting low frustration tolerance is not to make fun of followers, but to confront their irrational thinking and show them that indeed they can stand much more than they think they can.

One of the requirements for graduation at USNA is that every midshipman make a jump from a 10-meter board into the swimming pool, simulating jumping overboard from a ship. If you've never stood on a 10-meter platform looking down, let us assure you, it's a long way to the water. When I (GPH) was a midshipman we had to jump into the old Natatorium pool, which had a small platform at the top of the building situated among the rafters. On the day we had to jump, one of my classmates just couldn't bring himself to leap. After he climbed up to the platform and became panicky, he decided that rather than go into the water, he would climb through the rafters, over to the bleachers, and down through the stands on the other side of the building. Of course, we all thought he was crazy because it was much safer to jump into the water than to crawl through the rafters high above the bleachers. After several more trips up to the platform and after being ordered not to climb through the rafters, he finally jumped.

When a follower begins complaining about a drill, it may be time to remind them of the men of the USS *Forrestal* or the USS *Samuel B. Roberts*. The question, of course, would be, "How could those sailors fight fires, explosions, and certain sinking for hours on end if you cannot even repeat this simple drill? How is that possible?" When your crew begins to say to themselves, "I don't enjoy this much, but I can sure as hell tolerate it, and it just might save my life one day soon," then you've got a crew you can work with.

We are writing this chapter on December 5, 2003. At approximately noon today, many of the midshipmen from 13th company have begun their traditional relay run from Annapolis to Philadelphia carrying the official Army-Navy game ball. Today temperatures hover in the 30s with wind and freezing rain. Nonetheless, these midshipmen will carry the ball, running in small groups relay-style, the full 120 miles to the stadium. They won't complain. In fact, they consider it an honor to be part of the Army-Navy tradition. And tomorrow, with up to a foot of snow expected, the entire brigade will spend four to five hours standing in the snow, rain, and wind cheering on their team. The conditions will be utterly miserable but you'll not see them whine or become sullen. Navy midshipmen develop outstanding frustration tolerance.

THE GOUGE

We hope we've made the point about why we drill midshipmen so much at the Academy and what the ultimate objective really is. When they get to the fleet, they will be responsible for completing numerous drills and evolutions with their sailors or Marines. They'll run the drills over and over again, because one day their lives will depend on it. Do drilling and over-learning for reflexive execution apply outside the military? We think so.

In the civilian workplace, people want to know what to do to accomplish their jobs and how to do it right. And no one works in a vacuum; most of us must contribute as part of a team. Although some team members learn more quickly than others, the leader has to ensure that the weakest link in the chain knows how to complete his or her job correctly. Every member of the team has got to pay attention to detail, work with the team, and competently execute his or her duties so that the entire team succeeds. Leaders must work tirelessly with their "crew" until they are confident in the team's proficiency, then leaders must work to maintain that proficiency. The onus is always on the leader to lead by example and ensure that the team has direction, training, preparation, and frustration tolerance.

9

LEAD BY EXAMPLE

Retired Admiral James Holloway III (USNA class of '43), served in three wars, was the first captain of a nuclear-powered aircraft carrier (USS *Enterprise*), and went on to become the twentieth Chief of Naval Operations. While a first-class midshipman in the early 1940s, ADM Holloway described a curious incident that took place on the yard. He had been sitting on a bench with his fiancée just a month shy of graduation:

> As we got up to go our respective ways, Dabney to her bus and me to muster my platoon, I reached over to clasp one of her hands in both of mine as I told her how much I looked forward to seeing her June week. Suddenly, at this moment, out of the bushes behind us rushed a Jimmy legs—a civilian campus cop—with his pad and paper ready.

Holloway was written-up for committing a "public display of affection"—something prohibited for midshipmen and Naval officers in most circumstances (especially in 1943). There are obvious exceptions (e.g., departing to sea or returning home). This offense resulted in Holloway's confinement to his room the following weekend. Although most of us would consider the offense petty and the punishment too stringent, Holloway found that he could not argue with his company commander's rationale while adjudicating his case. When his punishment was meted out, the company commander looked him in the eye and said, "As a first-class-man, soon to be an officer, you should set a better example!"

At Navy, midshipmen learn to become intentional models. They learn that serving as an exemplar to followers is an inescapable fact of leadership. Modeling is nonnegotiable. Like it or not, you will exemplify leadership to those you lead. Midshipmen not only serve as exemplars to their peers and subordinates, but also to the many civilians who visit the Yard. Ask most midshipmen how many times they have been stopped by strangers in the Yard and requested to pose for photographs and they will sigh; the honest answer for most will be "Too many!" Although midshipmen will sometimes good naturedly commiserate about what a "pain" these requests can be, they will heartily honor them every time. And on good days, they might even see themselves through the visitor's lens—perhaps as the next Tom Cruise in *Top Gun*.

The question for midshipmen is this: How deliberate will you be in the exemplar role and what kind of example will you ultimately offer? In this chapter, we highlight several of the key lessons midshipmen must learn about leading by example. As each midshipman rises in rank and responsibility—both on the yard at USNA and in the fleet as officers—they will occupy positions of increasing rank and authority. And with advancement comes the steadily accelerating burden of visibility. Leaders have always been visible. Their behavior—public and private—is scrutinized at a level commensurate with their stature.

And if midshipmen are scrutinized, commanding officers and admirals live life in a veritable fishbowl. While in the history department and again while serving as a battalion officer, I (GPH) was constantly observed and judged by my actions both on the job and in my off time at the Academy. At the Academy, on rare occasions, I have seen an officer stumble in setting a good example for the midshipmen. The midshipmen, of course, notice immediately and that leader's capacity to lead is palpably diminished. I recall a particularly rainy and cold football game one year. The weather was atrocious and chilly rain slashed the midshipmen in the stands. Nonetheless, a very senior officer in the chain of command passed the word that he didn't want midshipmen to put their collars up because it would "look unruly" to the crowd and the TV audience.

Unfortunately, midway through the second half, that same senior officer was observed by the entire brigade to have put his collar up to help keep out the elements. Needless to say, this egregious breach of leadership by example was not lost on the brigade. In fact, it was the topic of conversation in numerous leadership classes the following week. Setting the example is an inescapable obligation for leaders; it is an inalienable facet of every job in the fleet. Excellent leaders accept this and use their visibility to enhance the organization.

THE POWER OF OBSERVATIONAL LEARNING

Famed psychologist and researcher Albert Bandura offered one of the most intriguing and influential experimental examples of the power of models in his pioneering "Bobo Doll" study. In this classic experiment, Bandura took very small children and exposed them to adult models (actors) that were playing (e.g., beating, kicking, slapping) violently with a five-foot-tall inflatable punching toy—a Bobo doll. The children were young enough not to have had any previous exposure to the toy. Not surprisingly, children who first observed these violent models, when given the opportunity to play with the Bobo doll themselves, did so in a remarkably violent manner. In contrast, children without violent modeling engaged in significantly less violence with the dolls. This effect has been replicated time after time in all varieties of follow-on studies. The take-away message is clear. Human beings are excellent observational learners; we learn how to be adults, spouses, and even leaders by watching important models.

Of course, skills and attitudes gleaned from observation are not always immediately manifested. Learning in which new behavior is acquired but not carried out or demonstrated until later is known as *latent learning*. Naval officers in the fleet, when asked to pause and reflect upon their leadership approach and the source of their primary leader behaviors, often report some surprise at discovering they are emulating the example offered by a USNA company officer, a division officer, or a department head on their first ship.

When I (GPH) first met my plebe year squad leader, a midshipman named Jay Johnson, I was very impressed. He was everything I thought a midshipman should be. His demeanor, deportment, and his sense of fairness and concern made a lasting impression on me. Although I only had him as a squad leader for my first semester at the Academy, I kept up with his career through *Navy Times* and "scuttlebutt" I heard around the fleet. It came as no surprise to me, when President Clinton named Jay Johnson as Chief of Naval Operations in 1996. Midshipman, and later, Admiral Johnson, through the example he set, was the type of officer who made you want to strive to become a fine Naval leader.

LIKE IT OR NOT, YOU WILL BE A MODEL

Those of us who are parents can relate to the concept of latent learning. Most parents can recall instances of being angered or horrified by their own children's utterances of a four-letter word or a socially inappropriate behavior— only to realize that this was precisely what they had modeled themselves. I (WBJ) once went to a car dealership with my youngest son, Stanton—then a two-year-old—only to discover the dealer did not put prices on his cars but required customers to "inquire" about the price. I got Stanton back in the car and, as I drove off, loudly referred to the dealer as a "shyster." For the next two years, every time I drove by the dealership with Stanton, he would spot the dealer's sign, point his finger accusingly, and yell "Shysters!"

In order for observational learning to occur, the observer must do four things in sequence. These include

1. Pay attention and observe the most salient elements of the model's behavior.
2. Remember the behavior later.
3. Reproduce the action.
4. Have motivation to both learn and later carry out the behavior.

In the military, learning from exemplars is absolutely essential to achieving the mission. In many circumstances, a platoon sergeant or division chief has a short period of time to demonstrate damage-control procedures, the correct firing of a weapon, or the plan for seizing a building occupied by an enemy. Observers in these circumstances rely on their model to be efficient, accurate, and patient.

Sometimes observational learning has to happen in one shot. More often, we learn to lead over time from watching both excellent and lousy exemplars; observational learning can show us what not to do just as effectively as how to do things the right way.

Sometimes learners are unaware that they have learned something essential about leadership. At other times they are cognizant of both their models and the lessons learned. Consider the following quote from a midshipman journal in one of my (GPH) leadership courses. It was written in the days following the Columbia shuttle disaster.

> The space shuttle (Columbia) tragedy has shown us another important factor in leadership. The country has been through a great deal over the last two years and suddenly, on Saturday morning, we awoke to more terrible news. When the Russian submarine Kursk sank, one of the key criticisms of President Putin was his refusal to cut his vacation short. For days after the tragedy, he stayed at his vacation home on the Black Sea. This is in stark contrast to the actions of President Bush. While on a weekend retreat to Camp David, he was informed of the tragedy. Even though he could do nothing tangible by returning to the White House, he did anyway. And in so doing, he helped stabilize the entire nation. Perception is everything. He was working in the White House, he appeared on television, and he was clearly leading the country. When times get tough it is important to consider symbols. President Bush offered a symbolic model of caring, commitment, control, and strength.

Whatever your opinions concerning President George H. W. Bush, it is hard to argue against the fact that in this instance he offered a strong example to the rest of the country—and, most important from our perspective, a model for up-and-coming leaders like midshipmen at the Naval Academy. Clearly, this student is aware that he learned something central about leading from observing the president at work.

SOME COMPLEX LEADER TASKS CAN ONLY BE LEARNED BY WATCHING

When I (WBJ) was leaving active duty, my replacement at the medical center at Pearl Harbor was asked to spend some time on ships and submarines to familiarize herself with fleet operations and the daily lives of the sailors she would be treating in the clinic. Several months later, she relayed that one of these cruise experiences had nearly turned deadly. Embarked for the day on a guided missile cruiser, her ship was involved in a war game exercise just off the coast of Oahu. At some point in the exercise, one of the other ships was to fire a missile at a floating target. Unfortunately, on this day, the missile missed the intended target and "locked on" to the ship to which my colleague was assigned.

She later recounted a period of no more than three minutes during which the crew was called to battle stations, countermeasure missiles were fired to attempt to knock the incoming missile out of the air, and the ship began taking evasive action on the surface to dodge the incoming projectile. In the end, automated machine guns, which pop up on the deck as a last-ditch line of defense, managed to hit and destroy the missile with only seconds remaining to impact. The crew breathed a collective sigh of relief. My colleague was too traumatized to sleep well for the next few days. But the story reminded me that being a CO on the bridge of a ship in battle is one of the most challenging and complex roles any leader will ever occupy. In the minutes after the incoming missile was detected, imagine the array of rapid-fire decisions and orders the CO had to issue. No time for consulting protocol. This is where you put it on the line. You either know how to react or you don't. You can either apply all the manuals and classes in an instant or you can't. And in combat, the outcome will be black or white. There is no room for in-between success here.

In the military, as in business and organizational leadership, some of the most important and essential leader roles are profoundly complex. And the *only* way to really master them is by observing a master at work. You can read all the manuals you want, but when missiles are in the air and closing, how does the seasoned CO blend knowledge of navigation, seamanship, weaponry, combat tactics, and management of his or her precious human resources (junior officers and senior enlisted) in the ensuing 30 seconds? We're sorry, but no officer in the fleet can thoroughly describe this for you. You have to be there and you have to see how it's done. And the more complex, nuanced, or dangerous the end goal is, the more essential it is to have a competent model demonstrate the unique blend of skill and knowledge required to do it right. Before flying a fighter plane, putting a submarine through an emergency surfacing drill, performing brain surgery, or delivering a controversial takeover bid to a hostile board of directors, you'd better be sure you've seen it done correctly.

ON BEING AN INTENTIONAL MODEL

At Navy, midshipmen who excel in academic achievement, athletic accomplishment, military bearing, and execution of key leadership duties within their own companies are chosen to serve for a semester of their first-class year as "stripers" or brigade-wide leaders. Equivalent to a student-body president and related offices held within other universities, striper billets are selected by a panel of officers. Midshipmen are selected for striper roles not only for their own benefit, but also for the benefit of the brigade as a whole. These stripers gain a unique opportunity to exercise leadership on a relatively broad scale (4000 of the nation's brightest young officers-in-training become their followers). The clear and immediate return for USNA is that these excellent role models will become powerful exemplars of what it means to succeed in positions of military leadership. The most effective stripers are deliberate and intentional about leading. They take their roles seriously and recognize that they are always "on duty" as models.

Midshipman Juliann Gallina, the first female brigade commander, expected some controversy when she assumed her position as the top brigade midshipman. But she exemplified what being a "striper" is all about. Midshipman Gallina penned an essay that summarized her intentions:

> I can readily say my Academy experience has been influenced by the fact that I am a woman, but I would never concede that it has made my experience more difficult....Since I-Day, I have pushed myself and my peers to surpass the perceived limits of women merely by accepting the daily challenges of being a midshipman.... I truly doubt (if) I would have pushed my limits if I had attended another school. I did not push these bounds merely for the sake of proving myself to others, but rather because the U.S. Naval Academy demands performance from all midshipmen. I have done jobs I have been asked to do, and as a result, my perceived boundaries have crumbled.

MACRO AND MICRO MODELING

Excellent leadership demands intentional modeling. On both the *macro* (command or organization-wide) and *micro* (individual relationship) levels, the best leaders realize they will influence their followers by their demeanors and actions and set about using this influence for the betterment of the organization and the individuals in it. At the macro level, a leader's attitudes, actions, and communication with subordinates set the tone for the organization's entire climate. On the micro level, excellent leaders mentor immediate followers within the boundaries of their time and resources.

My (GPH) youngest son, Shawn, recently set an example on the micro level. Shawn had been in Baghdad for eight months when he was given the opportunity to go on two weeks R&R back to Germany and his family. Right before he was to depart, he learned that the wife of one of his troop members was experiencing problems with her pregnancy. Shawn didn't hesitate to give the young soldier his seat on the plane home. Although Shawn was looking forward to spending two weeks home with his family, the right thing to do was to get his young soldier home to his wife.

We have discovered that accomplished leaders often find events—even bad ones—as opportunities to teach and model good leadership. One of the midshipman in my (GPH) leadership course described feeling simultaneously distressed and awed by the behavior of his extracurricular club's officer representative—a Navy lieutenant. While traveling with the team in another state, the officer cautioned the midshipmen under his supervision to abide by USNA rules during their after-event free time. Unfortunately, some of them violated travel policies and this behavior was reported to USNA authorities. Rather than place all the midshipmen on report, this officer took full responsibility for the misbehavior and insisted that the investigation focus on him. He framed the violations as a failure in his own leadership and did his best to shield his midshipmen from scrutiny while taking the flack himself.

Although this maneuver is career threatening, and although the officer never said a word to the midshipmen about his efforts to take the blame himself, every one of them knew the details. And they all felt miserable about it—especially those whose behavior was to blame. This story had a powerful impact on the midshipmen members of this team. In the words of the student who described these events, "He is showing us that when we are in charge, we will be held responsible for what those under our command do." Clearly, this officer's efforts at intentional modeling paid off. The lesson is one that none of these future leaders will ever forget.

Think of the intentional leader as a willful and deliberate teacher. He or she actively seeks opportunities to model crucial skills and leader behaviors as a means of guiding, developing, and mentoring. And it is essential that modeling be done in the right spirit. Rather than an opportunity to pompously prove one's superiority, good modeling emanates from a sincere interest in helping followers absorb the skills, techniques, and procedures essential to their success as well as that of the organization. Rather than modeling arrogance, the ideal model is caring, transparent, and willing to admit foibles and failings. The excellent model is also modest and imbued with a good sense of humor and humility.

Consider the age-old tradition of "hundredth night" at USNA. Hundredth night marks the evening of the hundredth day until graduation. On this night, the first-class are in a celebratory mood and ready to start counting the days until their USNA travails will end. And on this night, tradition requires that plebes and first-class midshipmen switch places for a few hours (from before dinner until study hour commences). Most first-class midshipmen handle the ensuing torment gracefully. Their plebes force them to stand at attention, offer chow-calls, drop for push-ups, and all manner of lovely revenge from the plebe's perspective. It is a night for plebes to vent pent-up frustration at the upperclass, and for upperclassmen to absorb this good-naturedly and with equanimity.

On occasion, however, a first-classman will refuse to participate. He or she is branded a coward by the plebes. More importantly, his or her own classmates will often express anger or shame at the lack of good leadership and respect displayed in this avoidant behavior. The message is clear: Excellent leaders lead by example. They are not afraid to sacrifice (in this case pride) for the benefit of their followers and for the good climate of their command.

LEADER BEHAVIOR GOVERNS COMMAND CLIMATE

Perhaps the most compelling reason for leaders to take seriously our admonition to be intentional when it comes to *being* an example is the consistent finding that the leader's attitude and behavior have a profound effect on the climate within the entire organization. Leaders who manage to transform follower behavior and attitudes hold power not through coercion but as a result of their own display of competence and character. When leaders provide an impressive example of job competence, communicate an inspiring corporate vision, and use copious helpings of empowerment and praise with subordinates, they set a positive tone for the entire command. Sometimes a public display of commitment to one's followers will inspire a deep and abiding loyalty. Consider this quote from Andrea Phelps (USNA, 1985) regarding her graduation ceremony at the Academy.

> President Reagan spoke at our graduation, which was an awesome thing in and of itself. Those of us fortunate enough to be in the top 100 graduates were assured that the president would be handing out our diplomas. The rest of our classmates would not have that honor. After President Reagan finished with the first 100 graduates, he was shown to his seat to watch the remaining procession. As soon as he understood that he was not going to be shaking every graduate's hand, he ordered the program to be altered so that he could in fact personally congratulate each graduate. We know that he was probably dead tired with blisters on his hand after it was over, but his gesture had an unbelievable impact on our class and our families. We were all ready to charge into battle for him: sometimes the smallest considerations have the biggest impact on your subordinates.

Since President Reagan showed this great consideration for the class of 1985, all members of every class since have been personally handed their diplomas by the presenter, whether it be the president, vice-president, secretary of defense, or a service chief. When I (GPH) attended my first graduation upon my return as a leadership fellow, the anchorman (standing last in the graduating class) mightily bear-hugged President Bush as the president gave him his diploma. Of course, we all expected the Secret Service agents to intervene immediately, throw him to the ground, and handcuff him, but the president took it all good naturedly. However, every anchorman since has been cautioned that hugging the commander-in-chief is not appropriate behavior for a soon-to-be commissioned officer.

Stephen Covey describes climate-creation from the perspective of principle-centered leadership: "The basic role of the leader is to foster mutual respect and build a complementary team where each strength is made productive and each weakness made irrelevant." Because who you are as a leader has everything to do with your public and interpersonal behavior, it is essential that the leader exercise patience, keep promises, and refrain from gratifying his or her own anger through harsh or unkind remarks. Followers need a model of self-restraint and emotional self-regulation if this is to become part of the command culture.

At USNA, we work to help our midshipmen appreciate the fact that real influence as a leader comes from modeling positive support, genuine consideration, and behavior that is congruent with one's policies and standards. This is what we call *transformational leadership,* and research suggests that transformational leaders create enduring loyalty and growth in subordinates because they identify with the leader. Because the leader is seen as genuine and supportive, followers truly "own" allegiance to the leader's directives. Coercion is not required. One of Navy's coaches set a great example for his midshipmen in this area. As one plebe described:

> Being a plebe, I was getting use to taking crap, so when we showed up at wrestling and were told to mop the mats every day, I thought nothing of it. However, our new coach stepped in very quickly and assigned the job to a different class each week. It was a small gesture that made a big impact. Our coach let us know that everyone was part of the team and would be treated with the same respect. While it seems trivial, it has also helped build team unity, because now everyone shows up early when it's their turn to mop so that their classmates don't get stuck doing all the work and their teammates can start practice on time.

And there is something else about leaders who create the right kind of command climate. When given the opportunity to besmirch the reputation of a colleague or capitalize on their own popularity at the expense of a superior or subordinate, they pass. The principles of congruence and integrity demand that I not undermine a shipmate. Again, consider the words of USNA graduate Andrea Phelps:

My squad leader for the first part of plebe summer did not yell at us that much, but you could tell he cared about us and our development. When he quietly said that he was disappointed in us, we all felt disappointed and wanted to try harder for him. My squad leader during the second part of the summer was a screamer. Although I could not put my finger on anything in particular that he said or did, I sensed that he did not really care about our development. When our first squad leader reappeared for the academic year and saw that my classmates and I were discouraged, he suggested to us that we should learn from whatever leader we had—all of us have a lesson to teach. Some leaders present a model that we should emulate. Others show us what not to do when it is our turn to lead.

Finally, leaders who are conscious of the examples they offer refuse to model or reward cynicism. Cynicism in organizations is a prominent concern these days. It emerges in an organization when there is a mismatch between expectations and experience. People often enter an organization, the Navy included, with an implicit psychological contract or a set of expectations about what the organization will be like and how they might benefit from their commitment to it. When expectations go unmet and followers perceive the contract to be violated, negative attitudes and behaviors ensue. One recent superintendent at USNA aptly described cynicism as "idealism with a broken heart."

Cynicism in a military command can result in lowered productivity, high turnover, reduced attention to the development of junior personnel, and most important, hampered ability to complete the mission. Excellent role models in the leader role have got to do three things to stamp out cynicism quickly:

1. Leaders must identify cynical attitudes among followers.
2. Leaders must make sure followers have appropriate expectations upon entering the organization and then follow through to insure that promises are kept and reasonable expectations are met.
3. Leaders must not only refuse to become cynical themselves (especially when their own expectations about leaders go unmet), but they must also kindly confront it in subordinates and convey sincere expectations for enhanced performance.

THE GOUGE

There is no getting around the fact that real leaders lead by example. Subordinates expect leaders to set the standards, however high, and abide by them. For a leader to do anything else is incongruent, insincere, and disheartening for those who follow. The old adage, "Never ask your followers to do something you wouldn't do" has never been more relevant than it is today. In the military, as in civilian corporations, asking a follower to do what you as leader will not do is betrayal. Outstanding leaders appreciate the potency and power of deliberate modeling. They go first and ask followers to come along.

At the Naval Academy, we try to instill the salience of leading from the front from day one. Midshipmen have entered a profession where exemplars of leadership, integrity, and honesty must be beyond reproach. Followers in the Navy trust that their leaders will know what to do in life or death situations and how to survive and be victorious in combat. Their lives depend upon it. They also trust that their leaders will live by their words and their examples.

The captain of a ship at sea has power far beyond his or her contemporaries in the civilian world, but that same captain owes followers an example to set course by. The leader must do his or her utmost to sustain that example and live by it. "Leading by example" sounds simple enough, but it is far harder to put into practice. It starts with thoughtful modeling and requires consistency and self-sacrifice.

10

IQ IS NOT ENOUGH

Anyone can become angry—that is easy. But to be angry with the right person, to the right degree, at the right time, for the right purpose, and in the right way—this is not easy.

ARISTOTLE, THE NICOMACBEAN ETHICS

Lieutenant Commander Barney "The Bull" Kauffman took over as commanding officer of the temporary personnel unit at a major naval base in the Pacific. Far from delighted with his new command, Barney recognized that this was a career-ending tour. A surface-warfare officer by training, Barney should have been department head for a combatant ship and preparing for orders as executive officer aboard a cruiser or destroyer in the near future. Instead, he had failed to land desirable department-head orders and was now relegated to a fairly irrelevant unit on the base. A series of less than stellar officer fitness reports had helped seal his fate in this regard.

Within the first few hours of the change-of-command ceremony, LCDR Kauffman's division officers and chiefs understood they were in for a bumpy ride. The new CO began calling in his junior officers and senior enlisted men within 30 minutes of taking command (no standing down, no getting to know his staff, no celebration, no affirmative comments regarding the good work the crew had been doing recently under very short-staffed and demanding conditions). His meeting with the executive officer, a junior lieutenant, typified his interactions with his subordinates. Without first reading any of the command records or recent performance data, the new CO began reading her the riot act for allowing one of her petty officers the morning off for a medical appointment and for not attending to some litter he had noticed near the entrance to the building that morning. At one point, he became enraged and slammed his fist on the desk, insisting that all future requests for leave or medical time off would have to go directly to him for approval.

He then stared at the lieutenant and said, "I don't know how you screwed up or whether you're just a lame officer but the fact that you're here instead of out there (pointing to the row of ships tied up at the pier) tells me you're no rocket scientist." When the lieutenant began to become tearful, the CO rolled his eyes, sighed derisively, and said, "Oh God, I've got a gusher for an XO!"

Over the course of the ensuing months, personnel in the command became increasingly disheartened and unhappy at work. They walked on eggshells and generally avoided the command suite for fear of coming to the CO's attention. At weekly command formations, senior enlisted personnel and officers cringed in anticipation of humiliating and sometimes scathing comments by the CO regarding all that they had failed to accomplish in the previous week. They also learned to tell their subordinates just to deal with illness or problems at home because the CO was unwilling to approve most requests for special leave or nonemergency medical care. He never asked about his personnel's families and clearly did not even know the names of many of his enlisted leaders.

As often happens in such situations, various members of the command sought "intelligence" about their CO from colleagues in commands where he had previously served. They discovered that his nickname "Bull" was bestowed as a result of his consistent reputation as a "bull in a china shop." Often impulsively angry, entirely lacking in tact, and prone to offending nearly everyone he worked with, "the Bull" had few supporters among his colleagues and fewer still among previous subordinates.

To make matters worse, the LCDR appeared genuinely surprised and confused when the proportion of both officers and enlisted personnel putting in retirement, discharge, or transfer requests reached an all-time high. He blamed his chiefs for creating a "bad climate" and failing to motivate effectively. When LCDR Kauffman failed to select for CDR and was forced to retire early from the Navy, he was both bitter and bewildered. It appeared that he truly did not understand what went wrong in his career and why colleagues and subordinates appeared to dislike him.

TECHNICAL EXPERTISE AND INTELLIGENCE ARE NOT ENOUGH

WHY LEADERS MUST BE EMOTIONALLY SKILLED

Although "The Bull" is a fictional composite of several officers we have known during the course of our careers (we are happy to report that very few were USNA alumni), he stands as a glaring example of what can go wrong in leadership when the leader lacks emotional intelligence. All too often, organizations equate technical competence and intellectual horse-power with general capacity for leadership. This is an erroneous connection. In point of fact, leaders can possess outstanding technical expertise (e.g., mastery of engineering systems, accounting savvy, business planning) and demonstrable intellectual prowess, yet be entirely ineffectual as leaders. So what's missing here? What was "the Bull" so painfully lacking when it came to relating to followers? Daniel Goleman and others would simply call it *emotional intelligence* (EI).

At USNA, brains are one commodity never in short supply. With mean SAT scores well over 1300, the vast majority of midshipmen graduated near the top of their high school classes. Nearly all of them received awards and honors for scholastic achievement. In the class of 2006, only 1214 students were admitted from a pool of 12,333 highly qualified applicants. If leader acumen were based exclusively on sheer intellectual power, it would be fair to predict that USNA graduates would be among the best natural leaders our country had to offer. We believe they are, but not only because of IQ. At Navy, we strongly emphasize emotional intelligence—both during admission and during the midshipman's development into a Naval officer.

Since the 1940s psychologists and other researchers have recognized that intelligence is about more than just cognition. Raw brainpower is not a strong predictor of real-world success. Several affective (emotional), personal, and social factors appear essential to functioning excellently in an interpersonal world. These ingredients are crucial when it comes to accurate prediction of a person's overall capacity and probability for success in the leader role. In pointing out the necessity for both expertise and empathy, Pagonis described it this way:

> There are millions of technocrats out there with lots of facts in their quivers and little leadership potential. In many cases, what they are missing is empathy. No one is a leader who can't put himself or herself in the other person's shoes. Empathy and expertise command respect.

In fact, IQ alone is a woefully inadequate predictor of job success. Research on the predictive utility of cognitive intelligence shows that it accounts for only 10 to 25 percent of the variance in performance among leaders. This is not impressive. We often see this phenomenon at play at USNA. At times, some of the brightest young plebes in an entering class—those who can ace highly technical engineering classes with a minimum effort—are the very ones who struggle interpersonally.

Although the Navy needs very smart engineers driving its ships and submarines, it needs leaders with more than technical smarts. In a fascinating study of Naval officers out in the fleet, Bachman found that the most effective Naval leaders were warm, outgoing, emotionally expressive, and sociable (in contrast to a leader who is cold, aloof, distant, and interpersonally disengaged). Bachman's research report was appropriately titled "Nice Guys Finish First." In fact, research from a range of settings confirms that business clients want to do business with someone who will genuinely listen, will take the time to engage them, attend carefully, and really work at understanding what they need and what they want from the business relationship.

So what exactly is *emotional intelligence*? The term was originally coined by researchers Salovey and Mayer who defined it as "a form of social intelligence that involves the ability to monitor one's own and others' feelings and emotions, to discriminate among them, and to use information to guide one's thinking and action."

Emotional intelligence (EI) has to do with a leader's ability to work with others and effectively lead change. EI requires the ability to establish trust, to communicate warmth and positive regard for others, and the capacity to delay gratification and avoid impulsivity in any form. In the military, as in any other organization, EI becomes increasingly important as one advances in rank. In the Navy and Marine Corps, everyone who makes admiral or general is bright, cognitively gifted, and technically proficient. But to rise to flag rank, one must also demonstrate interpersonal savvy and the ability to form relationships with a range of followers.

We mentioned Admiral Halsey in a previous chapter. He was often described as a gung-ho admiral with a gregarious personality and a very personable leadership style. His sailors felt that he was a part of them—a comrade and not just a leader. After Pearl Harbor Halsey took the fleet's frightened and disillusioned sailors and instilled new faith in them. He joined with them emotionally and used emotion to lift them and make them believe again. They loved him for it.

Goleman discovered in numerous research studies that EI proved to be twice as predictive as IQ and technical expertise when it comes to leading others. When I (GPH) was XO of a squadron, my CO was a very bright, intelligent guy, but he just couldn't connect personally with the sailors in the squadron. It wasn't that he didn't try, but he was not skilled emotionally and whenever he tried to connect, it seemed fake and contrived. During the whole year I served under him, he never once called me by my first name. I was always XO. That he called me XO around the squadron was fine, but he also called me XO at social gatherings. It didn't go unnoticed. Several of my department heads commented on this fact to me personally and asked why he never called me by my first name.

EVEN MILITARY OFFICERS NEED
EMOTIONAL SOPHISTICATION

If you've ever seen George C. Scott in the movie *Patton* (or any number of famous war movies depicting generals and admirals), then you might believe that a real military leader has only to be tough as nails—driving his troops hard and kicking ass when necessary (usually quite often) in order to get the job done. These Hollywood stereotypes have no time for feelings (their own or anyone else's) and they seem only to express one emotion—anger. These military characters seem to possess the impulse control and empathy of five-year-olds. (Consider the scene from *Patton* in which the general slaps a traumatized young soldier in the face for being a coward.)

There are several problems with these depictions of high-ranking leaders. First, they are largely inaccurate. Yes, admirals and generals can be salty and battle-hardened. But if they're effective and successful in the modern military, they also possess good interpersonal skills. Some of the most important interpersonal skills are empathy—the ability to stand by another and genuinely understand his or her situation—and the ability to delay gratification and do hard things that also happen to be right. Although it is true that in the throes of combat, interpersonal savvy will be less relevant than war-fighting proficiency, bravery, and the ability to get your followers to act on command, the proportion of time the average officer spends in combat is utterly minuscule in comparison to the time spent managing and leading in noncombat situations.

This is why we work hard at building leaders with emotional intelligence at USNA. Far from being incongruent with or counter to cognitive intelligence, EI serves to channel and express the leader's ability in productive and socially facilitating ways. If you could decide between a brilliant but emotionally retarded superior officer and one who was reasonably intelligent but emotionally engaged, which would you choose?

Research in the fleet confirms that most sailors want the latter. "Give us the expressive, warm, and genuinely interested CO any day," say the majority of followers. "Leave the cold or poorly self-regulated leader for someone else, thank you."

Another great Navy leader, Admiral William P. Mack, was concerned about his marines and sailors right to the end. A World War II hero, beloved by his sailors and later superintendent of the Naval Academy, Admiral Mack recently passed away and was buried at the Naval Academy cemetery. He had requested a simple service with little ceremony and no formal funeral guard. The reason? He was concerned that sailors and marines would have to "stand around waiting in the cold" at his graveside. Emotionally intelligent leaders are concerned about and attuned to the welfare of the people they lead. And emotional connection in no way hampers mission accomplishment. More often, leader EI directly facilitates getting the crew to do the hard stuff happily.

ON MARSHMALLOWS AND LEADERSHIP

In the Academy's introductory course in leadership and human behavior, plebes are introduced to some of the consistent research findings bearing on EI. For example, consider the infamous marshmallow experiment with four-year-olds. Researchers invited children one by one to sit in a room with a marshmallow in front of them. They are told that if they can wait to eat the marshmallow until the researcher returns from running an errand, they will get two marshmallows when the researcher returns. Now the torment begins. With the scientist out of the room, some kids grab the marshmallow and devour it immediately. But others are determined to wait. They stare into space, make faces, lay their heads on the table, and engage in all manner of self-distraction in hopes of holding out for a greater reward. Follow-up studies with these same children many years later reveal some fascinating findings. Those four-year-olds with the fortitude to hold out for the second marshmallow generally grew up to be better adjusted, more popular, adventurous, confident, and dependable as teenagers. Children who gave in to temptation immediately were more likely to be lonely, easily frustrated, and stubborn. They score significantly lower on their SATs and are more prone to teen pregnancy and substance abuse.

Emotional intelligence describes qualities like understanding one's own feelings, empathy for the feelings of others, and the regulation of emotion in a way that enhances living and leading. And, of course, EI describes the ability to control impulses and delay gratification. Midshipmen learn that EI is a key tool for getting along with others, taking control of life, thinking clearly, and making good decisions. A great example of what we mean came from a first-class squad leader last year. He did a very simple thing. He bought birthday cakes for his plebes on their birthdays. He remembered what it was like to be a plebe. With the cakes, he showed them that he understood.

Part of the leadership curriculum is designed to give midshipmen a solid emotional education. The vast majority of them come to the gates of Annapolis with strong EI features already in place. Without EI, it is unlikely they would ever gain admission to the Naval Academy. Remember, nearly all of those admitted are active leaders in high school and they have delayed gratification effectively in the past. (They often chose to study when social opportunities came calling.). Once on board, we want them to become more self-aware, more self-regulated, and more talented when it comes to reading and responding to the emotional and social climate in individual relationships and in a workplace. We also work at helping them make the link between their own emotional quotient (EQ) and the probability of success as a leader. In the leadership curriculum, we cover the five essential components of EQ:

1. Self-awareness
2. Self-regulation
3. Motivation
4. Empathy
5. Social skill

SELF-AWARENESS

One of the painful truths about leaders like "the Bull" (not Halsey) is that they are not at ease with themselves; they are often entirely out of touch with who they are. An emotionally smart leader must be self-aware. Goleman and others describe the self-aware leader as familiar with his or her own emotional tendencies and proclivities. Self-aware leaders understand how emotional states steer their behavior and how their emotional responses affect others in both their personal and work relationships. Self-aware leaders are self-acquainted. They are insightful regarding their own psychology. And self-knowledge brings confidence, realistic self-appraisals, and genuine and open interaction with others. In addition, the self-aware leader is nondefensive: When I know myself thoroughly, I have less to fear.

Anxiety among leaders is typically born of concern about the unknown. The leader who can neither identify internal emotional states nor predict how these will impact self or others creates a risky, unstable, and, therefore, more anxiety-provoking emotional context for everyone involved.

At USNA, midshipmen are given personality test feedback, peer feedback regarding their leadership skills, and assessments from superiors regarding their interpersonal and leader performance. During leadership courses, they are required to engage in self-reflection, journal writing, and insight-oriented in-class exercises. We consider it essential that these young officers in training achieve a high degree of self-awareness. Questions they must be able to answer include: What are my standout personality features? How do I react when stressed? How comfortable am I in front of others? How well do I acclimate to new environments? When angry or grieved, how well do I identify and manage these emotions? If you can't easily answer these and other questions bearing on self-awareness you shouldn't be leading followers in the fleet.

There is something else about self-aware leaders. They understand and appreciate their relative weaknesses just as thoroughly as they appreciate their strengths. As a result, they are typically of good humor when it comes to admitting what they do not do well.

When I (GPH) was commanding officer, I was touring the hangar deck one day and saw a showerhead that was installed on the wall. It was there for emergencies in case one of my sailors spilled something acidic or flammable on themselves. I thought to myself, "I wonder if it works." So I walked over and pulled on the chain and sure enough it worked. As the water came gushing out, I looked down and saw that there was an electrical cord running along the deck right next to me. I thought to myself, "That was pretty stupid."

At the squadron Safety Council the next day, I relayed my story to everyone in attendance, knowing as I told it that they were all thinking to themselves, "Man, was that stupid!" But I wanted them to realize that even though we had a showerhead there for safety reasons, it really was a potential safety hazard. I also wanted them to see that even the CO could fall victim to mistakes and inattention. Later that afternoon as I was walking the hangar deck, I noticed that the electrical outlet had been moved and a big red circle drawn around the showerhead. I praised the safety officer when I saw him later for being so conscientious. He just smiled and said, "Gee Skipper, we didn't want you to electrocute yourself!" A self-aware leader is transparent about things he or she struggles with and is known for self-deprecating humor.

When our department head, Captain "Corky" Vasquez checked on board several years ago, he met with several of the civilian professors in the department and said, "I'm not sure why they selected me for this job. When I was a midshipman, I pretty much majored in Lacrosse [of course there is no such major]. I'm no scholar but I'm humbled and delighted to be here." Corky's self-deprecating style won him instant popularity with his followers. In fact, Corky was tremendously self-aware. He never made pretenses about being something he was not.

In addition to understanding themselves, self-aware leaders play to their strengths. They quickly learn how not to set themselves up for failure. They look for jobs and performance arenas in which they can shine. They are clear about what they value, and their life and career decisions are congruent with these values and talents.

Consider the case of Commander Ward Carroll. A career F-18 flight officer, Ward came to USNA as an instructor and director of the Academy's master's degree program in leadership. Close to 20 years in the Navy had taught Ward that his gifts resided in the creative arena. A frustrated writer, Ward made the decision to honor his strengths and start writing about life as a Naval aviator. He also decided to wrap up his career as a Naval officer. He recognized and gracefully accepted the fact that he was not a good match for a long career in senior Navy leadership positions. In 2001 Ward published his first novel, *Punk's War*, to rave reviews. He has never looked back. Today, CDR Carroll is retired from the Navy, the author of several excellent military novels, and a man who both appreciates and honors his strengths and weaknesses.

SELF-REGULATION

We have all worked for an emotionally unregulated leader. Some revered military commanders were known for venting large helpings of rage on followers as a means of "motivating" them for improved performance. Called "screamers" by subordinates, they may "go off" when the crew does not perform to expectation, or sometimes merely because they are annoyed or frustrated. Although this approach may work once or even twice, a pattern of such disregulation in the emotional realm is nearly always counterproductive. Admiral Ernest King, Chief of Naval Operations during World War II, was sometimes this type of leader:

> King was an exacting and demanding boss. His treatment of subordinates depended largely on how well the subordinate knew his job and stood his ground. He could be ruthless toward

a subordinate whom he considered incompetent, not hesitating to humiliate an officer before his juniors when that officer failed to perform up to King's high standards. On the other hand, a subordinate who knew his business, did his job well, and was not afraid to stand up to King when he knew he was right got along very well with him. But I have seen King unmercifully browbeat certain staff officers who showed fear of his wrath. King must have seemed a paradox to those who knew him. He condemned some mistakes and tolerated others. Sometimes he was ruthless, other times kind. When a seaplane sank overnight at its moorings at French Frigate Shoals because of high winds, King was furious. The entire squadron would remain there, said King, weeks if necessary, until the sunken aircraft was salvaged. After days of futile efforts King relented and let the squadron return to Honolulu.

We likely all recall the case of the infamous "hockey dad" several years ago. This poorly regulated man became incensed with the father of another player and proceeded to confront and then attack the man. The altercation ended with the explosive father's beating the other man's head against the ice and killing him—all in front of the boys on the team. In the diagnostic literature there is a clinical category for this behavior—*intermittent explosive disorder*. Persons with this condition may be involved in episodes of "road rage," assault, battery, domestic violence, and even child abuse. In more mild versions, the explosive person may become verbally assaultive at the drop of a hat, often leading to relational or employment problems. In sum, even occasional explosive behavior is not desirable or impressive. None of us admires the out-of-control or raging leader.

Of course, some impulsive emotional responses are easier to control than others. Anger is among the toughest. Anger is an emotion with genuine evolutionary value. It appears when one feels threatened or wronged and a primitive drive for self-protection and protection of one's property kicks in. Physically, the body responds with a burst of brain neurotransmitters that arouse both hypersensitivity and aggressiveness. Fear has adaptive value too, and so long as it does not overwhelm or occur for sustained periods, it may spur one to fight or escape real danger. Problematically, anxieties—anticipatory worry about situations or events that are not truly dangerous—are always counterproductive. Emotional intelligence does not indicate a lack of anger or anxiety, but it does suggest awareness and control of these primitive affective states.

Although many organizations, the military being no exception, have been slow to change expectations about senior leaders in this regard, change has indeed come. In the old Navy, flag officers that might rage and even threaten subordinates were labeled "eccentric" but often tolerated. I (WBJ) once heard a retired flag officer state clearly that "a good leader has got to break a little china," by which he meant become enraged, storm around, and use bursts of intense anger to get the attention of the crew. There are several problems with breaking china and we try to make sure every midshipman at Navy appreciates them.

First, the emotionally disregulated leader creates a climate of fear and avoidance among subordinates. Rather than spur enhanced performance, the chronically angry and punitive leader actually undermines it. Research on leader emotions shows that when leaders are prone to expressing negative emotions, their subordinates rate them as less effective than more regulated leaders.

Second, this aversive leadership climate paradoxically sabotages not only the mission, but also the leader him- or herself. Seeing a leader as explosive and unpredictable generates anxiety and avoidance in crewmembers; this crew is more likely to withhold critical information. When something is wrong with the ship, or when a subordinate has made an error, the angry leader is less likely than the regulated leader to hear about it before it is too late. How many explosive COs have gone down because subordinates were unwilling to risk providing discrepant (but accurate) information about the ship's being off course, about a questionable sighting on the surface ahead, or about the capacity of the main engines to handle a demanding pace? Unreasonable COs do not always receive immediate and potentially lifesaving corrections from subordinates.

In my (GPH) second squadron, we were deployed to the western Pacific (WESTPAC) and had been tracking a submarine for about a week. The sub was travelling to its area of operations and had to transit the Malacca Straits. All submarines must transit the straits on the surface, so one of our crews was flying overhead at night visually tracking the running light on the sub's conning tower. Well, the sub pulled a fast one on the crew. It dumped the running light overboard and submerged. Not realizing what had happened, the crew continued to orbit the running light burning on the surface of the water until they realized they had been had. The sub got away. When the crew returned to base, our commanding officer exploded in an angry and unnerving tirade. He was livid.

A couple of months later, another enemy sub was spotted en route to relieve the one that had eluded us. At an All Officers Meeting, the CO asked the officers what crews wanted to go and track this one. After his display of anger the previous time, no one raised a hand. So he said, "Okay, all five lieutenant commanders' crews will go." Well, every LCDR could see the writing on the wall very clearly. If a lieutenant commander lost the submarine this time, he or she could kiss making commander good-bye.

Since I was a LCDR, my crew was among them. Just before we were ready to take off, the CO came aboard the aircraft and gave us a great inspirational send-off. He said, "If you lose him, don't come back!" What a guy! My crew did happen to be on-station when the sub tried to pull the same trick, but my radar operator saw the maneuver right away. We hung on and continued to track the sub after it submerged. It was a great crew effort despite the CO. And most important, we got to go back to base.

A third problem with emotional disregulation is the fact that it communicates a great deal about the maturity and stability of the leader. Raging is something two-year-olds do. We call it throwing a tantrum at that age, but the behavior is really the same. Losing one's temper can be quite gratifying and satisfying on a very primitive and regressive level, but it really constitutes emotional immaturity and even laziness. It is much harder to control one's emotional responses than it is to vent them immediately.

Finally, poor self-regulation can lead to extremely poor decision making and even failures in integrity. The enraged leader may physically grab a subordinate (we've seen this happen) and become the subject of a board of inquiry or even courts-martial. Similarly, an emotionally needy, depressed, or lonely leader may blur boundaries with a subordinate and become involved in a sexual relationship (we've seen this happen too) on the job. The leader with poor impulse control may sacrifice integrity at the altar of immediate gratification.

In contrast to these examples of poor self-regulation, we work to create Naval and Marine Corps leaders with the capacity for controlling or redirecting their disruptive impulses and moods. The objective is not to create robotic and emotionless military leaders, but rather leaders who are characteristically calm, cool-headed, thoughtful, self-reflective, comfortable with ambiguity, and willing to delay gratification. These are the behaviors that protect their integrity and create a climate of trust and confidence in followers.

On the bridge of a ship, the CO had better have junior officers who will disagree or provide discrepant information without hesitation. This is not a sign of disrespect; on the contrary, followers who are confident in the CO's capacity for self-regulation are the most willing to risk providing discrepant information for the good of the ship. These subordinates know their leader can handle it. They are used to being praised in public and corrected in private.

If your crew won't speak up, prepare for disaster. Consider the case of the USS *Greeneville,* which sank the Japanese school ship *Ehimi Maru* off the coast of Hawaii. The CO was a very competent officer. In fact, many described him as a rising star in the submarine community. His crew thought very highly of him and they were proud to be members of the *Greeneville.* Some observers; however, point out that his major leadership flaw was the demand to be in control of every evolution that went on in the sub. He was a hands-on leader in the sense of running all aspects of the sub. He was in control so often that the crew came to depend on him for almost everything that went on during almost every exercise or maneuver.

On the day of the accident, the *Greenville* was taking some VIPs on a short familiarization cruise off the coast of Oahu at the request of a former Commander-in-Chief of the Pacific Fleet. The captain wanted to show the VIPs what he and his crew could do, so he took them through some very exciting maneuvers. The problem was that the CO was doing everything himself. To do it all, he had to take some short cuts. Acclimated to the CO's leadership style, the crew remained silent when things started to go wrong and some procedures were overlooked. While demonstrating an emergency surfacing drill, he actually took over the sub from the officer-of-the-deck and went against the advice of his XO.

As the Greeneville surfaced, it sliced through the hull of the *Ehimi Maru,* which sank within minutes. Nineteen people were lost. The subsequent investigation found that the captain, although a very competent CO, had created a command climate characterized by excessive reliance on one man—the CO. His crew had become dependent on the skipper and he had allowed them to do it. The lesson: If you want your crew to speak up and take initiative, don't micromanage and never allow them to think you're omnipotent. It takes a crew of more than a hundred smart people—all taking initiative and doing their jobs—to avoid disaster in a submarine.

SELF-MOTIVATION

Navy midshipmen are notorious for demonstrating one of the key facets of emotional intelligence even before they check on board. As a group, they are perpetually driven to achieve—beyond both their own expectations and those of others. This is a group of successful men and women who love to accomplish goals for the sheer pleasure of succeeding and pushing their own bars higher. Research on EQ shows that the most successful leaders harbor an abiding love for the work itself—external reward takes a back seat to achievement. At USNA, midshipmen thrive when challenged; they show a genuine love for overcoming obstacles. They take tremendous pride when a hard task is successfully handled.

In fact, many a USNA leader has learned that these bright and motivated students are best kept from having idle time (perhaps this at least partially explains the rigorous around-the-clock schedule midshipmen endure). A couple of days before the Army-Navy game this year, the commandant of midshipmen walked into his conference room and discovered a full-size submarine torpedo occupying the spot normally taken by his conference table. Another commandant discovered a three-story-tall Frosty the Snowman adorning the roof of Bancroft Hall. Before another Army-Navy game a class removed all the contents from their company officer's (an Army officer) office and set up his belongings in a head (restroom). Another time a class filled a company officer's office with aluminum cans from floor to ceiling. Prior to the old power plant's demolition, my (GPH) class painted the following on the building's huge smokestack, "If the stack goes, we go with it." The point is that when you put 4000 bright, creative, and achievement-oriented students in one spot, you'd better provide lots of opportunity to achieve and accomplish, or they will be driven to create their own challenges.

The emotionally intelligent leader wants to be pushed and challenged to higher and higher levels of accomplishment. He or she can easily become fatigued and uninterested in rote and traditional approaches to the job. In contrast, license to use innovation and novel strategies for getting to the finish line seems to energize this leader.

Once again, consider the strategy employed by CDR Abrashoff of the USS *Benfold* when the crew was growing weary with the constant demands for scraping rust and painting the ship to prevent decay. Rather than grind his crew through these repetitive and menial tasks, he asked them to strategize alternatives. In the end, he turned to an external supplier of heavy-duty paint and stainless steel bolts. The net outcome was that the Benfold saved the Navy thousands of dollars, radically reduced the frequency with which the ship required painting and scraping, and freed the crew to pursue more meaningful and mission-relevant endeavors.

As far as innovation and novel strategies go, one of my (GPH) submarine classmates became a legend in his own right during a hurricane. When Hurricane Hugo hit Charleston in 1989, he was commanding officer of a submarine that was tied up to the pier in Charleston. The sub was undergoing some repairs and was not fit to go to sea but was in danger of suffering severe damage if it remained pier-side. Obviously, he didn't want to put his sub in harm's way, so he got enough systems working to take the sub out into the middle of the river, submerge, and ride out the hurricane on the bottom. He achieved quite a bit of fame among East Coast submariners for his exploit.

And there is something else about the self-motivated leader. He or she views the source of success and failure as internal. We call this the *internal locus of control* and it is prevalent among high achievers. Whereas many leaders give in to what social psychologists call the *self-serving bias* (attributing successes to internal factors, but attributing failures to uncontrollable external events and circumstances), the self-motivated leader believes firmly that his or her actions will determine the ultimate outcome in any scenario. Leaders like this remain optimistic even when the chips are down and the odds are long. They harbor an abiding belief that they can overcome nearly any adversity and win in the end. A strong sense of internal motivation is a cornerstone of emotionally intelligent leadership.

EMPATHY

One of the things I (WBJ) look forward to each summer is teaching a short intensive course in counseling skills for the 15 new company officers (Navy lieutenants and Marine Corps captains) who will each take up leadership duties for a company of approximately 120 midshipmen in Bancroft Hall. I teach this course as part of a master's degree program in leadership that each new company officer must complete before reporting to the Hall. As the last course in a very intensive graduate program, students sometimes see the counseling class as a low hurdle—an easy wrap-up to the year. Then they get to empathy and their outlook often changes. In my course, students are required to both understand and demonstrate interpersonal empathy in mock counseling sessions. These accomplished military officers are often surprised to find that genuine empathic communication is much harder than it looks.

Empathy is the ability to accurately recognize and understand the emotional messages of others. Empathy hinges on excellent listening skills, attention to both verbal and nonverbal communication, and the ability to hear both the overt and covert messages in a person's language. Midshipmen learn a sequence of empathic listening skills that include: actively attending to the message, comprehending and interpreting what is being communicated, responding in a manner that reflects correct comprehension and understanding, and, finally, storing the message in memory for use in subsequent interactions. Empathic leaders understand their people and communicate this understanding effectively. Empathy is always incomplete until the leader demonstrates that he or she has gotten the message and genuinely understands how followers are feeling.

Every leader will face a situation in which empathy will play a crucial role. When I (GPH) was CO, one of my junior officers came to my room and asked if he could speak to me. We had been on deployment for about four months and he stated that he had to go home for a short visit. I could see that he was upset, so I asked him why. Normally, officers were only allowed to go home in case of an emergency. He told me that he had not heard from his wife since we had left. I attentively listened to his story, asked him some questions, and decided that I would let him go home. I let him know that I would do anything I could to help him out and assured him I understood his anxiety. But I was also concerned about his emotional state as a pilot. I had seen situations in which pilots who were having family problems were responsible for crashes and loss of life.

The young officer went home and, sure enough, when he got to his house he discovered that his wife had moved out and taken everything but his recliner. It was a big blow for him. When he returned to the squadron, I talked with him frequently. When he told me he was ready to go flying again, I put him back in the cockpit.

In my (WBJ) course with company officers, there are a number of common errors that occur when first learning empathic skills. First, empathy is not sympathy. One need not become overinvolved in the feelings of others, nor should the leader actually "feel" follower emotions in the way the followers experience them. Empathy merely requires accurate understanding. Second, new leaders are often too quick to jump to solutions before fully understanding the problem. My Marine Corps officers sometimes have literally to bite their tongues to keep from saying, "Here's what you're going to do!" in the fist two minutes of a counseling session. They must learn to balance good listening with a natural propensity for getting to the solution.

At USNA, we are not training professional counselors, but many counseling skills—and empathy is at the top of the list—are connected to successful leadership. Great leaders can sense, understand, and then communicate understanding of follower viewpoints and reactions. When a fatal aviation accident occurs and the remaining crew is reeling with emotion, or when a battle group that has been patrolling the Persian Gulf for six months gets word its duty has been extended and that the crew will not make it home to families until after Christmas, the empathic leader anticipates and acknowledges the crew's feelings as a sign of both respect and understanding before helping them to move on and get the job done. When a leader is emotionally savvy enough to read emotions in others accurately and anticipate probable emotional reactions, the leader is more likely to prepare a successful response in advance.

Another great hero expressed this self-awareness under the most extreme conditions.

> While enduring torture in a Vietnam prison, then-Captain William Lawrence composed a poem in his head, which later became the state poem for his native Tennessee. While imprisoned, he cre-

ated a system through which teams of prisoners were assigned to work with any U.S. soldier who needed help or couldn't function on his own. And he helped them live through physical, psychological, and verbal abuse. "I always felt that in the military there must be an innate mutual trust and respect. Officers must have a deep and abiding concern for others, particularly those in difficulty or distress." He quoted physicist Albert Einstein who said, "Only a life that is lived for others is a life worthwhile."

A final note about empathy: There are few leader skills more conducive to developing and retaining talent. Empathic leaders at USNA often become known as "star-makers" or talent developers. In the fleet, empathic CO's are significantly more likely to have high retention rates. Their subordinates report greater job satisfaction. They feel understood and respected by their leader, even when they disagree with some of the leader's decisions. At Navy, we are not training psychologists for the fleet, but we are training leaders with a knack for excellent listening, genuine understanding, and solid communication in relationships with followers.

SOCIAL SKILL

The final component of excellent emotional intelligence may seem obvious but it is nonetheless crucial to success in leading. Goleman described social skill as "friendliness with a purpose," by which he meant the capacity to kindly and effectively move people in the direction you want them to go. Socially skilled leaders have many friendships and connections. They are natural networkers and bridge-builders, and people often respond positively to their outgoing style and friendly, engaged demeanor. Now, military leaders do not have to be socialites or dyed in the wool extraverts to be emotionally sophisticated. They do need to have real relationships, to be skilled at discovering and then building upon common ground between constituencies, and they need to be effective at persuasion.

Think of one's social skill as the framework or schema through which all the other important pieces of EI get put into practice and are expressed interpersonally. Excellent leaders can establish good working relationships with a wide range of people and they appear to genuinely enjoy interacting with them. They are poised, gracious, and attentive enough to communicate sincere interest in the lives and concerns of those they lead.

THE GOUGE

The ability to deal with emotions—both one's own and those of others—is the heart of emotional intelligence. Officers and leaders with EI seem to easily harmonize, persuade, and forge relationships with a wide array of followers and colleagues. Emotional intelligence is the key to being a team player and a good leader. It may be one of the most underrated facets of effective leadership. Although cognitive intelligence and technical proficiency are essential components of leading effectively, more often, it is the subtle elements of interpersonal skill that predict which leaders will rise to the top.

Emotionally intelligent leaders are self-aware; they are familiar with their emotional states and insightful about how these states affect others. Emotionally intelligent leaders are also self-regulated. They own emotional ballast and can effectively refrain from rageful explosion or sullen withdrawal in favor of more facilitative responses. Leaders with good EI are self-motivated—able to delay gratification in order to achieve some higher purpose. Finally, excellent leaders are empathic and socially skilled; they are a pleasure to interact with and they use their interpersonal savvy to build bridges and encourage followers.

11

THE THREE D'S
OF EMPOWERMENT:
DECIDE, DELEGATE,
AND DISAPPEAR

When USNA graduate Captain Mike Manazir (class of 1981) took command of the USS *Sacramento* in 2003, he disoriented his executive officer (XO) and the entire officer wardroom by immediately instituting a command style based on empowerment. Used to having the previous CO run most elements of the ship from bow to stern, these officers were unaccustomed to a captain who trusted them to do their jobs unencumbered. In the words of Captain Manazir:

> My first task upon arrival was to turn the ship over to the XO and department heads (DHs). It took a while for my XO to grasp that I really wanted him to run things with me as overseer, but in a matter of weeks, the ship's performance and reputation increased many-fold. I could trust the officers to do all the right things and, as a group, capture all the little points. Great results. It is apparent to me now that delegation increases the self-worth of those delegated tasks and enhances the company product. Just ensure that your leadership vision is simple and articulated clearly. I asked my wardroom to maintain excellence in every area and to communicate effectively down to the most junior enlisted. That's it. I haven't given a lick of additional vision and they have crafted the schedule, gotten the ship squared away, and done an excellent job taking care of all our

sailors. I find that I can just focus on the mission at hand, safety of the ship, and rewarding the sailors verbally and otherwise for their efforts. I stay way above the fray. I find out what I need to know from the XO or one of the department heads, and then go back to what I am doing. Trusting them and seeing the results has given me confidence that they've got my back covered and I don't need to worry much. I also keep my work hours limitod. I find this gives the DHs and the crew a chance to operate without me in their hair until they have all their ducks in a row. The best advice I ever got about empowering came from Rear Admiral Goodwyn. He said "Decide, delegate, and disappear." I have found that this works.

In many ways, Captain Manazir's approach to empowering his followers is precisely what we want Navy midshipmen to grasp as they prepare for the fleet. Leadership defined by visioning, trusting, and getting out of the way is diametrically opposed to leadership characterized by micromanaging, distrusting, and demanding. Consider the following reflection from one of Captain Minazir's 17 department heads when Manazir was XO board the aircraft carrier USS *Carl Vinson*:

Captain Manazir delivered the vision and told us to go and do it. He immediately took charge of the situation; let everyone know he was in charge, then let his subordinates deliver. He didn't pressure you before a deadline, simply expected you to do your job and knew you would. Captain Manazir wasn't a screamer. He praised a lot and always said "Thank you." Always. The end result was that DHs wanted to give him solutions, and good ones.

This approach takes a lot of confidence and a lot of trust. Of course one of the things that Captain Manazir had going for him was that his department heads and his executive officer came through. Although this may not always be the case, experience shows that an empowering approach is most likely to stimulate maximal performance from good followers. The most efficient leaders tell followers what they need, let them perform, and then use loads of reinforcement to encourage and correction to shape even sharper performance.

THE PARADOX OF EMPOWERED FOLLOWERS: GETTING MORE BY MANAGING LESS

Around the globe today, CEOs and organizational leaders are feeling the heat. Stockholders want results, times are uncertain, and every decision appears risk-laden and ominous. In the military, in business, and in college and professional sports, leaders go down quickly when results fail to meet expectations. The obvious temptation for leaders is to react to these circumstances by ratcheting up personal control and oversight of all elements of the company's operations. Threatened leaders can become domineering, tyrannical, and even bullying. They can fall prey to the notion that iron-fisted control and leadership through intimidation will buy results. In nearly every circumstance, they are wrong.

We here in the Washington, D.C., area have watched this play out with the beloved Washington Redskins and its disenchanted owner, Daniel Snyder, during the last four years. A highly successful businessman, Snyder amassed a fortune at a very young age from his telecommunications business—enough to buy his boyhood dream team, the Washington Redskins. He also thought he could purchase it and then demand instant success. But according to press reports and the team's abysmal record, a micromanaging approach to football operations has been extremely unsuccessful. Embracing a very brash and abrasive approach to doing business, he insists on hands-on control of all aspects of football operations. He is reportedly unwilling to listen to those who know football best and this has cost him and his team millions of dollars. He has personally fired people all the way down the ladder in the organization, and he has hired and sacked highly talented and well-paid coaches because none of them have instantly taken his team to the Super Bowl. Without a radical change in his style, this is the type of leader who might never be successful in football because he cannot seem to let his coaches and subordinates do their jobs, no matter how talented they may be. Sadly, Daniel Snyder may be an example of how to un-empower subordinates.

In this chapter, we highlight the necessity of empowerment for effective leadership. Empowering leaders share a number of behavioral habits in common. Empowering leaders offer unconditional and consistent praise and support. They see their followers as valuable, not because of their work, but because of who they are. They will follow through with punishment when it is deserved, but they never relish it and often work to find an outcome that teaches the lesson without slaying follower esteem and motivation.

An essential element of the empowering leader's psychology is an abiding assumption that their followers are generally good, trustworthy, willing to do the right thing, and ready to perform at or beyond expectations. Followers are notorious for confirming the benevolent assumptions of empowering leaders.

While I (GPH) was stationed in the Azores, on New Year's Day we suffered a powerful earthquake that measured over 7.0 on the Richter scale. Hundreds of people were killed; thousands of homes were destroyed; and there was a tremendous loss of livestock when the stone fences holding them in came crashing down. Our sailors responded magnificently. For the first few days, we all worked trying to rescue people and get them food, shelter, and clothing. As the months went on, our sailors continued to perform their own jobs during the day, but after hours and on weekends they were out with the locals on their own or in small groups, rebuilding homes and fences and trying to locate livestock.

Initially amazed, it dawned on me that these sailors were doing exactly what they should be doing—exactly what the CO had empowered them to do. Even though they were accountable to continue performing their military duties, these American sailors were "serving" in the most complete sense. An empowering style allowed them to enrich the people of the Azores and make the U.S. military and all Americans proud in the process.

One of the rich by-products of the empowering style is the freedom for followers to fail. Because the commanding officer has turned over day-to-day control of the ship to those who know the ship best—the crew—there exists the possibility that the crew will fail and disappoint or even sink the CO. But this risk is essential for the leader to bear. CDR Michael Abrashoff discovered this aboard the USS *Benfold*:

> I worked hard to create a climate that encouraged quixotic pursuits and celebrated the freedom to fail. I never once reprimanded a sailor for attempting to solve a problem or reach a goal. I wanted my people to feel empowered, so they could think autonomously.... Empower your people and at the same time give them guidelines within which they are allowed to roam. I called it my line in the sand: I had to be in on any decision that

could kill someone, injure someone, waste taxpayer money, or damage the ship. But short of that, anyone on my ship should try to solve any problem that came up.

What is the fruit of empowerment? Followers of these leaders feel delighted when they perform well in the skipper's eyes and alternatively feel deflated and dejected when they believe they have let the skipper down—not because they fear wrath or reprisal, but because they genuinely want to please the leader. This is the enduring paradox of empowerment. By creating a vision and some firm parameters within which followers can function, and then turning them lose to do their jobs without interference or scrutiny, leaders reap tremendous benefit in the form of follower loyalty, commitment, and performance.

Toward the end of my (GPH) command tour, the commodore came to me and said that the P-3 community was beginning a huge transition of squadron aircraft and one of my aircraft was to be among the first transferred to a West Coast squadron. He indicated very firmly that he wanted the aircraft transferred in the best shape possible. Understanding that the heat was on me, I was tempted to oversee the project every step of the way. Then I realized my crew members were the experts and I decided to turn the task entirely over to them.

I went to my maintenance department, which was extremely busy already getting prepared for our upcoming deployment overseas, and described the task. I told them the plane had to look brand new. I also told them I had complete confidence in their ability and then I departed on a two-week detachment overseas. As soon as I landed back at the base two weeks later, the entire maintenance department met me. They wanted me to see the outcome of their work as soon as I returned.

It was absolutely amazing. The inside of the plane was entirely redone, and I am convinced the entire aircraft was in better shape than when it had initially left the manufacturer's plant. It was comparable to that '55 Thunderbird classic that someone rebuilds and then never drives again. We were never going to fly the plane again. Yet, the look on their faces as I toured the plane told the tale. Even though they were getting ready to deploy and were extremely busy, the commodore had wanted a plane that everyone would remember in that transfer, and they were proud to be left alone to deliver something remarkable.

This was also a remarkable learning experience for me. By telling a talented crew what I needed from them and then confidently leaving the country, I conveyed a clear message of trust. Empowered, they didn't disappoint. When it comes to controlling the day-to-day operations, less is more. I explained to them the requirement, left, and let them do it on their own.

In the balance of this chapter we consider the essential components of empowerment.

EXPECT GREAT THINGS: THE PYGMALION EFFECT

A striking finding from research in leadership and psychology, often termed the *Pygmalion effect*, is that followers frequently rise (or fall) to the level of a leader's expectation. Consequently, wise leaders set high expectations and communicate genuine belief in the crew's capacity to meet the challenge and succeed. Of course, they simultaneously provide resources and sustained encouragement so that followers have what they need to get the job done. On the other hand, some leaders—perhaps distrustful or suspicious by nature—assume incompetence in the crew and communicate low expectations of performance. They should not then be surprised when the crew withholds effort or sabotages the leader's objectives.

On occasion, a follower will let you down. In imperfect organizations (all of them), this is a guarantee. The question for the empowering leader is how to respond in a way that instructs without humiliating or sabotaging future performance. During one of my (GPH) maintenance department's inspections when I was CO, I felt so confident about their ability to pass that I didn't give them much guidance and felt little need to worry. My maintenance department had performed at the top before and received the highest grades possible in every other inspection.

The afternoon before the inspection was completed, the top inspector came to my office and said he had discovered a problem with one of the divisions. He was letting me know so I could have the division work that night to fix things rather than get a low grade on the final report. I thanked him and called for the lieutenant commander in charge of the division. When the LCDR came to my office, I asked what the problem was and what she expected to do about it before the final inspection in the morning. She said she would take care of it and departed.

Well, in the morning, when I received the final report, her division had failed because I had been warned about the discrepancies but nothing had been done about them. It turned out that after she left my office, she met with her division, told them there were some discrepancies left to fix, and then departed. Her division didn't think it was that big a deal and departed shortly after she did. Nothing got fixed. It was the one time during my command tour that a junior officer ultimately let me down. The division was totally embarrassed by their performance. They understood fully that they had let the rest of the squadron down. The LCDR never lived down this performance among her peers.

Sometimes, as an empowering leader, you get burned, and even empowering leaders have to take some lumps. Yet, reverting to micromanagement cannot be an option. In this situation, I showed honest disappointment while refusing to demean the officer involved. This appeared to have maximum effect. I know she was horrified and deflated, as were her chiefs and junior officers. I asked for better work and I got it thereafter, which left me to continue reinforcing all the good things going on in my squadron.

It is difficult to overstate how significant the leader's assumptions about the team really are. Why? Whether you intend to or not, your belief about the officers and crew will be communicated in your actions and demeanor. Expect competence and success and you'll probably get it. The crew will see themselves through your lens. Your favorable opinion and flattering view will become their own, and they won't want to let you down.

Consider this reflection from an officer on Captain Manazir's ship during his XO tour on the USS *Carl Vinson*.

> Everyone wanted to please him because he made them believe they could please him. He assumed that each of us was a specialist in our area and that we knew what to do. Then he just expected us to go do it while giving us lots of praise and any resources we needed to do the job. He was always positive about us and always praised in public. He'd get on the 1MC and tell us that we were doing great work. The ship became the most qualified ship of its kind in the Navy. We won all the awards for

ships in our class and it was because we saw ourselves as the best crew in the Navy. We were something special. That's how he made us feel.

PRAISE, PRAISE, AND THEN PRAISE SOME MORE

Studies of organizational retention consistently show that one of the top reasons for people to leave an organization is limited recognition and praise. Employees can handle relatively low pay, workplace adversity, and even the dearth of creature comforts on board a ship or submarine at sea so long as they are relentlessly affirmed. This is a crucial point, and more commanding officers may fail at this component of empowerment than any other. If you want to create a group of loyal and successful followers, never miss an opportunity to praise their efforts—in public.

When I (GPH) was going through prospective-CO school in Norfolk, I had a brief on the number of medals a CO was allowed to give away in his/her squadron each year. As a commanding officer, few things are as potent as awarding medals to recognize your troops. A wise woman who had worked for Commander Naval Air Forces Atlantic for over 30 years gave the brief about the medals. "Depending on the size of your squadron," she said, "you could give away 5, 10, or 15 of these medals a year." Then she added something I would not forget. She said, "And I'm the only one who counts."

I smiled when I realized that what she was telling us was that if we had deserving sailors, and had already used up our quota, we should put in for the extra medals anyway because she was the only one who counted them all and no one ever asked her if someone had used a couple more than they were rated. I never abused her confidence, but strangely, I did seem to lose count occasionally on exactly how many medals I gave out each fiscal year. It was the best piece of advice that any civil servant ever gave to prospective COs.

Once a vision is created and the leader hands over responsibility to the crew, his or her job is to fuel their subsequent efforts, and reinforcement constitutes very high-octane fuel. Empowering leaders understand that followers may not get it right the first time, so they shape or praise successive approximations to the goal. Rather than rage at failures, they find something positive in performances that fall short, point out necessary corrections, and then empower followers to get back at it. The net effect of consistent praise is a work force that feels confident and efficacious. Yes, they are free to fail, but they rarely do. The work environment is characterized by excitement, positive emotion, and sincere expectation for success.

An interesting by-product of empowering leadership is an increase in discretionary time. When the crew is doing the job of running the ship, the CO simply has more time to find people and performances to praise. Quite often this praise is public. At other times, praise and recognition of one's followers happens behind the scenes.

When a destroyer captain and USNA graduate (who wishes to remain anonymous) learned that one of his best chiefs intended to leave active duty, he was disappointed. The chief was an excellent performer and a fantastic model for enlisted sailors. He was one of the many senior enlisted leaders who had risen to the level of the captain's expectations and had made his department one of the most efficient in the Navy. About this time, the captain noted a call for nominations for an award given annually to a stellar chief petty officer. The problem was that the nomination needed to come from one of the nominee's subordinates. No problem. The captain wrote up the entire nomination package, found a subordinate of the chief's who happily agreed to submit it, and the package was on its way. Several months later, the commanding officer was delighted to walk into the chief's workspace and formally announce that the chief was the recipient of this prestigious award. Later that afternoon, this chief requested that his retirement papers be pulled. He was deeply moved by the award and decided to stay on active duty. The empowering leader finds a range of methods for rewarding and honoring followers. In fact, when it comes to bringing up a crew, this may be job number one.

PUNISH SPARINGLY AND RELUCTANTLY

A final word about praise: Research shows that it consistently beats the alternative—punishment. That is, from single-cell organisms to human infants to midshipmen and bright naval officers, we learn more quickly and effectively when reinforced for correct responses or near approximations than when we are punished for incorrect responding. While praise bolsters motivation and self-esteem, punishment is associated with shame and a negative self-view.

In one unfortunate example of the effects of sustained punishment without reinforcement, a former commandant at USNA (the officer tasked with overseeing the day-to-day activities of the entire brigade of midshipmen) took over and immediately decided that he needed to begin controlling the small details of running the brigade. In addition, he offered little praise or reward when individuals or groups achieved great things. His philosophy was that no praise was required when midshipmen performed as he expected. However, when things went wrong, punishment and restriction were doled out in large helpings.

The paradox here is that we work hard to teach midshipmen the mechanics of creating a praise-rich environment. This environment is always more positive, pleasant, energizing, and productive than one saturated in punishment. Sure enough, it wasn't long before even the top midshipmen leaders had trouble motivating their midshipmen to do anything but avoid punishment. Morale hit new lows, performance began to drop, and discussions in leadership classes regarding the effective and ineffective use of punishment and reward became increasingly energized.

Morale in the brigade ebbs and flows with the coming and going of various commandants and their shifting views on reinforcement. As we write this chapter in the winter of 2003 through 2004, we are delighted to report that the current commandant truly "gets it" in this regard. Rarely does a day go by that the commandant is not sending e-mails to the entire brigade and the USNA community extolling the achievements of various midshipmen or the brigade as a whole. When there is a big win in football or when the brigade shows excellent spirit or a can-do attitude in achieving a task, praise is forthcoming and extra liberty is often thrown in. The response in terms of both effort and morale is stunning.

Perhaps worst of all, consistent punishment without ample reinforcement leads to hopelessness, or what Seligman describes as *learned helplessness*. You will recall from an earlier chapter in this book that Seligman is famous for the seemingly sadistic shocked dog experiments. Canines that were randomly shocked from the floor of their cages would eventually lie down and accept the shocks. Later, when moved to a cage in which they could simply step over a wall into an adjoining cage with no shock, they made no effort to do so. They had become cognitively helpless. Punished randomly and without apparent opportunity to end the punishment, they gave up.

How often have CEOs and commanding officers used a punishment-rich environment to run their organizations? Too often, we think. When leaders punish without creating desirable alternatives to the wrong behavior, helplessness ensues. The proof of this leadership style is typically evident in poor morale, low retention, and failure to accomplish goals. Although punishment is occasionally unavoidable, it should be an exception in the truly empowered organization.

UNLEASHING ACHIEVEMENT VERSUS DEMANDING OBEDIENCE

During the fall leadership course for plebes at USNA, students watch footage from the original social psychology experiments on obedience conducted by Stanley Milgram of Yale University. In these experiments, ordinary citizen volunteers from the New Haven area were erroneously led to believe that they were "teaching" a student (a confederate of the experimenter) by administering electric shocks when the student gave incorrect responses to memory recall tasks.

Although no shocks were actually being delivered, the elderly male student screamed and pleaded for the "teacher" to stop. He complained of a heart condition and eventually stopped responding altogether. Nonetheless, the teacher was told to continue administering what he or she believed to be increasingly severe and dangerous electrical shocks. Shockingly (pun intended), a full two-thirds of these healthy and normal citizens went all the way, complying with the experimenter's request to deliver the full range of shocks to an apparently unconscious or possibly even deceased student.

We show midshipmen this clip as a means of highlighting the profound power of obedience to authority. Each of us is capable of unethical, inhumane, and even genocidal behavior if ordered to act so by a convincing authority. Of course, obedience is a double-edged sword in the military. Obeying lawful orders and adhering to the chain of command are essential to the good order and discipline of military units. Obedience is also crucial for achieving the mission in difficult circumstances. The military can never be a democracy.

Here is the question we want our leaders-in-training to ask: Why do subordinates obey? What makes them do the job in spite of all the adversity? In the military, part of the answer will always be that they have sworn an oath to serve, and service demands honoring rank and following orders. Yet there is much more to it.

While some followers are motivated to obey primarily out of fear, others find obedient service to be a pleasure. When serving the commanding officer is a genuine and natural response of gratitude for empowering and motivating leadership, the CO has created a venerable fighting force. Rather than wielding coercive power and threats to achieve performance, the empowering leader assumes followers want to work, want to innovate, and want to achieve. The empowering leader works to fan these flames of internal drive whenever possible.

The best company officers at the Naval Academy are the ones who truly let the first class midshipmen run the company. If the company commander is perceived as merely the "mouth" for the company officer, he/she will accomplish little. But if the midshipmen in the company see that the first class leaders truly have an input into running the company, then that company inevitably is one that works well together, plays well together, and is usually in the running for "Color Company" honors.

One of the many commodities never in short supply at USNA is the psychological need for achievement. Achievement motivation correlates with expending great effort in order to accomplish a task—simply for the satisfaction of accomplishment. Psychologist David McClelland's research reveals that those high in need for achievement are naturally more competitive, enjoy taking responsibility for problem solving, and experience a deep sense of pleasure in regard to accomplishing tasks.

The young officers we prepare for the fleet are all high achievers. They were high achievers before they arrived at USNA, and they will continue to be driven by this need long after their Naval careers end. Many followers are also likely to be curious and creative. They savor challenge, puzzle solving, and the stimulation that tackling a new problem offers.

In this way, we share a great deal in common with the primates. In a famous set of experiments with rhesus monkeys, Harlow discovered that they would go to great lengths to figure out how to open a latch even when there was no reward forthcoming for so doing. Sometimes the freedom to put one's talents to work is reinforcement enough.

The wise leader understands achievement motivation and is careful never to coerce or command when simply offering a challenge plus encouragement to "go for it" will suffice. Interestingly, the followers of empowering leaders often get most energized about the most difficult problems—so long as the leader communicates trust, support, and praise along the way.

PERSONAL TRAITS OF EMPOWERING LEADERS

In order to really delegate and disappear as a leader, one must be decidedly self-assured and secure personally. Giving subordinates real power without feeling personally or professionally threatened takes confidence. The less secure a leader is —the less at ease with him- or herself—the more anxiety provoking relinquishing power will be.

It is especially important for new leaders to appreciate the limits of their knowledge and skill and to defer to seasoned experts. This must be done with humility, trust, and without any pretense to absolving oneself of ultimate responsibility for the outcome. At USNA, midshipmen learn that as junior officers, the gravest error they can make is failing to utilize the hard-won wisdom of the fleet's senior enlisted leaders. Doyle Borchers (class of 1965) learned the virtue of humble empowerment:

> An old chief boson's mate pulled me aside just before commissioning. He said, "Sir, I bet you think you know everything about the Navy." Of course I replied very confidently that I did and that I was ready for the fleet. He sat me down and said that if I wanted to be a success as a naval officer, when I got to my first squadron and was assigned my first job as a division officer, I should get with my leading chief and ask him to have a cup of coffee with me. The chief would probably roll his eyes and mutter to himself, "Here we go again." Then I should tell the chief that I didn't know anything about the real Navy and that I expected

him to run the division and help me learn the real ropes. My job was to take care of him and the sailors in the chain of command, and his job was to keep me informed and up to speed. Well, I took that advice and it was the best advice I ever received.

In addition to being personally secure and reasonably humble, empowering leaders are often known for their consideration. Considerate leaders are friendly and supportive of followers. They generate a variety of methods for communicating concern about individual followers' personal situations and showing appreciation for the work they do. In fact, the capacity to personalize recognition and care is a primary feature of empowerment. And in military commands or large companies, this is no easy task. Again, consider reflections on consideration from the CO of the USS *Sacramento*, Captain Mike Manazir:

I realized early in my command tour that simply knowing each sailor's name paid huge dividends. That was the most frequently noted facet of my tour there. It occurred to me that it was embarrassing for me if I didn't know a sailor worked for me (there were about 300 of them). This effort apparently went farther as a leadership tool than I expected: "He knows my name!" I tried to do the same thing when I became an aircraft carrier XO. Of course there I didn't know about 3000 of the sailors by name, but I knew a lot. I spent as much time as I could walking the decks and talking to sailors. When I left the ship, several of them noted that these interactions and conversations about their lives and their work were often the highlight of their day. And I tried to thank them all a thousand times a day. When I get on the 1MC I am always positive. I never lambaste the crew as a whole. I recognize good performance and achievement, mention names whenever I can, and specify the negatives I want attacked in the greater context of overall good performance.

Yet another slice of empowerment is the willingness to protect subordinates. Although empowering leaders habitually relinquish control of the ship to the crew (delegate and then disappear), protection is a responsibility that must always remain with the leader. And make no mistake, efforts at empowerment will have zero effect if followers believe the leader will hang them out to dry for innovations gone awry or occasional failures.

I (GPH) remember after we had returned from my last deployment, I was sitting in my office when I heard a commotion out in the administrative office. Then there was a brusque knock at my office door. Two Naval criminal investigative agents entered my office with one of my sailors in handcuffs, followed by my XO and command master chief. They abruptly sat down and informed me that they had arrested one of my sailors on charges of breaking and entering a barracks room and stealing from his fellow sailors.

Now, I knew this sailor very well, and was sure he had not committed the crimes with which he was being charged. As I questioned the agents, I knew they had the wrong man. They told me they had eyewitnesses to his crime and were just there to inform me that he was being arrested. Unwilling to relent so easily, I asked them when the alleged crimes had taken place and then called in one of my personnel petty officers. I asked her to bring the manifests from the flights returning from deployment. As I looked over my flight manifests, I ordered the agents to let the sailor go. He had not even been in the states when he was accused of committing the crimes. The agents were shocked. The handcuffs were taken off my sailor and he was released to me. Having faith in my sailors was one of the things I prized most about leading, and they rarely let me down. The lesson in this incident was that if the leader will go to the mat for the crew, the crew breathes a collective sigh of relief and gets busy fulfilling the mission. They are emboldened and reassured when they have confidence in their leader.

Consider this comment from Captain Manazir's administrative officer aboard the *Carl Vinson*: "When a department head had a problem or made a big mistake and knew the CO would be furious, we'd go to XO (Manazir) and he'd say, 'Let me tell the CO. It's better if I take the heat. That's the leader's job, to take the heat, to take responsibility. After a couple of those types of incidents, Manazir's department heads knew they had Manazir in their corner." Leading from the front instills lots of confidence, lots of motivation, and lots of productivity too.

Although many of the critical elements of empowering leadership can be taught and honed, one facet of empowerment has more to do with a leader's fundamental personality style than the others; it is a difficult thing to teach. We are referring here to the natural tendency to respond to novel or difficult situations with positive emotion or affect. Labeled *positive affectivity* by researchers, it describes a set of behavioral and emotional habits that make the leader confident and effective as one who empowers.

Leaders with positive affectivity maintain relative equanimity in the face of adversity and they are able to forgo opportunities to rage and blame the crew for failures. In fact, followers describe these leaders as perpetually optimistic, positive, and satisfied with themselves and their lives. They are transparently secure and appear genuinely happy much of the time. This emotional flavor rubs off on followers and positively infects the entire workplace.

I (GPH) personally felt that this had a lot to do with being genuinely happy with your present life and position. When I was a commanding officer, I never asked, "Will this get me promoted?" before making a decision or taking action. I was truly delighted to be in the position I had been given and felt fortunate that I had an opportunity to serve as CO. Several of my department heads and chiefs commented to me that this attitude was evident and that it helped my sailors feel more confident in accomplishing the mission; they never thought I was using them for my own personal gain or glory.

I felt then, and I still do, that this should be the way every leader approaches his or her leadership position. Be content where you are and let people see it. Paradoxically, the leader who cares more about people than promotions is probably most likely to get the sort of productivity from followers that leads to promotion.

Far too often, followers are exposed to a leader on the opposite end of the affectivity continuum, the leader characterized by negative affectivity. This leader's exchanges with followers are defined by sullen or angry affect and negative reactions to challenges and novelties. The negative leader is frankly incapable of empowerment because suspicion and distrust or anxiety-based control occupies a central and pervasive place in his or her psychology.

During my (GPH) second squadron tour, we had a CO who often displayed copious amounts of negative affectivity. When I arrived in the squadron, our maintenance department was having some trouble keeping the planes fully repaired. I didn't think this was anything new because this was during a timeframe when repair parts were few and far between. Every squadron was having trouble keeping planes in repair. But our CO didn't see it that way. He took the drastic measure of cancelling the entire flight schedule one day, firing the maintenance officer, moving from the CO's office to the maintenance officer's office, and taking control of the maintenance department.

This was not only totally humiliating to the maintenance officer and the entire maintenance department, but it also sent a message to the larger squadron. We had an impulsively angry CO who demanded control, took drastic measures to get his point across, and if he fired the maintenance officer, would probably fire anyone who did not deliver instantly, regardless of circumstances. I learned a lot from this CO about how to disempower your people.

In fact, we have seen two notable subtypes when it comes to negative affectivity.

- *Paranoid.* The paranoid leader is unconsciously and constantly suspicious, distrustful, and unwilling to assume benevolence and good intentions on the part of followers. Chronically fearful of sabotage from within the crew's ranks, this leader assumes ill will among subordinates and responds in kind as a means of self-preservation. Having assumed the worst of followers, this leader has no alternative but to seize control, demand constant evidence of obedience and loyalty, and undermine the crew's internal motivation through punishment, constant scrutiny, and, at times, even ridicule. If you have ever seen the movie *The Caine Mutiny*, then you know that Captain Queeg is an excellent example of the paranoid leader. The paranoid leader is unwilling to empower because relinquishing any power is simply too threatening.

- *Obsessive-Compulsive.* Equally incapable of empowerment, but for different reasons, the obsessive-compulsive (or as Freud would say, "anal retentive") leader is notoriously rigid, ordered, driven by ritual, and anxious about failure. Although not suspicious of subordinates, this leader is too anxious to let others do important work and feels compelled to check and double check followers' work. Personal rigidity translates into tight control and the effective destruction of spontaneous and autonomous thinking within the crew. Obsessive-compulsive leaders are masters when it comes to killing synergy, creativity, and excitement in the workplace.

EMPOWERMENT AS "SUPERLEADERSHIP": CREATING SELF-LEADERS

Each fall the Naval Academy officers and faculty greet a new crop of wide-eyed 18-year-old men and women. To say these plebes are "wet behind the ears" when it comes to the tasks of adulthood, let alone the tasks of leading in combat, is an understatement. It is fair to say that looking into these young faces each fall is among the most hopeful and frightening things a seasoned officer can do. Hopeful because this crop represents the best our nation has to offer. Frightening because we have only four years to help these young people make the transition from high school student to combat leader.

In May of their fourth year at Annapolis, each of those who weather the course of study and training at USNA must be capable of effectively leading a diverse Naval division or Marine platoon into hostile territory.

In the end, the only certain indicator that a midshipman is ready to become an officer is evidence of the capacity for self-leadership. Just as parents work for years to mold sons and daughters who are self-policing, self-motivated, and self-directed adults, so too do excellent leaders understand that leading subordinates to lead themselves is the sine qua non of outstanding leadership. A first-class midshipman must be self-governing to succeed at Navy and an officer must be focused on preparing his or her unit to lead itself.

We once again refer to the heroic story of Commander Gilmore, the commanding officer of the submarine USS *Growler* during World War II. You will recall that CDR Gilmore, in the middle of an intense battle, calmly gave the order to clear the sub's bridge, and, refusing safety for himself, remained on deck while his men went below. Having suffered fatal injuries during the attack, CDR Gilmore gave the order to "Take her down." Gilmore was lost at sea but his well-trained crew, inspired by the courageous fighting spirit of their dead captain, safely brought the *Growler* to port.

Most of what we have described as empowerment in this chapter can be distilled to the concept of superleadership first proposed by Manz and Sims. Superleaders are focused on making their crews self-guiding. Rather than bending the wills of subordinates, superleaders seek avenues for sparking their needs for accomplishment and releasing their talents. Superleaders encourage followers to take on responsibility, exercise initiative, and govern themselves in the workplace.

Leaders in this vein see their job as defined by moving followers from dependence on the leader to independence. Self-guided followers participate in and even initiate goal-setting. They are motivated and psychologically committed. Empowered, their excitement about the mission energizes the organization. In a nutshell, one can identify superleaders from the company they keep. Eventually, sharp, self-motivated, internally driven, and deeply loyal followers will surround these leaders. In the military as in business, this makes for a formidable combat team!

THE GOUGE

During the war with the Barbary pirates, an irascible American Navy commodore named Edward Preble began a naval tradition of empowering subordinates that has continued to this day. Sent to the Mediterranean to protect U.S. maritime interests, Preble initially complained to the Navy Department that they had sent him "nothing but a pack of boys" to help him fulfill his duties. Preble was a hard, demanding, and strict disciplinarian. During the passage to Gibraltar, Preble had an opportunity to examine "his boys" and they him, and neither liked what they saw. A stoic New Englander, Preble contrasted significantly with his protégés who were young, glory-bound, and full of spirit.

However, it wasn't long until Preble realized that "his boys" were brave, smart, and loyal—even if green in battle. As they battled the Barbary pirates and went on to achieve significant naval victories Preble discovered that he could count on his crew to perform. He set about sharing the mission and then letting them take their rightful place in the chain of command. By the end of the war against the Barbary pirates, Preble had fashioned a core of a young, energetic officers, who would eventually lead the nation's Navy into the War of 1812 and set sturdy Naval traditions that would guide the Navy over the following century.

Preble's boys included naval heroes like Stephen Decatur, William Bainbridge, and many others. Although it is often difficult to empower and trust, Preble, like leaders in any organization, quickly discovered that you couldn't fight pirates alone.

Naval leaders, commanding officers, and business leaders oftentimes find themselves with an intriguing dilemma. Subordinates are often self-motivated and high-achieving. More than anything, they want to be trusted and encouraged. They want the freedom to be creative, take risks, and even to make blunders. They want the satisfaction that comes from achieving the mission and the pride that results from pleasing a respected leader.

When leaders are reluctant to give up control, they communicate distrust and marginal expectations. When they micromanage they sabotage innovation and energy. They stunt follower development and create an atmosphere void of self-leadership. When followers are given the opportunity, when they are empowered, they will often exert tremendous effort for their leader. But when stifled, indifference and demotivation quickly become the norms.

12

CREATE UNITY BY PRIZING DIVERSITY

Few Americans realize that our Navy is a direct product of centuries of British Naval tradition. The majority of the Colonial Navy's heroes learned their sailing and professional seamanship skills in the Royal British Navy. It is not surprising then that when John Adams penned the Navy's first official regulations, he borrowed many of the British Navy's traditions and customs—including its emphasis on an officer's sense of personal honor.

One of the early similarities between the British and American navies was uniformity of racial and ethnic background among officers. Exclusively Caucasian and often from privileged families, the officer corps contrasted sharply with enlisted crewmen who were often quite diverse. On some American vessels, more than half the enlisted crewmen were direct immigrants from foreign countries.

Although a significant number of African-American sailors enlisted in the early Navy, they were limited in the professional ratings for which they could apply (e.g., cooking and serving food). This divergence in opportunity between black and white sailors continued through WW II. Prior to WW II, two black men were admitted to the Naval Academy, but neither graduated. The first black American to graduate from USNA was Wesley A. Brown (class of 1949). In 1965, there were only 9 black midshipmen in the brigade, and by 1974, the number had increased to 178.

Although the USNA brigade today is quite diverse and generally representative of the American population, the Academy, like any organization, has had to work at deliberately integrating previously excluded groups. Along the way, many leaders stepped up and helped create unity of spirit and mission among widely diverse men and women. In this chapter, we highlight many of the lessons learned in the process and the big picture we want our midshipmen to grasp when it comes to creating a high-functioning team from an eclectic mix of followers with diverging racial, ethnic, gender, and religious backgrounds. In business as in the Navy, it is clear that excellent leaders must find ways to help diverse followers coalesce into a unified force.

EARLY USNA GRADUATES PRIZED DIVERSITY

When Paul Richmond graduated from USNA during the height of World War II, he was devastated to learn that serious vision problems would keep him from getting orders to a combat ship. Instead, the Navy assigned Ensign Richmond to shore duty. In short order, he was assigned a job he never could have anticipated and, perhaps, a job that a lesser officer may have balked at accepting whole-heartedly. He was assigned as one of the primary training officers for the Navy's first class of commissioned black officers. Historian Paul Stillwell writes this about Richmond's reaction to his unusual orders:

> So deeply ingrained was the Naval Academy ethic that an officer energetically carried out the duty ordered, even if it was not something he asked for.... In the Naval Academy tradition, he said "Aye, aye, sir" and set out to make them the best-trained officers he could. It was not a grudging project on his part. He developed a genuine admiration for these men who came to be called the "Golden Thirteen."

Ensign Richmond is an excellent model of the sort of leader the Naval Academy seeks to generate—one who follows well and accepts challenges with genuine tenacity and who, in turn, leads with tolerance and sincere admiration for the contributions of all followers—in short, a leader who recognizes and promotes the value of a diverse workforce.

Of course, after the Golden Thirteen were successfully commissioned as the first black officers in the Navy, their tribulations were far from over. In many ways, they were just beginning. All 13 men later described substantial racism and resistance to their very presence in the fleet. When Ensign Samuel Barnes entered the officers club in Okinawa, every white officer stood up and quietly exited, and when Ensign Gene Cooper walked across a military base, many white sailors refused to render a salute.

During those difficult years, many of the Golden Thirteen took heart from the presence, support, and example of another USNA graduate, CDR E. Hall Downes, who ran the Naval Training School at Hampton, Virginia. An excellent leader, and a man thoroughly supportive of the Navy's policy of opening the officer corps to black citizens, CDR Downes modeled acceptance and collegiality while using his rank to extinguish racially motivated resistance. Consider some of the comments made by members of the Thirteen:

> When we first got there, he asked us all where we were from and what our experiences had been. The next time I talked with CDR Downes, he knew my name, where I was from, and what schools I had attended—all that I had told him before—without hesitation. The fact that he would make the effort to learn so much about us and remember it indicated genuine concern. He instilled a sense of pride and dignity, reminding us frequently that we were men (Ensign Frank Sublett). I thought he was the epitome of a military officer. My image of good leadership was developed primarily from him. You don't have to be a screamer. You do need to be concerned about the people under you, and he always was. As for racial slurs, he was death on them, just wouldn't tolerate anything untoward (Ensign John Reagan).

It is perhaps especially important that CDR Downes did not tolerate subtle or overt expressions of racism. In adopting this command policy he sent a powerful message to both white and black officers in his charge that divisiveness would not be tolerated and that the larger mission (winning the war) must be the unit's focus. CDR Downes understood that achieving the mission would require a clear sense of unity and respect among all officers in the service.

As an example of CDR Downes's approach to racial slurs and events, consider a story relayed by Ensign Gene Cooper who returned to work for CDR Downes after he was commissioned. One night, Ensign Cooper was assigned to pick up a Navy captain at the local airport. When the captain spotted Ensign Cooper's bars, he immediately demanded to see the commanding officer of the base. The captain then informed CDR Downes, "If I had known there was a Negro officer on this base, I would have asked not to be sent here." Ensign Cooper reported that CDR Downes was infuriated. He called back to Washington and had the captain's orders changed to Alaska! This act of protection, and many like it, helped assure the Navy's first class of black officers that many of the organization's leaders were serious about making them belong.

LEADING EFFECTIVELY IN DIVERSE ORGANIZATIONS

The United States military generally, and the Naval Academy specifically, serve as microcosms or samples of American culture in all its racial, ethnic, and religious diversity. At present, the population at large and the population at Annapolis are increasingly diverse and decidedly multicultural. It is safe to say that diversity is an element of our culture that will only expand. It is therefore safe to assume that successful leaders in any organization will be those who openly embrace elements of diversity while showing particular acumen when it comes to bringing a wide range of followers together in ways that promote both personal and professional unity.

Outstanding CEOs of some of our country's most enduring and successful corporations (e.g., IBM, Proctor and Gamble, Johnson and Johnson) are famous for understanding that the lives and productivity of employees from minority groups are powerfully shaped by the place or culture in which they work. These builders saw their role as creating an environment—in effect, a culture—in their companies in which diverse employees would be secure and integrated, and thereby do the work necessary to make the business succeed.

In a military command or in civilian business, culture can appear invisible, but it is always powerful. It encompasses the patterns of thinking, speaking, and behavior among members and it is typically transmitted to succeeding generations through ritual and indoctrination. When midshipmen check aboard at USNA, they enter a military culture that often seems bizarre, enigmatic, and even terrifying. Within four short years, the culture is rarely noticed by these same midshipmen.

Of course, the culture at USNA, like the culture in any organization, is notoriously slow to change and strongly resistant to any crack or modification in its form and structure. Military sociologist Maddi Segal finds that across businesses and across time, integrating previously excluded groups into an organization's culture is always difficult. Early on, negative attitudes, discriminatory behaviors, social isolation, and overt harassment often await members of the newly admitted group. The greater the inertia and tradition associated with the organization's culture, the greater the anticipated resistance.

The question for leaders is this: How can you most effectively integrate all members of a diverse group—especially previously excluded minority members—while minimizing negative fallout and building a sense of unity and cohesion? Creating a culture that applauds diversity and models tolerance is a responsibility that rests squarely on the shoulders of the leader.

At the Academy, we feel that integrating midshipmen into the culture as quickly as possible is the best way to make that adaptation, and that is one of the reasons why plebe summer is so demanding and intense. Fatigued, bewildered, and desperate just to survive, plebes have no time to concentrate on how their new shipmates are different. The only relevant question is: "How on earth can we all get through this and succeed?" This is the same question they will ask over and over again as combat leaders in the fleet.

INTEGRATION AT USNA:
LEARNING FROM FAILURES AND GETTING IT RIGHT

As a sample of the American population, USNA has episodically struggled to integrate previously excluded groups, change its culture, and move ahead with a more diverse and enriched mix of future officers. There are many examples where efforts at integration have gone well.

In 1945, for example, Wesley Brown became the first black midshipman at USNA. His experience must have been lonely but his role in shaping Academy culture was profound. President Jimmy Carter remembered when midshipmen Brown joined the brigade:

> Although he was two classes behind me, we both ran cross-country during the year that we were at the Academy together. My primary memory of him is that he was always judged on his performance and he always crossed the finish line ahead of me. A few members of my senior class attempted to find ways to give him demerits so that he would be discharged, but Brown's good performance prevailed and he became the first African-American to graduate from the Naval Academy. I learned from Wesley Brown.

Brown, however, described his experiences like many other midshipmen who had gone before and have since followed him. Plebe summer was hectic. The new customs, discipline, regulations, forced memorization, and new skill requirements were frustrating. At the beginning of the academic year, Brown started to run into some trouble. A small group of midshipmen tried to "fry" him (give him demerits) for every minor infraction. He was in serious conduct trouble by Christmas. As a result, his grades began to slide, which heightened his anxiety. He was assigned mentors to help him out, and by the time the "Dark Ages" (the period between Christmas and the start of spring) was over, he began to get his bearings. He felt that the novelty of being a black midshipman had run its course and by the end of the year both his academic and conduct grades had improved significantly. Brown eventually graduated in the upper half of his class.

Today, African-American, Asian-American, and Hispanic-American midshipmen are thoroughly woven into the culture at USNA. But efforts at integrating previously excluded groups have not always gone as well. At times, USNA leaders have been challenged to significantly alter the Academy's culture in short order and in the face of significant resistance.

BRINGING WOMEN ON BOARD

When Congress passed legislation in 1975 requiring that the three service academies begin admitting women the following year, an observer at

USNA, or either of her two sister academies, might have thought the sky was falling. This egregious congressional violation of academy culture met with the vehement outrage and resistance that normally accompanies sudden integration and cultural change. On July 6, 1976, 81 women plebes arrived for Induction Day at USNA. Four years later, 55 of these women graduated and received commissions. Life for these intrepid women was anything but pleasant. As Durning observed:

> The 81 women who entered the U.S. Naval Academy in the summer of 1976 were breaking precedent and attempting to function in a male ethos with virtually no female role models. Their small numbers ensured that all their actions would stand out and be subject to over-evaluation, and the initial attitudes of male midshipmen toward coeducation were known to be generally unfavorable. Problems of assimilation were expected, involving both sexes.

The inaugural class of women midshipmen encountered strong resentment and opposition from their male counterparts. They were often isolated, shut out, and insulted or harassed. When Sharon Hanley Disher, one of the women in this inaugural class decided to write a book about the experience more than a decade after graduation, she was surprised to discover that many of her female classmates wanted nothing to do with the project. In the preface to her excellent book, *First Class*, Disher writes:

> Reliving those four years was too difficult—almost impossible for some. The scars were deep, the skeletons too painful to drag out of the closet, even 16 years later. What could be so bad? I remembered the taunts and the insults. I remembered the defeminizing uniforms and haircuts. But I love the Naval Academy. I always have and always will. It reinforced in me self-confidence, leadership, and assertiveness.

Hostility from male midshipmen sometimes took the form of pranks. Such pranks appear to have reached their zenith on December 8, 1989, the week before the Army-Navy game, when midshipman Gwen Dreyer was handcuffed to a urinal in a men's bathroom while others laughed and photographed her. At the time, most midshipmen and some leaders at the Academy assumed it was just another Army-Navy prank. But her parents were justifiably outraged, as were Congress and the Department of the Navy. This incident served to stimulate several investigations and reviews. It also served to warn the Navy that more than a decade after women had joined the brigade of midshipmen, the USNA culture remained fractured with regard to making women part of the team.

Stronger leadership was needed to unify a mixed-gender Navy and Marine Corps team. Perhaps the real leadership tragedy of the Gwen Dreyer incident is the fact that midshipman Dreyer resigned from USNA a few months afterward. A combination of media attention and continued resentment from male colleagues made the environment toxic for her. Not only was USNA diminished by her resignation, the country we are mandated to serve was deprived of a fine naval officer—largely because leaders had proven unable to thoroughly unify the brigade.

One of the sad ironies of the difficulty with integrating women into the Academy culture is the fact that women have been crucial players in naval service for hundreds of years. During the eighteenth and nineteenth centuries, women served as nurses, cooks, and even combatants on naval ships. During WW I, 11,880 women served as yeomen, and during WW II, 350,000 women served in some form of military service. When Congress overturned the combat exclusion law in 1993, women won access to combat ships and aviation squadrons. Thousands of women have since served in combat positions and have shown outstanding professionalism and skill in hostile conditions.

Not surprisingly, women midshipmen have performed exceptionally well academically, athletically, and militarily. And many of them have gone on to achieve great things. Consider Class of 1981 graduate Wendy Lawrence, who became the first of four female graduates to become astronauts. She is the veteran of three space shuttle flights, as well as a superb naval aviator and leader.

The challenge for Navy leaders was to make it clear to everyone in the culture that women were serving and dying in combat. They are shipmates in the most complete sense, and their presence at USNA and every other training center in the military is long overdue. In any organization, successful leaders discover methods for making the integration of previously excluded groups personal: "She's not just any woman, she's your shipmate and she just might save your life or give her own one day."

Sharon Disher, one of USNA's first women graduates, recounted how a statement made to her by a woman midshipman 20 years after Disher's own graduation helped her recognize just how much things had changed for women. The young midshipman stated, "Ma'am, we're different than you, we wear our class rings." The symbolic importance of this statement was not lost on Disher. Somehow the culture at Navy had changed enough in two decades that women were truly members of the brigade. They were integrated and bonded enough that the class ring symbolized achievement, pride, and connection.

INTENTIONAL ACCULTURATION

One of the myths bearing on leading a diverse group of followers is that a leader must choose between two polar options when working to create a unified culture: Option one is to remain entrenched and intolerant of members from new or minority groups, while option two, assimilation, requires that the primary culture adopt or accept new members' culture and habits entirely.

In fact, we work hard to remind midshipmen that the most effective route to leading a diverse mix of followers is a third or in-between option: *acculturation*. Effective leaders seek acculturation in their organizations by helping followers to talk the language and appreciate the values and traditions of various subgroups while remaining rooted in their own language and values. In our leadership courses, the term *cultural intelligence* is often used to refer to the process of creating such an acculturated fighting force. Leaders in business and the military must constantly acculturate or run the risk of stagnation and rigidity. This organization will alienate newcomers and important new subgroups. Sadly, it may have to be broken or shut down for change to occur.

In order for a Navy ship or a Marine Corps unit to embrace a common mission and become cohesive on and off the battlefield, leaders must instill a set of common command values. Two of the universal human values articulated by Kidder are especially relevant to leading diverse groups—unity and tolerance. The value of unity holds that all persons play a role in the larger collective. Unity is often an essential part of the esprit de corps of military units, and no effective fighting unit is lacking an emphasis on community and allegiance to the group. A closely related value, tolerance,

223

is also critical to prizing diversity and working as a unit. Tolerance insists that one cannot impose values on others and that each member of the collective is entitled to respect and dignity.

USNA graduate Mike Abrashoff found unity and tolerance to be essential ingredients in leading a diverse crew as CO of the USS *Benfold*. Although "diversity" training had been a staple of the ship's training schedule, an assessment of the crew revealed that women and minority sailors sometimes experienced racial prejudice or harassment. So Abrashoff shelved the program and began leading what he referred to as "Unity Training" for the entire crew. Here he emphasized the crew's commonalities and personally modeled utmost respect and absolute fairness to all crew members. When an instance of racism or sexism was reported, he addressed it swiftly and firmly.

The trick for a leader is to get his or her people to stop focusing exclusively on the differences among them and to start focusing on the things they share. In the Navy, these include a sobering military mission, a fundamental commitment to serve the people of the United States, and an abiding and reverent determination to "Beat Army." Leaders would be well served to help their followers take the words of Reuben Snake, Nebraska tribal chief, on board: "The spirit that makes you stand up and walk and talk and see and hear and think is the same spirit that exists in me—there is no difference. So when you look at me, you're looking at yourself—and I'm seeing me in you."

WHAT LEADERS CAN DO

Although we have hinted at some of the steps leaders can take to stem divisions and create unity in diverse and multicultural organizations, we conclude this chapter with some specific leader recommendations. In the end, the success or failure of a military command or civilian business will hinge to some extent on the leader's capability as a unifier—an inspiring model who can create a vision, display respect and fairness, protect new organizational members, create acculturation, and make amends when the organization has failed minority groups. In a nutshell, here is what we want new Navy ensigns to consider as they begin their careers as culturally sensitive combat leaders.

FIRST, BUILD A UNIFYING VISION

Earlier in this book, we emphasized the salience of creating a vision for followers. Nowhere is this more significant than in a diverse group—a group that can become distracted by differences and contrasts. At USNA, Academy leaders effectively get midshipmen focused on their status as shipmates, not only to current midshipmen, but all those past and future. Midshipmen quickly differentiate themselves from Air Force, Army, and students at every civilian college in the land. They quickly begin to see themselves as future Navy and Marine Corps officers. When they stand 4000-strong in the stadium during a football game—each dressed identically and each cheering madly for the team—an observer would note very little division and no apparent emphasis on standing out among individuals.

At Navy, midshipmen receive a vision—a future ideal—that each of them can share in. And leaders themselves are unflinchingly committed to this vision. In order to integrate minority groups and previously excluded members into the brigade or into business, leaders must help all members find a convincing vision. It must be centered on common goals and the clear need for cooperation versus competition if the vision is to be realized. A well-conceived unifying vision also serves to motivate and energize a diverse working group.

The USNA mission statement clearly puts everyone at the Academy, from the superintendent on down to the barbers in the midshipmen shops, on the same page with regard to our end goal. Our job is to produce professional war-fighters for the United States, and all members of the Academy community are committed to that goal regardless of race, background, gender, or religious belief. Everyone in our organization must be treated fairly and honorably to accomplish and complete the mission.

When leaders at USNA in the late 1970s realized that one of the things most demoralizing to female midshipmen was the combat exclusion law preventing women from serving on combatant vessels, they went out of their way to attempt to change this law. One approach was to push the envelope and place female midshipmen on as many combatant ships as possible. Eventually, these included cruisers, destroyers, and helicopter assault ships. This public display of support for a small and often excluded subgroup of the brigade served to create a vision that included *all* members of the brigade as future combatants and equal contributors to the mission of the military. Today, female midshipmen may choose to become surface warfare officers, combat pilots, and Marine Corps officers. Our vision is clear: Men and women equally share the burden and the honor of preparing to go to war.

GIVE PUBLIC SUPPORT TO MINORITY GROUPS
AND REINFORCE WORDS WITH ACTION

If there is one factor that above all others is utterly essential to creating a unified organizational culture, it is the example set by leaders. When a previously excluded group seeks entry, integration is typically doomed to failure without the strong and consistent support of the primary leader. After synthesizing research in this area, Segal concludes that top leadership must be committed to making integration work, *and* that he or she must communicate this publicly and repeatedly.

Excellent leaders are active and outspoken advocates for integration and unification. They model fair treatment of all members regardless of gender, race, religion, etc., and they are careful to choose diverse models for emulation and recognition. Thoughtful leaders use gender-inclusive language and reject any humor that may come across as sexist or racist— even when no members of minority groups are present. They are also cautious to avoid "protecting" a subgroup in such a way as to disadvantage them by protecting them from challenges or failing to give corrective feedback. Clearly, the public behavior of the leader is directly related to the ultimate success of the organization at integrating minority groups and pursing a common goal.

Since women were first admitted to USNA, a string of Academy superintendents has worked to use position and public authority to hasten integration and weaken efforts to undermine it. Admiral William Lawrence, the superintendent to first welcome women to USNA, worked tirelessly to speed their acceptance into the brigade. He spoke often to male members of the Academy and made it clear he would not tolerate any undignified behavior toward women, and, further, that anybody who communicated derision or harassed women in private but not in public was the "ultimate coward." ADM Lawrence also frequently attended and supported the fledgling women's athletic teams. His presence at the finish line of the women's varsity rowing competitions had a significant and inspiring impact on the members of the team. More importantly, his stalwart support was duly noted by men in the brigade.

In 1987, Superintendent Admiral Marryott wrote a memo dispersed to the entire USNA community making it crystal clear that he would not tolerate any instance of sexual harassment. He wrote, "This issue has my strongest personal interest. I will deal with instances of sexual harassment and discrimination swiftly and surely. I expect the same from the chain of command." His words, and later, his follow-through made it clear he meant business.

Finally, in 1995 Admiral Larson eliminated *The Log*, an underground publication by a few midshipmen that, while intended to be humorous and irreverent, often included disrespectful and disheartening comments about women. Although *The Log* had been published by midshipmen for decades, Admiral Larson understood that allowing such a publication to continue would constitute implicit tolerance for discrimination and disrespect of female midshipmen. In the end, *The Log* was deemed unacceptable and contrary to the ultimate inclusion of all midshipmen that the Academy was determined to achieve.

WHEN APPROPRIATE, APOLOGIZE AND SEEK RECONCILIATION

Sometimes an organizational unit can create a unified and acculturated climate only to be undermined from above—by leaders who themselves set a lousy example and tolerate the very discrimination smaller units have worked diligently to eradicate. Such was the case for USNA in 1991 when, at the annual Tailhook convention for Naval aviators, some 90 women were sexually molested as they attempted to pass along a hallway filled with more than 200 drunken Navy and Marine Corps aviators.

Although it is still unclear how in the world events at this meeting could have gotten so entirely out-of-hand, a subsequent Inspector General report revealed that numerous senior leaders in the Navy ignored progressively deteriorating standards of behavior during the decade preceding the fateful 1991 convention in Las Vegas. Further, many of them were aware of the numerous absurd and juvenile traditions associated with the meeting. These included extreme intoxication and the now infamous "gauntlet" in which unsuspecting women would be groped and even bitten in hotel passageways.

Tailhook 1991 represents one of the most thoroughly humiliating failures of Navy leadership on record. Not only were several flag rank officers present at the convention, many of them were present in the hotel during the debauchery that ensued. Worse yet, many of them later denied any responsibility for these events. It is utterly clear that the Navy aviation community had thwarted Congressional mandates to thoroughly and respectfully integrate women into the service, and that those in charge were directly to blame. As one junior officer present at Tailhook later put it: "I don't think that anybody saw anything that they felt hadn't happened in the past. And so…if it had been allowed to happen in the past, they'd just let it go."

Even in light of all the egregious and stupefying leadership malpractice demonstrated at Tailhook, perhaps nothing about the events and subsequent investigation remains as demoralizing as the failure on the part of any senior leader to immediately come forward, take full responsibility, and sincerely apologize. This is the sort of serious leadership and accountability we expect from midshipmen at USNA, yet no officer had what it took to fully appreciate the damage this debacle had done to the Navy community and to set a genuine course of apology and reconciliation. Most of them appeared far too concerned with distancing and protecting themselves.

In order to unify a diverse crew, a commander has got to take responsibility for the inevitable failures and missteps that accompany any process of integration and culture change. In fact, such apparently unsavory events give the leader a chance to publicly reaffirm commitment to unification and to take swift corrective action. Both elements are essential to keeping integration on track. An example of such willingness to humbly admit failure and make necessary changes was offered by Admiral Elmo Zumwalt during his tenure as chief of Naval operations.

During the early 1970s, when race relations between black and white sailors were at an all time low, there were two highly publicized incidents of racial violence aboard the U.S. aircraft carriers *Kitty Hawk* and *Constellation*. In both cases, physical altercations between black and white sailors resulted in physical injuries and destruction of property. In one case, a detachment of USMC guards was called in to disperse the crowd with force, and the situation came close to producing a national tragedy. On both ships, black sailors perceived injustice and inequity in both the reward and punishment systems. They also reported fewer opportunities and little tolerance from many white shipmates. There were powerful feelings of animosity on both sides.

While many senior Navy leaders and investigation reports blamed the unrest and subsequent altercations on poor discipline, inaccurate recruiting ads, and other extraneous factors, Admiral Zumwalt, then the senior officer in the Navy, had a very different take. He called a meeting of all his top brass in the Navy and Marine Corps and proceeded to tell them that the Navy had failed to meet its equal opportunity goals, and that it had failed its black sailors and marines. He made it crystal clear that he wanted "whole-hearted" implementation of every facet of the Navy's equal opportunity program. He also launched a wide-reaching program of race-relations training throughout the Navy.

Admiral Zumwalt took full responsibility for the events on those aircraft carriers. He read the altercations as a failure in leadership. Rather than blame the sailors, he asked their leaders why they were not making integration work. In addition to handling race relations, Admiral Zumwalt is also considered a great crusader for female sailors, and the opportunities for women were greatly enhanced under his stewardship.

CREATE OPPORTUNITIES FOR EXPOSURE TO DIVERSE GROUPS

A strange thing happened during the 1976-1977 academic year at USNA (the first year women entered the Academy). A study of attitudes about women showed that those male students with the greatest level of interaction with women midshipmen—all the men in the plebe class—developed progressively and significantly more positive views of their female comrades (e.g., they were more likely to agree that women could stand the stress of command responsibility and that women should be considered for important command positions). It was clear that mere exposure to women midshipmen helped break down stereotyping and traditionalism in attitudes that might otherwise stymie integration of a new group.

Male plebes shared the suffering of plebe summer with women. They shared classes, they marched together, and they endured the indignities of being "trained" by upperclassmen throughout the year. When May came

229

and the plebe class conquered Herndon as one, the women in the class had moved from the "them" of September to the "us" of May.

In contrast, upperclassmen (those with the least direct contact with female midshipmen) remained relatively hardened in their negative views about women in the service. Unfortunately, a few alumni fostered this resentment and were partially responsible for the negative reactions to women in the brigade. Since then, forward-looking alumni have made it a point to downplay those "old school" attitudes, and insist that all alumni get "on board" with the fact that women are a significant and beneficial part of the Academy and the Navy. Today, a midshipman who harbors and communicates antagonistic views about women colleagues is told in no uncertain terms to get with the congressional mandate to fully integrate women or get out.

The lesson for leaders is this: In order to blend previously excluded groups into your organization, arrange interaction between polarized and unfamiliar groups from the start. Social psychology researchers have recognized the unifying effects of simple proximity for years. Whether integrating racial, ethnic, gender, or religious groups, the secret is simple: Get them to work together—preferably on a super ordinate goal or compelling mission.

And there is something else. Research shows that when members of a majority group have contact with high-status members of a minority group, prejudice toward all members of the minority group tends to decline. At USNA in 1976-1977, one of the companies in Bancroft Hall had a female company officer, a lieutenant. Not surprisingly, male midshipmen in this company reported significantly more positive attitudes toward women in the military. The lesson? Wise leaders are deliberate about giving minority groups representation high in the leadership hierarchy in the organization.

And here is one more lesson about exposure to previously excluded groups: Sometimes the reason for the exposure is less important than the outcome. Consider the case of my (GPH) cousin Mike, an enlisted Marine in Vietnam. While serving as a member of an elite reaction force during the war, Mike was involved in an accidental explosion and lost both of his arms. Following a lengthy recuperation, adaptation to false limbs, and completion of a college degree in the face of great obstacles, he was offered a job at IBM.

Sometime later, I was reading *Time* magazine and noticed an IBM ad with a photo of Mike's torso and artificial arms. The advertisement was trumpeting IBM's progressive hiring practices. At the time, it appeared to me, personally, that my cousin's disability was being exploited by the company. As one of the first seriously disabled veterans hired by the company, he was in the limelight whether he wanted this status or not. But a funny thing happened. Mike worked hard and surprised a lot of people. Far from just a handicapped poster guy, he turned out to be an exceptional employee and a top-notch leader (leave it to the Marines). Over the years, he worked his way up the IBM corporate ladder. Along the way, IBM's view of handicapped employees changed. The reason for my cousin's hiring became less important than the impact of his employment on the organization and on opportunities for other men and women with physical disabilities. It's all about proximity.

In order to blend diverse subgroups into a unified organizational force, leaders must get them to work together. Although it is unreasonable to expect early contacts to be exclusively positive, it is reasonable to expect things to get better with sustained proximity and consistent interaction. Excellent leaders persist in this vein and find an inspiring vision to keep diverse followers looking ahead instead of to the side or to the rear. Although we cannot promise our young leaders that the work of unifying diverse groups will be easy, it will pay dividends in the form of a tolerant, inclusive, and productive workforce.

THE GOUGE

From its inception, the United States Naval Academy has had a single job to do—training combat leaders for the Navy and Marine Corps. And while this mission has never wavered, the USNA community has occasionally struggled with unity and cohesion within the brigade of midshipmen—often sparked by the need to integrate previously excluded groups. Although USNA is akin to nearly any other organization in this regard, its highly public position has made it the focus of more attention and scrutiny over the years than is typical of most institutions.

The Navy, along with its sister services, has devoted tremendous energy to tackling the problem of blending diverse groups and thoroughly integrating the Academy. Portions of the journey to this end were rocky and painful for the early participants from new groups. They were remarkably courageous. And most will tell you that the effort was well worth the outcome.

Combat leaders must lead effectively in all conditions and with a cadre of widely diverse followers. To do this, they must find avenues for creating unity and cohesion at all costs. Differences of race, ethnicity, gender, and religion must be recognized, respected, tolerated, and, we would say, prized. But differences cannot become the focus. An effective combatant ship and an effective organization must attend to the business at hand. Followers will do this when the culture at work is denoted by genuine respect and reciprocal dignity.

When a leader prizes diversity and creates a powerfully unifying vision, individual members of the team feel safe and can get about the business of fighting the war—whatever that may be. Outstanding leaders are publicly and consistently supportive of minority group members. They work hard at creating opportunities for exposure and interaction among diverse subgroups and when things go wrong or a group is marginalized, they take responsibility, make amends, and correct the problem.

The bottom line is this: Tolerant and unifying leaders beget tolerant and unified workplaces. When it comes to reacting to previously excluded groups, your followers are watching your example.

THE FINAL GOUGE

Since 1845, the United States Naval Academy has been in the business of building top-flight leaders for the nation's Navy and Marine Corps. All USNA graduates must be prepared to lead in combat successfully, and every graduate must be deserving of the president's complete trust. At Navy, midshipmen are developed morally, mentally, and physically. They are imbued with the highest ideals of duty, honor, and loyalty in order for USNA to provide graduates who are dedicated to a career of Naval service and prepared to assume the highest responsibilities of command, citizenship, and government.

Many of the essential leadership lessons promulgated within the walls of the Naval Academy are equally salient for leaders in business and organizational settings. Those invested in becoming outstanding leaders would do well to consider the 12 leadership lessons elaborated in this book. Excellent leaders in combat, industry, or government attend to these timeless and sometimes hard-learned lessons:

- **Lesson 1: Leaders Are Made.** The idea that leaders are born and that leadership traits are innate is an outdated notion unsupported by research. More than 150 years of experience in developing combat leaders show that the art and science of leading well hinges less on genes and common sense and more on training, tenacity, and supervised experience. Leadership-facilitating traits include drive, intelligence, motivation, integrity, and self-confidence, while leadership-inhibiting traits include argumentativeness, insensitivity, narcissism, fear of failure, perfectionism, and impulsivity.

- **Lesson 2: Take Oaths and Make Commitments.** Effective leaders learn to make commitments to organizations, causes, and followers. They identify personally with the mission and find meaning in staying the course when things get tough. The most effective commitments are based on intrinsic values, not external rewards. Wise leaders understand that hard work and sacrifice enhance commitment and that loyalty and commitment thrive when followers' primary needs are met.

- **Lesson 3: Follow First.** No leader can succeed without first mastering the art of excellent following skills. Outstanding followers demonstrate a number of salient characteristics and habits: (1) they are self-governing, internally directed, and able to fully manage and motivate themselves; (2) they understand the importance of learning their jobs well and demonstrate a commitment to competence; (3) they are unequivocally loyal to the commanding officer; (4) they are honest and forthright when it comes to delivering news to the boss, yet judicious in the time and place for such input; (5) they take full responsibility for slipups; (6) they are willing to act proactively to nip problems in the bud.

- **Lesson 4: Character Counts.** Nobody leads with authority and credibility unless personal honor and integrity are evident and unquestioned. Credible leaders are consistent; they are honorable and moral at all times, even when nobody is looking. Although adherence to timeless ethical principles is important, the strongest leaders exude personal virtues—internally located character qualities. Virtuous leaders are models of honor, courage, and commitment.

- **Lesson 5: Create Tri-Level Vision.** Successful leaders master the art of visioning; they create vision for the organization on three important levels. First, they hone a vision of self-as-leader that realistically incorporates both talents and vulnerabilities. Second, they expertly craft convincing visions of key followers—visions that buoy esteem and capitalize on follower strengths. Finally, visioning leaders craft a vision for the unit or organization writ large. They discern a corporate picture or an image of what the unit can become that wins over followers and stimulates commitment and achievement.

- **Lesson 6: Inoculate for Stress.** In order to perform well when catastrophe strikes or everyday stressors reach a critical tolerance threshold, top leaders prepare for stress via intentional exposure to brief but intense doses. Controlled exposure heightens protection against the corrosive effects of exhaustion, pain, and adversity. Effective leaders accurately appraise the threat associated with a situation and respond with calm, problem-focused strategies. Resilient leaders view themselves as capable of an effective response.
- **Lesson 7: Put Shipmates First.** Outstanding leaders place the needs of followers before their own. They enjoy reciprocal loyalty from colleagues and followers because they are consistently loyal first. They appreciate the fact that leading well is an act of sacrifice; that leading requires a sober acceptance of obligation to serve followers.
- **Lesson 8: Drill for Success.** To succeed in military combat or business ventures, seasoned leaders appreciate the significance of preparation. Drilling for every eventuality enhances confidence and, on occasion, saves lives. Practice, preparation, and more practice are the hallmarks of well-prepared and well-led organizations. When the crew is proficient and confident, the commanding officer knows the military unit is ready to do whatever job is assigned.
- **Lesson 9: Lead by Example.** Stellar leaders understand and accept the burden of visibility. They appreciate the power of modeling and recognize that followers will learn more by watching than listening. Refusing to be inadvertent or haphazard models, they find avenues for becoming an intentional exemplar. Not only are they conscious of providing a congruent example for the larger organization, they work at ensuring that their interpersonal behavior offers an example they want subordinates to replicate. Specifically, they model kindness, consideration, moral virtue, and patience.
- **Lesson 10: IQ Is Not Enough.** Genuinely "smart" leaders offer more than a high IQ and technical job-related expertise; they exude emotional intelligence as well. The emotionally sophisticated leader holds an advantage over less sophisticated leaders and typically enjoys significant loyalty among followers. To lead well, a leader must demonstrate emotional self-awareness, the capacity for effective self-regulation, thorough self-motivation, genuine empathic regard for others, and outstanding social skills.

- **Lesson 11: Decide, Delegate, and Disappear**. The best leaders appreciate the paradox of getting more by managing less. Rather than demand and coerce, they empower followers to perform. They have high expectations, but make benign assumptions about the crew and provide unconditional backup and support. They use praise and reinforcement copiously while resorting to punishment with genuine disdain and only as a last resort. Generally optimistic, kind, and encouraging, they are soon surrounded by independent, high-performing, and deeply satisfied followers.

- **Lesson 12: Prize Diversity**. Excellent leaders create unity by prizing diversity among followers. They create command cultures defined by mutual respect across gender, racial, ethnic, and religious lines. They model acculturation—appreciating the values and traditions of various subgroups. Unifying leaders communicate a unifying vision to diverse followers. They offer public and unequivocal support to minority groups, and when the organization falls short in honoring diverse groups, they are the first to apologize and seek reconciliation. Finally, unifying leaders create opportunities for increased interaction among polarized groups.

Endnotes

INTRODUCTION

Page 1: "*When Lieutenant Commandeer Dick Stratton...*" G. Atkinson, *The Boat School Boys* (Oct. 16, 2000), FreeRepublic.com, pp. 2-5.

Page 1: "*Third, don't despair when they break you...*" Ibid., p. 3.

Page 2: "*Lenient and humane treatment...*" Ibid., p. 3.

Page 2: "*For example, Jerry Denton...*" Ibid., p. 5.

Page 3: "*They have taught you too well McCain!...*" Ibid., p. 5.

Page 7: "*Since 1845, the Academy...*" Crane and J. F. Kieley, *United States Naval Academy: The First Hundred Years* (New York: Whittlesey House, 1945).

Page 8: "*For in my mind, there is but one...*" K. Montor, T. M. McNicholas, A. J. Ciotti, T. H. Hutchinson, and J. E. Wehmueller, *Naval Leadership: Voices of Experience* (Annapolis, MD: Naval Institute Press, 1987), p. 1.

Page 8: "*...one of the greatest things about winning...*" J. Clary, *Field of Valor: Duty, Honor, Country, and Winning the Heisman* (Chicago: Triumph, 2002).

Page 10: "*In many ways, their job...*" R. S. West, "The Superintendents of the Naval Academy," *United States Naval Institute Proceedings* 72 (1946): 64.

Page 11: "*...apprentice route to a commission in the Navy...*" Crane and Kieley.

Page 11: "*The first midshipmen of the regular navy...*" Ibid., p. 3.

Page 11: "*Jarvis clung to his station...*" Ibid., pp. 4-5.

Page 12: "*On September 13, 1842…*" J. Sweetman, *The U.S. Naval Academy: An Illustrated History* (Annapolis, MD: Naval Institute Press, 1979).

Page 12: "*… strong outcry from members of Congress…*" Ibid.

Page 13: "*He [a leader] should be the soul of tact…*" Montor et al., p. 7.

CHAPTER 1

Page 19: "*In an important* Harvard Business Review *article…*" W. G. Pagonis, *Leadership in a Combat Zone* (Cambridge, MA: Harvard Business School, 2001).

Page 19: "*In this chapter, we debunk…*" R. L. Hughes, R. C. Ginnett, and G. J. Curphy, *Leadership: Enhancing the Lessons of Experience*, 2d Ed. (New York: McGraw-Hill, 1996).

Page 20: "*Fall of my 3/c year,…*" Robert Niewoehner, personal communication, October 2002.

Page 21: "*We refer, of course, to Vice Admiral…*" W. Lord, *Incredible Victory* (New York: Harper Collins, 1998).

Page 21: "*When Halsey became seriously ill shortly…*" Ibid.

Page 23: "*I assumed that low pay…*" D. M. Abrashoff, *It's Your Ship: Management Techniques from the Best Damn Ship in the Navy* (New York: Warner Books, 2002), p. 13.

Page 25: "*It is by no means enough…*" J. Crane, J., J. F. Kieley, *United States Naval Academy: The First Hundred Years* (New York: Whittlesey House, 1945), p. 13.

Page 25: "*I boarded the USS* Hunt *to begin…*" J. McCain, *Faith of Our Fathers* (New York: Random House, 1999), pp. 135-138.

Page 26: "*If leadership is more than…*" A. Lau, "Military Leadership," in C. Cronin (Ed.), *Military Psychology: An Introduction* (Needham Heights, MA: Simon & Schuster, 1998), pp. 49-69; S. C. Wieczorek, *Leadership and Human Behavior,* 2d Ed. (Boston, MA: Pearson Custom Publishing, 2002).

Page 27: "*Possessing certain traits…*" S. A. Kirkpatrick and E. A. Locke, "Leadership: Do Traits Matter?" *Academy of Management Executive* 5 (1991): 48-60.

Page 27: "*…Below we highlight…*" S. Kassin, *Psychology,* 2d Ed. (Upper Saddle River, NJ: Prentice Hall, 1998), p. 11.

Page 31: "*Personality research on USNA midshipmen…*" R. Lall, E. K. Holmes, K. R. Brinkmyer, W. B. Johnson, and B. R. Yatko, "Personality Characteristics of Future Military Leaders," *Military Medicine* 164 (1999): 906-910; K. M. Murray and W. B. Johnson, "Personality Type and Success among Female Naval Academy Midshipmen," *Military Medicine* 166 (2001): 889-893; Kasin.

CHAPTER 2

Page 38: "*…as flashbulb memories*" R. Brown and J. Kulik, "Flashbulb Memories," *Cognition* 5 (1977): 73-99.

Page 43: *"Nearly half a century ago, psychologist..."* A. H. Maslow, *Motivation and Personality* (New York: Harper and Row, 1954).

Page 44: *"A prime example of this..."* M. Gelfand, "Time, Tide and Formation Wait for No One: Cultural and Social Change at the United States Naval Academy: 1949-2000," unpublished doctoral dissertation, University of Arizona, 2000.

Page 44: *"A POW exhibit..."* Ibid.

Page 44: *"At the Army-Navy game,..."* Ibid.

Page 46: *"...as vertical cohesion."* J. Shay, "Cohesion, Confidence, Command, Climate: Keys to Preventing Psychological and Moral Injury in Military Service." In G. R. Andersen and L.L. Christman (Eds.), *Leadership Theory and Application* (Boston: Pearson Custom Publishing, 2001), pp. 347-351.

Page 46: *"Vertical cohesion is rooted..."* Ibid.
Page 46: *"That is, to build loyal..."* S. Covey, *Principle-Centered Leadership* (New York: Simon & Schuster, 1991).

CHAPTER 3

Page 51: *"A Navy ship or submarine is..."* R. P. Vecchio, *Leadership: Understanding the Dynamics of Power and Influence* (South Bend, IN: University of Notre Dame Press, 1977).

Page 52: *"Sir/Ma'am, you now have 10 minutes..."* H. Turowski, *Plebe* (Kent, WA: Paradigm Press, 1994), p. 118.

Page 53; *"...you now have 2 minutes..."* Ibid.

Page 53: *"The memories of my years at the Naval Academy..."* J. Carter, "Distinguished Graduate Awards Ceremony Speech," Annapolis, MD, October 12, 2002.

Page 54: *"A study of the distinguishing..."* D. F. Whiteside, *Command Excellence: What It Takes to Be the Best!* (Washington, DC: Department of the Navy, 1985).

Page 56: *"Gentlemen..., whether you're cleaning boilers..."* G. Harper and S. Wieczorek, *Leadership and Human Behavior* (Boston, MA: Pearson Custom Publishing, 2002), pp. 204-208.

Page 57: *"In the section that follows..."* M. DePree, *Leadership Jazz.* (New York: Doubleday, 1992); R. L. Hughes, R. C. Ginnett, and G. J. Curphy, *Leadership: Enhancing the Lessons of Experience,* 2d ed. (New York: McGraw-Hill, 1996); R. E. Kelley, "In Praise of Followers," *Harvard Business Review* (Nov.-Dec., 1988); P. S. Meilinger, "Ten Rules of Good Followership," *Military Review* 47 (1994).

Page 58: *"Excellent followers think..."* J. B. Rotter, "Generalized Expectancies for Internal versus External Control of Reinforcement." *Psychological Monographs* 80, Whole No. 609 (1966).
Page 60: *"At Navy, as at other top-flight organizations..."* Meilinger, 1994.

CHAPTER 4

Page 69: "*The classes of 1950 to 1953...*" M. Gelfand, "Time, Tide and Formation Wait for No One: Cultural and Social Change at the United States Naval Academy, 1949-2000," unpublished doctoral dissertation, University of Arizona, 2002, p. 419.

Page 70; "*The Honor Concept was presented...*" J. Gantar and T. Patten, *A Question of Honor* (Grand Rapids, MI: Zondervan, 1996), p. 49

Page 70: "*...neither would my father...*" John McCain, *Faith of My Fathers* (New York: Random House, 1999), p. 58.

Page 71: "*...Students [midshipmen] need to understand...*" J. B. Stockdale, "The World of Epictetus." In C. Sommers and F Somers (Eds.), *Vice and Virtue in Everyday Life*, 3d Ed. (New York: Harcourt Brace, 1993), pp. 658-674.

Page 71: "*It is interesting that enforcement...*" Gelfand, p. 420.

Page 71: "*It was decided by...*" Ibid., p. 420.

Page 71: "*...purveyors of moral education...*" N. M. Meara, L. D. Schmidt, and J. D. Day, "Principles and Virtues: A Foundation for Ethical Decisions, Policies, and Character." *The Counseling Psychologist* 24 (1996): 4-77.

Page 73: "*They could have used...*" Trent Angers, "The Forgotten Hero of My Lai," *Acadian Profile* 18, No. 6 (March/April 1998).

Page 74: "*Virtue ethics calls...*" Meara, Schmidt, and Day, p. 24.

Page 74: "*In February 1982...*" Al Bell, "USS *Morton* Sea Stories," USS *Morton* 948 (org. p. 2-3).

Page 75: "*As the USS* Morton *was sailing...*" Ibid., p. 2.

Page 75: "*As the* Morton *approached...*" Ibid., p. 5.

Page 75: "*What are the virtues...*" W. F. May, "The Virtues in a Professional Setting, *Soundings* 67 (1984): 245-266.

Page 76: "*Notre Dame ethicist Naomi Meara...*" Meara *et al.*, pp. 28-29.

Page 76: "*War exacts great...*" John Allen, *Commandant's Intent* (unpublished personal document) (Annapolis, MD: Feb. 19, 2002).

Page 77: "*I will bear true faith and allegiance...*" United States Navy, *Core Values of the United States Navy* (Washington, DC: Author, 2003).

Page 78: "*If there is a common theme...*" Meara *et al.*.

Page 78: "*Those who serve...*" J. Carter, Speech delivered at the U.S. Naval Academy, June 1996.

Page 79: "*In a recent speech...*" J. P. Reason, "Trust as a Basis of Leadership." Address delivered to the brigade of midshipmen. Annapolis, MD.

Page 80: "*Integrity is...*" Stockdale, p 661.

Page 80: "*Stockdale recounts...*" Ibid., p. 662.

Page 81: "*The linkage of men's...*" Ibid., p. 662.

Page 82: "*I will support and defend...*" United States Navy (2003).

Page 82: "*Ramage pursued his targets...*" W. Cross, *Challenges of the Deep: The Story of Submarines* (New York: William Sloan Associates, 1959).

Page 82: "*One strategic bridge...*" Jennifer Sheppard, *Trident Newspaper*, Annapolis, MD, Oct. 11, 2002.

Page 82: "*Under continuous fire...*" Ibid.

Page 83: "*For conspicuous gallantry...*" USS Nautilus.org.

Page 85: "*I will obey the orders...*" United States Navy (2003).

Page 87: "*Late in the fall of 1992...*" William Garrett, *Character Development at the U.S. Naval Academy*, Annapolis, MD, autumn 1992.

Page 88: "*When a leader has...*" Festinger, *A Theory of Cognitive Dissonance* (Evanston, IL: Row Peterson, 1957).

CHAPTER 5

Page 93: "*A graduate from...*" D. Borchers, personal communication, Nov. 2002.

Page 94: "*When a leader creates...*" Shaskin, M., "Visionary Leadership." In W. E. Rosenbach and R. L. Taylor (Eds.), *Contemporary Issues in Leadership* (Boulder, CO: Westview Press, 1993).

Page 94: "*When USNA alumnus...*" D. M. Abrashoff, *It's Your Ship: Management Techniques from the Best Damn Ship in the Navy* (New York: Warner Books, 2002).

Page 95: "*For decades, Saddam Hussein...*" J. N. Mattis, *Commanding General's Message to All Hands.* Kuwait, March 2003.

Page 96: "*He was a man...*" J. Carter, Speech delivered at the U.S. Naval Academy. Annapolis, MD, June 1996.

Page 97: "*Every year, people...*" G. Posner, *Citizen Perot, His Life and Times* (New York: Random House, 1996), p.16.

Page 99: "*Plebe Summer...*" H. Turowski, *Plebe* (Kent, WA: Paradigm Press, 1994), p. 185.

Page 99: "*I noticed something...*" D. Bower, Class Journal Entry, March 2003.

Page 104: "*There is no greater...*" J. R. Allen, *Commandant's Intent* (Annapolis, MD: United States Naval Academy, 2002).

Page 104: "*The USNA experience...*" *Naval Academy Parents Club Newsletter, Colorado. From Yard to Blue Angels, a Week of Traditions,* 2000.

Page 106: "*Remember that followers...*" W. B. Johnson, R. Lall, J. M. Huwe, A. Fallow, E. K. Holmes, and W. Hall, "The Flag Officer Mentor Study: Did Admirals Have Mentors?" *Proceedings of the U.S. Naval Institute* (Dec. 1999): 44-46.

Page 106: "*When he asked me...*" J. Carter, Acceptance Speech, Distinguished Graduate Banquet, Annapolis, MD, Oct. 2002.

Page 107: "*An excellent corporate vis*ion..." Ibid.

Page 108: "*If you think the task...*" Grose, Captain, USMC. *Marine Corps Amphibious History Doctrine*, p. 1.

Page 108: "*Lieutenant Colonel "Pete" Ellis...*" Ibid., p. 1.

Page 108: "*...The Marines refused...*" Ibid., p. 2.

Page 108: "*Excellent leaders are...*" C. Deputy and D. Morris, D., *Leadership: Theory and Application* (Boston, MA: Pearson Custom Publishing, 2001), p. 126.

CHAPTER 6

Page 116: "*For the leader, stress...*" S. Kassin, *Psychology,* 2d Ed. (Upper Saddle River, NJ: Prentice Hall, 1998).

Page 118: "*The discipline...*" A. Metsger, "Reflections on USNA." In R. Zino and P. Laric (Eds.), *Tales from Annapolis* (New York: Omega Resources, 2000).

Page 120: "*Although this is the prototypical...*" R. Zino and P. Laric (Eds.), *Tales from Annapolis* (New York: Omega Resources, 2000).

Page 120: "*This session consists of...*" Ibid., pp. 160, 163.

Page 121: "*Now, more than 40 years after my graduation...*" A. J. McCain, *Faith of My Fathers* (New York: Random House, 1999).

Page 122: "*All leaders face...*" R. S. Lazarus and S. Folkman, *Stress, Appraisal, and Coping* (New York: Guilford, 1984).

Page 123: "*The second phase in the appraisal...*" Ibid.

Page 123: "*Lazarus and Folkman...*" Ibid.

Page 124: "*As in the case of intellect...*" S. C. Kobasa, "The Hardy Personality: Toward a Social Psychology of Stress and Health." In G. S. Sanders and J. Suls (Eds.), *SocialPsychology of Health and Illness.* (Hillsdale, NJ: Erlbaum, 1982), pp. 3-32.

Page 128: "*During a period of several days...*" P. Mass, "A Bulletproof Mind," *The New York Times Magazine* (Nov. 10, 2002).

Page 129: "*In dire situations...*" C. Deputy and D. Morris, *Leadership, Theory and Application* (Boston, MA: Pearson Custom Publishing, 2001), p. 305.

CHAPTER 7

Page 133: "*The Academy defines...*" Kristen Murdock, USNA Catalogue 2003-2004, p. 14.

Page 133: "*The abiding commitment to take care...*" Shannon Revell, *USNA Catalogue 2003-2004*, p. 22.

Page 134: "*Being a shipmate...*" R. B. Cialdini, *Influence: How and Why People Agree to Do Things* (New York: Quill, 1984).

Page 135: "*The most sacrosanct principle...*" A. J. McCain, *Faith of My Fathers* (New York: Random House, 1999).

Page 137: "*When Robert Greenleaf...*" R. Greenleaf, *Servant Leadership* (Mahwah, NJ: The Paulist Press, 1977).

Page 137: "*Those striving to be...*" S. R. Covey, *Principle-Centered Leadership* (New York: Simon & Schuster, 1990), p. 34.

Page 139: "*I served as first battalion commander for the fall...*" Andrea Phelps, personal communication. October 2002.

CHAPTER 8

Page 143: "*On the morning of July 29...*" www.chinfo.navy.mil/navpalib/ships/carriers/histories/cv59-forrestal/forrestal-fire.html; www.arlingtoncemetery.net/ussforr.htm

Page 147: "*Beyond drilling for parades...*" J. Conklin, "Reflections on USNA." In R. Zino and P. Laric (Eds.), *Tales from Annapolis* (New York: Omega Resources, 2000).

Page 147: "*During plebe summer, we had...*" Sam Nichols, personal communication. October 2002.

Page 150: "*During the 14 months before we sailed for Vietnam...*" Harold Moore, *We Were Soldiers Once...and Young* (New York: HarperTorch, 2002), p. 34.

Page 151: "*...In 1996, the government's...*" United States General Accounting Office, *Military Aircraft Safety Report*. GAO/NSIAD-96-69BR. (Washington, DC: Author, 1996).

Page 151: "*Damage control comprises...*" USS Enterprise (CV-6), *Operations Manual* (Washington, DC: Department of the Navy, 1940).

Page 152: "*Plebes were ordered...*" R. Zino and P. Laric (Eds.), *Tales from Annapolis* (New York: Omega Resources, 2000).

Page 152: "*But even the best prepared crew can face...*" C. Deputy and D. Morris, *Leadership: Theory and Application* (Boston, MA: Pearson Custom Publishing, 2001).

Page 157: "*Consider the manner...*" L. Brackenbury, *This Is a drill, This Is a Drill!* Press release from U.S. Navy Amphibious Group One, public affairs office, 2003.

CHAPTER 9

Page 161: "*As we got up to go our respective ways,...*" R. Zino and P. Laric (Eds.), *Tales from Annapolis* (New York: Omega Resources, 2000).

Page 163: "*Famed psychologist...*" A. Bandura, *Social Learning Theory* (Englewood Cliffs, NJ: Prentice-Hall, 1977).

Page 167: "*At Navy, midshipmen…*" E. J. Michell, *Leadership Selection at the U.S. Naval Academy: An Analysis of Brigade Leaders and Their Fleet Success.* Master's Thesis, Naval Postgraduate School, Monterey, CA, 1998.

Page 167: "*I can readily say…*" M. Gelfand, Time,Tide and Formation Wait for No One: Cultural and Social Change at the United States Naval Academy, 1949-2000, unpublished doctoral dissertation, University of Arizona 2002, p. 391.

Page 170: "*Leaders who manage to transform…*" K. S. Donahue and L. Wong, "Understanding and Applying Transformational Leadership," *Military Review* 14, no. 8 (1994): 8.

Page 170: "*President Reagan spoke…*" A. Phelps, personal communication, 2003.

Page 171: "*Stephen Covey describes…*" S. Covey, *Principle-Centered Leadership* (New York: Simon & Schuster, 1991).

Page 171: "*My squad leader…*" A. Phelps, personal communication, 2003.

CHAPTER 10

Page 177: "*Daniel Goleman and others would simply…*" D. Goleman, *Emotional Intelligence* (New York: Bantam, 1995).

Page 177: "*Since the 1940s…*" C. Cherniss, "Emotional Intelligence: What It Is and Why It Matters." Paper presented at the annual meeting of the Society for Industrial and Organizational Psychology, New Orleans, LA, April 2000.

Page 178: "*There are millions of technocrats out there…*" W. G. Pagonis, *Leadership in a Combat Zone* (Cambridge, MA: Harvard Business School, 2001), p. 7.

Page 178: "*In fact, IQ alone…*" Cherniss.

Page 178: "*Although the Navy needs…*" W. Bachman, "Nice Guys Finish First: A SYMLOG Analysis of U.S. Naval Commanders." In R. B. Polley (Ed.), *The SYMLOG Practitioner: Applications of Small Group Research* (New York: Praeger, 1988).

Page 178: "*So what exactly is emotional intelligence?*" P. Salovey and J. Mayer, "Emotional Intelligence." *Imagination, Cognition, and Personality* 9 (1990): 185-211.

Page 179: "*We mentioned Admiral Halsey…*" G. P. Harper and S. C. Wieczorek , *Leadership and Human Behavior*, 4th Ed. (Boston, MA: Pearson Custom Publishing, 2003), p. 134.

Page 179: "*Goleman discovered that in numerous research studies…*" Goleman, 1995.

Page 180: "*Another great Navy leader…*" Edward Reid, "A True Navy Hero," *Shipmate,* Annapolis, MD, April 2003.

Page 181: "*Part of the leadership curriculum…*" Goleman, 1995, 1998; Salovey and Mayer.

Page 184: "*King was an exacting and demanding boss…*" T. Buell, *Master of Seapower: A Biography of Fleet Admiral Ernest J. King* (Boston: Little, Brown & Co., 1980), p. 106.

Page 186: "*First, the emotionally disregulated leader...*" K. M. Lewis, "When Leaders Display Emotion: How Followers Respond to Negative Emotional Expression of Male and Female Leaders." *Journal of Organizational Behavior* 21 (2000): 221-234.

Page 190: "*Once again, consider the strategy employed...*" D. M. Abrashoff, *It's Your Ship: Management Techniques from the Best Damn Ship in the Navy* (New York: Warner Books, 2002).

Page 192: "*While enduring torture...*" Mary Felter, "Former Academy Leader Honored," *The Capital* (Nov. 28, 2003).

CHAPTER 11

Page 195: "*My first task upon arrival...*" Mike Manazir, personal communication, 2003.

Page 197: "*...the necessity of empowerment in effective leadership*" R. L. Hughes, R. C. Ginnett, and G. J. Curphy, *Leadership: Enhancing the Lessons of Experience*, 2d Ed. (New York: McGraw-Hill, 1996); J. A. Conger, *The Charismatic Leader* (San Francisco: Jossey-Bass, 1989).

Page 198: "*I worked hard to create...*" D. M. Abrashoff, *It's Your Ship: Management Techniques from the Best Damn Ship in the Navy* (New York: Warner Books, 2002).

Page 200: "*A striking finding...*" R. J. House, "A 1976 Theory of Charismatic Leadership." In J. G. Hunt and L. L. Larson (Eds.), *Leadership: The Cutting Edge* (Carbondale, IL: Southern Illinois University Press, 1977).

Page 202: "*Studies of organizational retention...*" Hughes *et al.*

Page 202: "*Once a vision is created...*" Hughes *et al.*, Conger.

Page 204: "*Perhaps worst of all, consistent punishment...*" M. E. P. Seligman and S. F. Maier, "Failure to Escape Traumatic Shock," *Journal of Experimental Psychology* 74 (1967): 1-9; M. E. P. Seligman, D. C. Klein, and W. R. Miller, "Depression." In H. Leitenberg (Ed.), *Handbook of Behavior Modification and Behavior Therapy* (Englewood Cliffs, NJ: Prentice-Hall, 1976).

Page 205: "*During the fall leadership...*" S. Milgram, "Behavioral Study of Obedience," *Journal of Abnormal and Social Psychology* 67 (1963): 371-378.

Page 206: "*One of the many commodities never...*" D. C. McClelland, *Power: The Inner Experience* (New York: Irvington, 1975).

Page 207: "*In a famous set of experiments with rhesus monkeys...*" H. F. Harlow, "Learning and Satiation of Response in Intrinsically Motivated Complex Puzzle Performance in Monkeys." *Journal of Comparative and Physiological Psychology* 43 (1950): 289-294.

Page 207: "*An old chief bosun's mate pulled me...*" D. Borchers, personal communication, 2003.

Page 208: "*In addition to being personally secure...*" Hughes *et al.*

Page 208: "*I realized early in my...*" M. Manazir, personal communication, 2003.

Page 209: "*Although many of the critical elements...*" Hughes *et al.*

Page 212: "*Most of what we have described as empowerment...*" C. C. Manz and H. P. Sims, "Superleadership: Beyond the Myth of Heroic Leadership." *Organizational Dynamics 19* (1991): 18–35.

CHAPTER 12

Page 215: "*Although a significant number of African-American...*" N. Miller, *An Illustrated History of the U.S. Navy* (New York: Macmillan, 1977), p. 156.

Page 215: "*The first black American...*" J. Sweetman, *The U.S. Naval Academy* (Annapolis, MD: Naval Institute Press, 1995), p. 208.

Page 215: "*In 1965, there were only...*" Ibid., p. 238.

Page 216; "*So deeply engrained was...*" P. Stillwell, *The Golden Tthirteen: Recollections of the First Black Naval Officers* (Annapolis, MD: Naval Institute Press, 1993), pp. 29-30.

Page 217: "*Of course, after the Golden Thirteen were successfully...*" Ibid., pp. 128-129, 154.

Page 217: "*When we first got there...*" Ibid., p. 90.

Page 218: "*As an example of CDR Downes's approach to racial slurs...*" Ibid., p. 90.

Page 218: "*Outstanding CEOs of some of our country's...*" T. E. Deal and A. A. Kennedy, "Strong Cultures: A New 'Old Rule' for Business Success. In J. T. Wren (Ed.), *The Leader's Companion: Insights on Leadership through the Ages* (New York: The Free Press, 1995), p. 281.

Page 219: "*Military sociologist Maddi Segal...*" M. W. Segal, "Women's Military Roles Cross-Nationally: Past, Present, and Future." In C. Deputy and D. Morris (Eds.), *Leadership Theory and Application* (Boston: Pearson Custom Publishing, 2002), pp. 279-280.

Page 220: "*Although he was two classes behind me...*" J. Carter, speech delivered at the U. S. Naval Academy, October 2, 2002.

Page 220: "*Brown, however, described...*" Sweetman, p. 207.

Page 220: "*At the beginning of the academic year...*" Ibid., p. 208.

Page 221: "*The 81 women who...*" K. P. Durning, *Women at the Naval Academy: The First Year of Integration.* NPRDC-TR-78-12. .(San Diego, CA: Navy Personnel Research and Development Center, 1978).

Page 221: "*Reliving those four years was...*" S. H. Disher, *First Class: Women Join the Ranks of the Naval Academy* (Annapolis, MD: Naval Institute Press, 1998).

Page 221: "*Hostility from...*" S. H. Goodsen, *Serving Proudly: A History of Women in the U. S. Navy* (Annapolis, MD: Naval Institute Press, 2001).

Page 222 "*Stronger leadership was needed...*" Ibid.

Page 222: "*One of the sad ironies...*" Ibid.

Page 223: "*One of the myths...*" G. F. Simons, C. Vazquez, and P. R. Harris, *Transcultural Leadership: Empowering the Diverse Workforce* (Houston, TX: Gulf Publishing, 1993).

Page 223: "*In fact, we work hard...*" Ibid., p. 10.

Page 223: "*Two of the universal human values...*" R. M. Kidder, "Universal Human Values: Finding an Ethical Common Ground." In J. T. Wren (Ed.), *Leadership Companion: Insights on Leadership Throughout the Ages* (New York: Free Press, 1995), pp. 500-508.

Page 224: "*USNA graduate Mike...*" D. M. Abrashoff, *It's Your Ship: Management Techniques from the Best Damn Ship in the Navy* (New York: Warner Books., 2002).

Page 224: "*Leaders would be well served...*" Kidder, p. 505.

Page 225: "*At Navy, midshipmen...*" Segal ; Simmons *et al.*

Page 225: "*When leaders at USNA...*"H. M. Gelfand, "Time, Tide, and Formation Wait for No One: Cultural and Social Change at the United States Naval Academy, 1949-2000," unpublished doctoral dissertation, Department of History, University of Arizona, 2002.

Page 226: "*If there is one factor...*" Segal.

Page 226: "*Excellent leaders are active...*" Gelfand, p. 352.

Page 227: "*In 1987, Superintendent Admiral Marryott wrote...*" United States Naval Academy, *Report to the Superintendent on the integration of women in the brigade of midshipmen.* (Annapolis, MD: USNA, 1987).

Page 227: "*Finally, in 1995, Admiral Larson...*" Gelfand, p. 399.

Page 227: "*Sometimes an organizational unit can...*" Office of the Inspector General, *The Tailhook Report* (New York: St. Martin's Press, 1993).

Page 228: "*Tailhook 1991 represents one of...*" Ibid., p. 87.

Page 229: "*While many senior Navy...*" "Zumwalt rebukes top navy leaders on racial unrest," *New York Times*, November 11, 1972, p. 1.

Page 229: "*He also launched a wide-reaching...*" Ibid.

Page 229; "*A strange thing happened...*" Durning.

Page 230: "*Research shows that when members...*" Ibid.

INDEX

INDEX

ABOUT THE AUTHORS

W. Brad Johnson is an associate professor of psychology in the Department of Leadership, Ethics, and Law at the United States Naval Academy. A faculty associate at Johns Hopkins University, Johnson's work has appeared in numerous journals and professional publications including *Consulting Psychology Journal, Military Medicine,* and *The Journal of Psychology.*

Gregory P. Harper is a graduate of the United States Naval Academy and a retired Navy captain and aviator. Captain Harper is a national security fellow at Harvard University, and is a former instructor at the U.S. Naval War College, as well as a former director of the National Joint Military Intelligence Center.